Enlightening without obfuscation

Science vs. Religion — doubt vs. religious experience: both outlooks are valuable in a reconciliation that makes sense and is fundamental to a full life.

God Unmasked;
The Full Life Revealed

Ernest Lane, M.D.

How can doubt and critical examination be reconciled with spirituality and religious belief? Is God a representation of the natural universe? Or a projection of the imagination at a cosmic level? These and other such questions are squarely put to readers of Ernest Lane's *God Unmasked; the Full Life Revealed*. He would have his readers "look beyond the agenda, desires and needs of the self."

Observing a drift toward crass materialism and an overindulged individualism, Lane argues that a full life requires a reconciliation between science and spirituality. His message is primarily for the skeptical minded who sense the need for a non-material dimension in their lives. Lane succeeds in bringing the reader through many a philosophical and theological thicket, skillfully avoiding the snares of cynicism. A book for the inquiring skeptic, *God Unmasked; the Full Life Revealed*, offers important insights for those in search of a life beyond mere hedonistic comforts.

Herbert K. Beals, Historian/Author of *For Honor and Country* and *Juan Perez, Northwest Coast*

This book has a surprising and unexpected power to inspire the reader to constructive introspection.

Geoffrey Hamilton, Researcher, educator and consultant/Author of *An Ultimate Truth*

Ernest Lane's book, *God Unmasked; the Full Life Revealed*, is an exploration of the concept of God which speaks to those of us who think of ourselves as Twentieth Century "scientific men." I see this book as being written for individuals who regard more traditional views of God as being somewhat superstitious.

The author's writing style is clear and concise. It provides a sense that one thoroughly understands what is being expounded. His statement and restatement of theological concepts, each time with a slightly different focus, indicates that the subject has been viewed from many sides and different angles.

I highly recommend this book, especially for those of us who tend toward rationalism but realize that science doesn't have all the answers and, indeed, does not ask the most important questions.

David Hiebert, Industrial Quality Control Representative

God Unmasked;
The Full Life Revealed

Answers You Don't Expect

The Questions:

Religious experience and doubt: can they be compatible?
Can the conflict between religion and science be reconciled?
Why is religious experience valuable?
How should I direct my life?

Ernest Lane, M.D.

Design and typesetting by Family Graphics, West Linn, Oregon
Cover design by Patrick Burke, Photography and Design, Tigard, Oregon
Poem illustrations by the author

HIGH GROUND PUBLISHING

Copyright © 1998 by Ernest Lane. All rights reserved. This book may not be reproduced in whole or in part, in any form (except by reviewers for the public press) without permission from the publisher.

LCCN: 98-85155

ISBN: 0-9654915-2-8

Publisher's Cataloging-in-Publication
(Provided by Quality Books, Inc.)

Lane, Ernest (Ernest Aaron).
    God unmasked : the full life revealed : answers you don't expect / Ernest Lane. -- 1st ed.
    p. cm.
    Includes index.
    "The questions: Religious experience and doubt: can they be compatible? Can the conflict between religion and science be reconciled? Why is religious experience valuable? How should I direct my life?"
    Preassigned LCCN: 98-85155
    ISBN: 0-9654915-2-8

    1. Psychology--Religious. 2. Religion and science.
I. Title.

BL53.L36 1998   200.1
                          QBI98-983

About the Publisher

High Ground Publishing, a division of Northwoods Consulting, has as its mission the publication of previously unpublished works **that recognize, uplift and celebrate the heroic nature of human life from a rational, reasoned and objective point of view, free of mysticism and magic**.

Manuscripts that meet these requirements will receive a serious evaluation. Adult nonfiction preferred, fiction considered. No poetry or books for children.

Manuscripts must include SASE if the author wants it returned.

No agents, authors only.

Copyright Permissions

Alighieri, Dante. From THE DIVINE COMEDY by Dante Alighieri, translated by John Ciardi. Translation copyright 1954, 1957, 1959, 1960, 1961, 1965, 1967, 1970 by the Ciardi Family Publishing Trust. Reprinted by permission of W. W. Norton & Company, Inc.

Armstrong, Karen. From A HISTORY OF GOD, by Karen Armstrong. Copyright © 1993 by Karen Armstrong. Reprinted by permission of Alfred A. Knopf, Inc.

Bachelard, Gaston. From THE POETICS OF REVERIE by Gaston Bachelard, translated by Daniel Russell. Translation copyright © 1969 by Grossman Publishers, Inc. Orig. Copyright © 1960 by Presses Universitaires de France. Used by permission of Viking Penguin, a division of Penguin Putnam Inc.

_____. From THE POETICS OF SPACE by Gaston Bachelard, translated by Maria Jolas. Translation copyright © 1958 by Presses Universitaires de France. Translation copyright © 1964 by The Orion Press, Inc. Used by permission of Viking Penguin, a division of Penguin Putnam Inc.

_____. From ON POETIC IMAGINATION AND REVERIE by Gaston Bachelard, translated by Colette Gaudin. Copyright © 1987 Spring Publications, Inc. Reprinted by permission of Spring Publications, Inc.

Barth, Karl. KARL BARTH; THEOLOGIAN OF FREEDOM. Ed. Clifford Green. Reprinted by permission of Sciences Religieuses/Studies in Religion. From Sciences Religieuses/Studies in Religion 7/2, Spring 1978. Trans. George Hunsinger.

Bates, Tom. Excerpts from "When Good Turns Bad," by Tom Bates of *The Oregonian* staff. The Oregonian © 1994, Oregonian Publishing Co. All rights reserved. Reprinted with permission.

Bellah, Robert N., et alia. HABITS OF THE HEART: INDIVIDUALISM AND COMMITMENT IN AMERICAN LIFE. Copyright © 1985,1996 Regents of the University of California. Reprinted by permission of the University of California Press.

Burke, Kenneth. PERMANENCE AND CHANGE: AN ANATOMY OF PURPOSE, THIRD EDITION, WITH A NEW AFTERWORD.

Copyright © 1984 The Regents of the University of California. Reprinted by permission of the University of California Press.

Camus, Albert. From THE MYTH OF SISYPHUS AND OTHER ESSAYS by Albert Camus, trans. Justin O'Brien. Copyright © 1955 by Alfred A. Knopf Inc. Reprinted by permission of the publisher.

Cassirer, Ernst. AN ESSAY ON MAN. Copyright 1944 by Yale University Press. Published by Yale University Press. Reprinted by permission of Yale University Press.

Cervantes. DON QUIXOTE by Miguel de Cervantes Saavedra, translated by Samuel Putnam. Translation copyright 1949 by The Viking Press, Inc. Used by permission of Viking Penguin, a division of Penguin Putnam Inc.

Dostoevsky, Feodor. From NOTES FROM THE UNDERGROUND: A Norton Critical Edition by Fyodor Dostoevsky, translated by Michael R. Katz. Translation copyright © 1989 by W. W. Norton & Company, Inc. Reprinted by permission of W. W. Norton & Company, Inc.

Eliot, T. S. Excerpts "East Coker," "The Dry Salvages," and "Little Gidding" in FOUR QUARTETS, copyright 1943 by T.S. Eliot and renewed 1971 by Esme Valerie Eliot, reprinted by permission of Harcourt Brace & Company.

Gardner, Marilyn. Excerpts from "'Entertain Me,' Says A Restless Nation as it Yawns Over Soccer" Reprinted with permission from *The Christian Science Monitor*. Copyright © 1994 The Christian Science Publishing Society. All rights reserved.

Giddens, Anthony. MODERNITY AND SELF-IDENTITY. Copyright © 1991 Anthony Giddens. Reprinted by permission of the Stanford University Press

Goethe, Johann Wolfgang von. GOETHE'S FAUST, PARTS I AND II, translated by Louis Macneice. Copyright 1951, 1954 by Fredrick Louis Macneice, renewed 1979 by Hedli Macneice. Reprinted by permission of Oxford University Press.

Haught, James; Excerpts from "Charting Terror in the Name of the Lord." Reprinted from the Charleston Gazette in *The Oregonian*. Reprinted by permission of James A. Haught.

Hawking, Stephen. A BRIEF HISTORY OF TIME. Copyright © 1988 Stephen W. Hawking. Reprinted by permission of Bantam Books, a division of Bantam, Doubleday, Dell Publishing Group, Inc.

Hick, John. AN INTERPRETATION OF RELIGION. Copyright © 1989 by John Hick. Published in the United States 1989 by Yale University Press. Reprinted by permission of Yale University Press.

Hoffer, Eric. THE TRUE BELIEVER. Copyright 1951 by Eric Hoffer, copyright renewed 1979. Harper Collins PublishersInc. Reprinted by permission of Harper Collins Publishers Inc.

Homer. THE ILIAD OF HOMER. Translated by Richmond Lattimore. Copyright 1951 by The University of Chicago. All rights reserved. Published 1951 by The University of Chicago Press. Reprinted by permission of The University of Chicago Press.

Hylton, Judith E. Music Theory I. Third edition. Copyright 1994 by Judith E. Hylton. Noteworthy Music. Reprinted by permission of Judith E. Hylton.

Jaynes, Julian. THE ORIGIN OF CONSCIOUSNESS IN THE BREAKDOWN OF THE BICAMERAL MIND. Copyright © 1990 by Julian Jaynes. Published by Houghton Mifflin

Leopardi, Giacomo. LEOPARDI: POEMS AND PROSE, ed. Angel Flores, transl. Edwin Morgan. Reprinted by permission from estate of Angel Flores

Maslow, Abraham H. RELIGIONS, VALUES, AND PEAK EXPERIENCES. Copyright © 1964 Kappa Delta Pi. Reprinted by permission of the Literary Estate of A. H. Maslow

Myers, David D. THE PURSUIT OF HAPPINESS. Copyright © 1992 by David G. And Carol P. Myers Charitable Foundation. Reprinted by permission of William Morrow & Company, Inc.

Putnam, Robert D. "It Isn't the Old Men who are Grumpy in America," printed in *The Oregonian,* 12-31-95. Reprinted by permission of Robert D. Putnam.

Rainwater, Janette. YOU'RE IN CHARGE: A GUIDE TO BECOMING YOUR OWN THERAPIST. Copyright © 1979 Janette Rainwater. Reprinted by permission of Janette Rainwater.

Reynolds, David K. PLAYING BALL ON RUNNING WATER. Copyright © 1984 by David K. Reynolds. Reprinted by permission of William Morrow & Company, Inc.

Spong, John Shelby. LIVING IN SIN? A BISHOP RETHINKS SEXUALITY. Copyright © 1989 by the Rt. Rev. John Shelby Spong. Reprinted by permission of Harper Collins Publishers.

Suzuki, Shunryu. ZEN MIND, BEGINNER'S MIND. Ed. by Trudy Dixon. Published by John Weatherhill, Inc. Protected by copyright under terms of the International Copyright Union; all rights reserved. Reprinted by permission of Weatherhill.

TAO TE CHING by Lao Tzu, a New English Version, with Foreword and Notes by Stephen Mitchell. Translation copyright © 1988 by Stephen Mitchell. Reprinted by permission of Harper Collins Publishers, Inc.

Tolstoy, Leo. THE DEATH OF IVAN ILYICH AND OTHER STORIES. Trans. By Louis and Aylmer Maude. Reprinted by permission of Oxford University Press.

Wallraff, Charles F. KARL JASPERS: AN INTRODUCTION TO HIS PHILOSOPHY. Copyright © 1970 by Princeton University Press. Reprinted by permission of Princeton University Press.

Weil, Simone. GRAVITY AND GRACE. Reprinted by permission of The Putnam Publishing Group from GRAVITY AND GRACE by Simone Weil. Copyright © 1952 by G. P. Putnam's Sons; renewed © 1980 by G. P. Putnam's Son.

_____. SELECTED ESSAYS/ SIMONE WEIL: AN ANTHOLOGY 1934-43. Translated by Sir Richard Rees. Copyright © 1962 Oxford University Press. Reprinted by permission of the Peters Fraser & Dunlop Group Ltd.

Audience for Book and Disclaimer

This book is written for the general public, including academics who I expect would find much of interest.

Any individual who reads this book agrees to hold the author and publisher of the book free from any liability. If you do not wish to accept full responsibility in the reading of this book, you may return it to the publisher for a refund of the price of the book. The author and High Ground Publishing, a division of Northwoods Consulting, shall have neither liability nor any responsibility whatsoever to any person or entity with respect to any loss or damage caused, or alleged to have resulted from, directly or indirectly, the information contained in this book.

The information contained herein is not intended to be perceived as a source from which to establish a particular religious practice. Neither is it intended to disenfranchise people of faith.

This book has as its mission the education and edification of the reader.

To George Victor

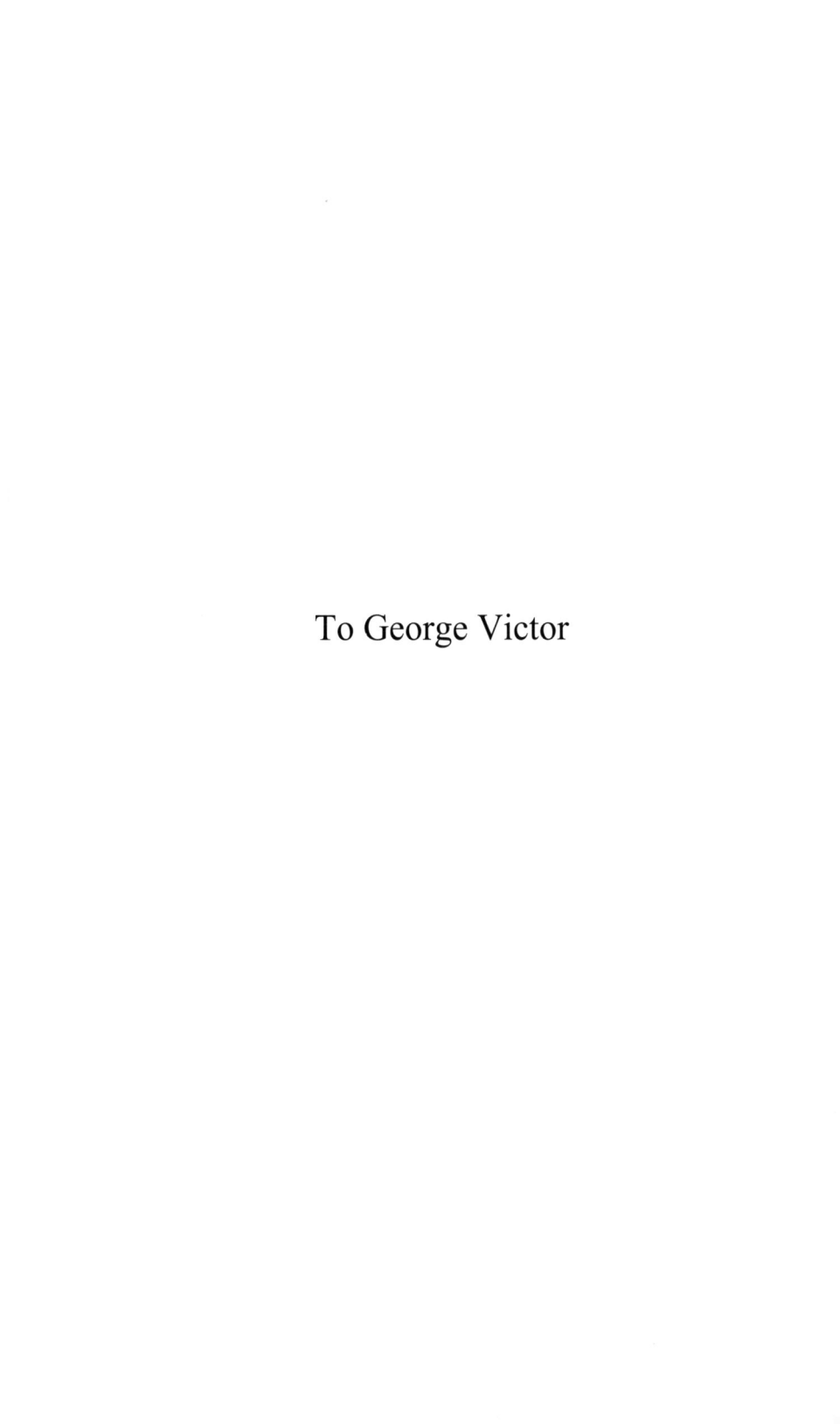

Table of Contents

Acknowledgments

Foreword

Part I: Initial Remarks   1

    Why This Book Was Written and For Whom
    Meaning?
    Localized Life; Enlarged Life
    Definitions
    Proof and Problems
    Preview

Part II: Full Life   23

Chapter 1 - Green Light   25
    An Unimportant Conversation About Importance
    Fantasia I
    Fantasia II
    Fantasia III
    Serious Note

Chapter 2 - Doubt: the Path to Truth   31
    Uncertainty Today
    Doubt and Truth
    Characteristics of Doubt
    Summary

Chapter 3 - Wonder, Thankfulness   43

Chapter 4 - The Swamp of Anguish; the Flow of Openness   53
    Overview of the Chapter
    Anguish
    Control
    Engaged Detachment
    Freedom
    Openness
    The Cleared Mind
    Word-symbols
    Imagination
    Summary

Chapter 5 - Review and the Realms of Being and Becoming   87

Chapter 6 - Self-absorption   89
       Absorption with Self
       A Commercial
       Many Paths
       Out of the Pit

Chapter 7 - Empathy, Anti-empathy, and Action   101
       Overview of the Chapter
       Definition of Empathy and Predisposing Factors
       Love
       Action and Anti-empathy
       Factors That Limit Empathy
       Self-negation
       The Interplay and Flow of Empathy and Action

Chapter 8 - Self and Society   119
       The Value of Social Organization
       Emotion and Freedom
       Television and "Emotion Junkies"
       Social Control and Excess Idealism
       A Balance

Chapter 9 - Integrity; a Fullness of Life   133

Chapter 10 - Nonsense   141

Part III: The Unmasking of God   143

Chapter 11 - Word-symbols and Imagination   145

Chapter 12 - Universe, Hope, and Value   157
       The Universe
       Unknowns
       Self and Universe
       Hope
       Value

Chapter 13 - Release From Doubt and Discernment   177
               Release
               External Authorization
               Word-symbols
               Self-righteousness
               Summary

Chapter 14 - God Unmasked   185
               Before Beginning
               The First Aspect of God
               The Second Aspect of God
               The Third Aspect of God
               Overview of the Three Aspects of God
               The Utilitarian Dilemma
               Objectivity and Subjectivity
               Doubt
               A Note on Ending This Chapter

Chapter 15 - Into the Air   205

Chapter 16 - Mysticism: the Strength of Ambiguity   213
               Mysticism, Ambiguity, and Freedom
               The Ineffability of Mysticism
               Accessibility to the Mystical State
               The Impetus Toward Realizing a Mystical State
               Individual Variation in Spiritual Receptivity
               Summary

Chapter 17 - Opposition   225

Chapter 18 - Individual Differences and Religious Practice   229
               Individual Differences
               The Natural World
               Anthropomorphism
               Self-righteousness and Doubt
               Opposition
               Integrity
               Silence

Chapter 19 - The Nature of a Religious Orientation 251
        Until I Die
        The Function of Religious Practice
        Self-righteousness and Doubt
        Components of a Religious Orientation
        God, Music, and Freedom
        Review

Chapter 20 - Soft 269

Part IV: Bringing It All Together 271

Chapter 21 - The Value of Continuity 273
        The Sense of Community
        Interpersonal Relationships
        A Defective Tool of Enormous Value
        Individual Continuity and Religious Practice
        Continuity and Humanism
        Review

Chapter 22 - Minimizing the Maximum 293
        The Cleared Mind
        Doubt
        The Focus on God
        A Balance, Phases, and Trust

Chapter 23 - Review 307

Chapter 24 - The Psychologic Body 311
        Overview
        A Metaphor
        Openness
        Freedom; the Cosmic Imagination; God
        Values
        Final Considerations
        Last, Short Verse

Works Cited 332
Index 336

Acknowledgments

I was most fortunate in receiving valuable input in the review of this book from a number of sources. They have provided insight into the content of the book as seen from a wide variety of orientations.

The editorial work done by Geoffrey Hamilton of Northwoods Consulting was exceptional. I very much appreciate his excellent critical advice. Hamilton's comments and suggestions have greatly increased the clarity and readability of this book. In addition, conversations with Geoffrey Hamilton led me to further develop the concepts that are presented herein.

The support of my wife, Leah, has been invaluable in completing this work. Also, she has provided certain valuable suggestions.

I am grateful for the evaluation of this book by Dr. Herbert Biskar, Ph.D., Psychotherapist. His input has been quite helpful. Dorothy Larco provided a very thorough critique of *God Unmasked; the Full Life Revealed*. In addition, I was fortunate in having the book reviewed and evaluated by several other interested readers from a wide variety of backgrounds: Rev. Woodley White, Presbyterian minister, Herbert Beals, historian, Trudy Evans, Registered Nurse Practioner, Prof. Jan Anderson, Professor of English.

Of special note is the review and Foreword by Dr. Jim Clemans, Ph.D., Physics. His comments revealed to me how a scientist views this manuscript. I also appreciate the evaluation of this book by another man of science, David Hiebert.

Foreword

As a scientist, for whom doubt and operating hypotheses are the coin of the realm, I found this book to be an engrossing, challenging conversation with a friend. Dr. Lane challenged me to revisit many of the debates of my youth. Is there a God? Why am I here? What pleasures me? His mature yet refreshingly self-effacing style was conducive to the very conversation that he wants to have with the reader. The conversation proceeded with frequent acknowledgment of the limitations of human knowledge and the value of doubt in sustaining a course in life that is consistent with this life's learning, while maintaining the flexibility to modify one's life view with new information. There was an attitude of willingness to adopt new approximations of the truth.

Dr. Lane describes a naturalistic concept of God as the imaginative representation of all existence. This understanding of God is pantheistic, and it includes a subjective dimension: the imagination. By the logic of Occam's Razor, which requires that assumptions introduced to explain a thing must not be multiplied beyond necessity, this naturalistic concept seems unnecessary. To the scientific mind, advocating something that is ineffable and beyond all meaningful delineation is not useful. Moreover, integrating a mindfulness of such concepts into my thinking would create interference with orderly thought, analysis, and understanding. I could not realize the value which Dr. Lane claims many would find from using the God concept.

I find wonder in how things work and develop. Expanding my understanding through discoveries is gratifying. I feel appreciation for those gifts of existence which give me the capacity to explore the nature of the physical world. An appreciation for the ability to explore and discover gives me a positive outlook; it is fulfilling and provides me with one of the pleasures of life. I believe that my appreciation is an expression of thankfulness, which validates for me Dr. Lanes's emphasis on the value of thankfulness.

In *God Unmasked; the Full Life Revealed* Dr. Lane points out how spiritual experience can release people from excess self-absorption. This has consequences at several levels. At the individual level, the push and pull of interactions between people may be more likely to eventually deteriorate into self-centered expressions of conflicting wills if they are excessively self-absorbed. Even the most enlightened of us may, occasionally, find our outlook degenerating into narrow self-interest without appropriate recourse to openness and empathy. After this "conversation" with Dr. Lane, I am more able to understand the value of religious experience for many. This book helped me to be more tolerant of the spirituality of others. Dr. Lane sets forth a hypothesis for how spirituality can be valuable in a complex world where many use less analytical approaches to dealing with doubt. This book gives me the perspective to properly respect, tolerate and support spirituality in others. This viewpoint helps me relate to the needs of diversity in the work-place and, in fact, in all walks of life.

Regarding society as a whole, Dr. Lane points out that the practice of religion has been associated with cruelties, wars, and injustices. However, he also notes that the positive aspects of religious practice should not be disregarded. I concur with his statement that there is a comity which we need in order to have a civil society, and I agree with his position that a reservoir of civility is supported by the release of many from excess self-absorption. Dr. Lane has indicated that this release can be provided by religious practice. The spirituality that Dr. Lane describes is valuable to the practice of religion in a way constructive to society.

Reading *God Unmasked; the Full Life Revealed* brought me to a fuller understanding of important aspects of life. This book has added depth and breadth to my understanding of the pleasures of existence.

Jim E. Clemans, Ph.D. Physics

PART I

INITIAL REMARKS

Initial Remarks

Why This Book Was Written and for Whom

Meaning?

Localized Life; Enlarged Life

Definitions

Proof and Problems

Preview

WHY THIS BOOK WAS WRITTEN AND FOR WHOM

There is a human need for spiritual experience and expression. This need plus an awareness of the problems associated with spirituality have led me to write this book. Also, I have wanted to find some plausible reconciliation between the scientific and the spiritual realms.

I will start this section by giving you some information about my background. My Jewish parents both died when I was an infant. My mother died of a blood clot to the lungs, and my father committed suicide three weeks later. At age seven my adoptive Jewish father died. After two or three months in a Catholic orphanage, I lived at times with my sister's family, who intermittently attended Methodist services. During my high school years I stayed with my adoptive mother, who, if she had been religious-minded, would probably have been Lutheran since she was Norwegian.

After military service I attended college and medical school. I am a general practitioner and have practiced medicine for over thirty years.

My exposure to a scientific background contrasts with my varied religious background. It has been a project of my life to reconcile the findings and orientation of scientific endeavor with those aspects of spiritual life which I find to be valid.

I will expand on this. In the course of my life I have found that a most valuable quality to have is an openness to truth. Furthermore, it seems true to me that, in the nature of events, in life as well as for existence in general, there is not only a pattern of consistency and predictability but also a certain amount of chance and haphazardness. There seems to be a chaotic aspect to the events of existence.

In my view, the occurrence of haphazardness as part of existence tends to mitigate against the belief in a supernatural consciousness. Random chance would seem to contradict the belief that a god intervenes in some purposeful way in the workings of the universe. Furthermore, I understand that various proponents of process theology consider the nature of existence as evolutionary and subject to both mechanism and chance. Though theologians of this persuasion do incorporate the dimension of chance in their orientation, they still believe in a supernatural purposefulness. To me, a supernatural manipulation of the universe for the well-being of human individuals does not seem to be true.

This can be carried a step further. Even if there were no amount of chance and haphazardness, even in the presence of an entirely deterministic causation, the concept of a supernatural consciousness managing the universe in order to fit some grand purpose does not seem likely. Purposeful activity by a god does not seem plausible to me, but, of course, this point of view is not something I can prove.

To many, the reality of the existence of a supernatural consciousness named God is just as valid as— or more valid than—my point of view. In fact, I recognize the worth of a spiritual orientation for believers in God. There is often an added dimension to life, a fullness of the spirit, that often accompanies a belief in God.

The substance of this book is a recognition of the value of a spiritual orientation and the presentation of a particular spiritual orientation which is consonant with an openness to truth. In this regard, we can consider the status of truth in the outlook of science. The scientific endeavor is the systematized development of that information which can tentatively be considered to be true. At the heart of scientific endeavor is an openness to new conceptions of the truth. On the other hand, a religious outlook usually involves beliefs which contradict that which can be believed on objective grounds. In addition, we can view the nature of religious practice beyond the commitment to that which is ordinarily unbelievable. Religious practice gives articulation to a sense of spirituality by fulfilling the need for wonder and for openness into the joy of enlarged awareness. The religious approach affords the possibility for joyful wonder and for thankfulness for existence. This wonder and thankfulness are sources of value. They give meaning to life.

In regard to an openness to objective validity, the outlooks of science and religion are, by and large, contradictory. This book seeks to reconcile these two outlooks, the scientific and the religious, in a way that preserves the validity of both.

I do not claim that the findings of this book are universally valid. These findings are true for me and quite probably for a number of others. To me they seem to be basic truths, constituents of a full life.

Furthermore, I feel that if religion could be put on a more valid basis, it could become valuable to many who think of the spiritual realm as meaningless. This book is written for those who tend to doubt the validity of spiritual experience but realize that there may be value in such experience. The book is aimed at those who have a skeptical frame of mind but sense a need for a spiritual dimension in their lives. It is not an exhortation or a call to spiritual exaltation. Rather, it is a delineation, a step-by-step look at the full life and the role of spirituality in that life. The discussion will not satisfy those who want an "emotional high." Hopefully it will fulfill the needs of some who want a broader underpinning, a foundation, for their lives.

Al: The word "delineation" does not sound joyful to me. I think of things of the spirit as being joyful.

I hear a remark. Who are you?

Al: I'll tell you in the next section.

I'm the author. You can tell me now.

Al: Please bear with me. At least, you could say if the information in your book can lead to a joyful spirit.

I'll answer your concern and expect to hear more from you soon, Al. The steps described are not plodding. Those who tend toward a skeptical approach to this subject may find the insights worthwhile and possibly even joyful. For skeptics to whom doubt inhibits an inclination toward the fulfillment of spiritual experience, this book presents an opportunity, a way to a new beginning.

To continue, this book is not for those who are confident in their particular expression of spirituality. To those who have found God and are secure in their knowledge, the information presented in this book will

Initial Remarks

likely seem like a weak substitute for spiritual expression. I would not expect that these individuals would find much of value in this presentation.

There is another limitation for this book. It does not deal with the important subject of mental illness. That subject is beyond the scope of this presentation. Rather, we start at a point at which psychologic problems have been, for all practical purposes, resolved and move from that point to the path of fullness of life.

I will indicate another reason why I have written this book. It involves personal experience. In 1940 I was eleven years old. World War II had started the year before, and in the following year our country would enter the war. In newsreels we had seen the sweep of German force through Czechoslovakia, Poland, Denmark, Norway, the Low Countries, and France. Germany was on the brink of invading England during 1940 before reversing course to invade Russia.

Also, we were aware of the German oppression of Jews. In newsreels we saw Hitler expounding his messages: German superiority, *ein Volk* (one people), human perfection, a robust Germany of superior people, in control of its destiny and dictating its will to surrounding countries. The news clips also showed the response of Hitler's audiences: energized and joyful as they listened to the passionate words of their leader, *der Führer*.

In that period of time I had certain dreams. I was a Jew in America, but what if my parents hadn't emigrated from Rumania? In my mind, the plight of Rumanian Jews was not different from that of Jews directly under Nazi control. I had dreams of fleeing into the woods and trying to survive winter in the wild while escaping from manhunts. There were dreams of being caught and dreams of life and death in a concentration camp.

Also, I had an opposite view of the German character. My brother-in-law was German-American; I believe his parents came from Germany. Part of the time during my youth I had lived with my brother-in-law and sister. Since they were twenty years older than me, they were parent figures to me, and their son and daughter were like brother and sister. My appreciation for my brother-in-law was very real. Although he was a strict disciplinarian, he was also a compassionate and outgoing person.

In sum, I had seen extremes in the expression of German character. On one hand I saw Germans as overbearing and aggressive in the expression of control and perfectionism; opposed to that I saw compassion and openness.

How could I resolve these contradictory views of German people? One way was to gain a better understanding of the desire for control and perfection. I recognized the inclination toward excess control and toward the extreme of perfectionism as being within the potential make-up of all humans, not just Germans. Also, I realized that there is value in the inclination for control and perfection if expressed to a reasonable degree and not carried to a destructive extreme. I have enlarged upon this subject in Chapters Four and Six.

One of the consequences of Nazi Germany's drive for control and perfection was the expression of extreme cruelty toward Jews; the Jews were seen as subhuman. I will elaborate further on the universality of the human potential for harm and destruction. In seeing a capacity for cruelty in all humans, myself included, I do not by any means want to imply an exculpation of the actions of Nazi Germany. However, with a broader understanding of the nature of human life, it is valuable to have a realization of the potential for destructive action by each of us. This realization may help to provide some understanding of harmful actions by ourselves or others. Although the perpetrators of cruelty should be punished, an awareness by the victims of the universal potential for cruelty may release those who had been subjected to such cruelty from lingering in an excess indulgence of self-righteousness and a sense of victimhood. Such indulgence in self- righteousness might further harm the victim.

One of the reasons I have written this book is to provide some delineation of the nature of a healthy interaction between the tendencies toward control, perfection, self-righteousness, empathy, and openness. These are addressed in Chapters Four through Eight. A later part of the book is concerned with the sphere of religion, and these qualities are of particular importance in various aspects of religious practice.

Also, I want to point to the utilization of an attitude of doubt toward propaganda in any form—social, political, whatever. The subject of doubt is taken up in Chapter Two.

MEANING?

"Something is wrong, you say? There is something more to life? What is that something?" I have heard this sort of mood expressed. Many feel that something is wrong with our outlook on life. It seems that many feel a lack of meaning. And, beyond that, although they may want some meaning for their lives, they sense that—ultimately, in view of the grand scheme of things—there is no meaning.

Several authors have described a lack of any meaning for existence. I will quote the British poet T. S. Eliot:

> There is no end, but addition: the trailing
> consequence of further days and hours... (37)

There is no end. No purpose or significance; that is the message. We are faced with this message and many are looking for something beyond the absence of meaning. Is this all there is? For many of us, it appears that the world, the universe, wheels on without direction. We perceive no fore-ordained goal.

One may say that the perspective of modern science has led us to this outlook; we will discuss that later. But it can be said at this time that the apparent aimlessness of the processes of the universe would seem to confirm a lack of any type of transcendental consciousness or concern.

The Italian poet Giacomo Leopardi describes this lack of transcendental concern in, "The Broom":

> Nature has no more care
> Or praise for human souls
> Than for the ants: and if she slaughters men
> Less terribly than them,
> This is no great wonder ... (lines 231-5)

> So nature, unaware of man and eras
> Man calls ancient, unaware of links
> From ancestors to sons,
> Stands always green, or rather sets her feet
> On such a lengthy road
> She seems to stand. Meanwhile kingdoms decay,
> Peoples and tongues die out: she does not see it:
> And man presumes on his eternity. (lines 290-7)

We still ask the question: What is our significance? What is the significance of our existence? Is there some guiding light to help us in finding the way to live and the direction to go?

We do not find a meaning of existence in that realm of information for which we can have objective knowledge. John Hick, philosopher of religion, expresses this when he states: "We live as part of a continuous flow of events no one of which nor the ensemble of which is self-explanatory. The occurrence of each one is explained by reference to other earlier or simultaneous events" (79).

Many ask about the meaning of existence. American philosopher William James cites the thoughts of the Russian author Leo Tolstoy (as translated into French by G. Dumas):

What will be the outcome of what I do today? Of what I shall do tomorrow? What will be the outcome of all my life? Why should I live? Why should I do anything? Is there in life any purpose which the inevitable death which awaits me does not undo and destroy? .... "But perhaps," I often said to myself, "there may be something I have failed to notice or to comprehend. It is not possible that this condition of despair should be natural to mankind." And I sought for an explanation in all the branches of knowledge acquired by men. I questioned painfully and protractedly and with no idle curiosity. I sought, not with indolence, but laboriously and obstinately for days and nights together. I sought like a man who is lost and seeks to save himself, and I found nothing. I became convinced, moreover, that all those who before me had sought for an answer in the sciences have also found nothing. And not only this, but that they have recognized that the very thing which was leading me to despair, the meaningless absurdity of life, is the only incontestable knowledge accessible to man. (131-2)

Al: I see what you are talking about. I get the message. Let's go on to the next chapter.

Wait a minute. I want to know who you are. And where are your quote marks?

Al: You mean, where are my quotation marks.

Yes, you know what I mean.

Al: Well, where are your quotation marks?

I don't need them. I am the author. Where are yours?

Al: *And I don't want italics either!*

You don't have to get emotional about it.

Al: Let me make a deal with you. If we forget about quotation marks and italics, I will make occasional interesting comments about the text.

Initial Remarks

Can I count on that? Your comments will be interesting and constructive, will they?

Al: I agree to that. In fact, you can quote me on that.

I still don't know who you are.

Al: I am Al. You are familiar with the term "et al," aren't you?

Yes.

Al: According to Merriam Webster's Collegiate Dictionary, et al means "and others" (1383). But that term is really referring to me. I am the Al they are talking about when they say "et al." I am the other person.

I'm glad you clarified that. Let's get back to the part that might be making you uncomfortable. We want to have a real feel for this. It is important. Concern about the meaninglessness of existence is a significant source of impetus toward a spiritual life. I would like to cite a couple of more authors.

Al: Well, I am getting depressed.

You will be happy by the end of this book.

Al: Can I count on that?

No, but I am an optimist. Please don't suffer too much with this next quote. The French philosopher Blaise Pascal could envisage the full horror of a world that seemed empty of ultimate meaning or significance:

> When I see the blind and wretched state of man, when I survey the whole universe in its dumbness and man left to himself with no light, as though lost in this corner of the universe, without knowing who put him there, what he has come to do, what will become of him when he dies, incapable of knowing anything, I am moved to terror, like a man transported in his sleep to some terrifying desert island, who wakes up quite lost with no means of escape. Then I marvel that so wretched a state does not drive people to despair. (88)

In her book, *A History of God*, the British theologian Karen Armstrong quotes the German philosopher Friedrich Nietzsche: "Everything that had previously given human beings a sense of direction had vanished. The death of God would lead to unparalleled despair and panic. 'Is there still an above and below?' cried the madman in his anguish. 'Do we not stray, as though through an infinite nothingness?' " (356)

Al: That is a triple quote: Armstrong quoting Nietzsche quoting the madman. That could be confusing.

Confusion would not be a bad alternative to meaninglessness. However, I will try to keep things clear.

Many have described despair over the lack of meaning in their lives. There is a desire for significance, for meaning, and a need to be relieved from doubt and despair. Armstrong states: "Human beings cannot endure emptiness and desolation; they will fill the vacuum by creating a new focus of meaning" (399).

LOCALIZED LIFE; ENLARGED LIFE

Let's look at the other side of things. Many who do not have some spiritual orientation are not in despair and are not concerned with meaninglessness. Regarding spirituality, we can see two opposite outlooks. One direction is toward finding some meaning in life. On the other hand, many seem to be unconcerned about meaning or spirituality.

For many, life may seem more-or-less complete: take out the garbage, have dinner, see a movie, work—all of life's activities. If there are not too many disturbing problems, life may go on without an apparent need for that spiritual orientation which can lift a person out of everyday life and into the sphere of an enlarged awareness of things.

In fact, in our modern life, the world beyond everyday life is available at all times with the push of a button. Television viewing is continuously available. Although not usually recognized as such, television becomes, in effect, a god for many. It is a ready source to transform the mind, moving the consciousness into ever new experience. But television is a false god. I will elaborate on the effects of television in Chapter Eight.

A fullness of life may not seem like an option to some people. Some individuals are not aware that it is possible to live a life that includes happiness. In addition, there are some people who seem to avoid happiness in the belief that they don't deserve it, probably due to some distorted psychologic mechanism.

Aside from those who have lives that are adequately fulfilling, at least for now, and aside from those who have no inclination to change unhappy situations or outlooks, let's consider the rest of us. For many of us, a life that would be centered totally on the self is incomplete. While involvement in work or projects beyond the self may be fulfilling, a need is often sensed for an additional dimension, an enlarged sense of awareness that encompasses something more. Many do sense that a completely self-centered life is generally a life that is inadequate or even self-defeating. We won't go into detail at this time; the subject of self-centeredness will be taken up in Chapter Six. However, I will point to a phrase used by William James regarding what can be considered as one of the more extreme outcomes of the orientation of self-centeredness: "self-loathing, self-despair; an unintelligible and intolerable burden to which one is mysteriously the heir" (143).

If we are able to release ourselves from excess self-absorption, it may then become possible to sense an awareness of something beyond our own goals, aims, and desires. For many, the avenue for a release from the attitude of self-centeredness is a path in the direction of spirituality. In this larger awareness we might find that the spiritual orientation is not only an answer to meaninglessness of existence; it is also a fertile source of wonder and mystery.

Armstrong provides an excellent overview of the nature of religion, and, in doing so, includes this role of wonder and mystery as a part of a natural tendency toward spiritual expression:

> Yet my study of the history of religion has revealed that human beings are spiritual animals. Indeed, there is a case for arguing that *Homo sapiens* is also *Homo religiosus*. Men and women started to worship gods as soon as they became recognizably human; they created religions at the same time as they created works of art. This was not simply because they wanted to propitiate powerful forces; these early faiths expressed the wonder and mystery that seem always to have been an essential component of the human experience of this beautiful yet terrifying world. Like art, religion has been an attempt to find meaning and value in life, despite the suffering that flesh is heir to. Like any other human activity, religion can be abused, but it seems to have been something that we have always done. It was not tacked on to a primordially secular nature by manipulative kings and priests but was natural to humanity. (*xix*)

I believe that many of us have an inclination toward a larger awareness. A sense of enlarged awareness may provide us with a new perspective on those aspects of life into which our minds may have become channeled. Also, when there is an imaginative dimension to our enlarged awareness, our thoughts can be free and not bounded by the particulars of everyday life and objective realities. We may be drawn into experiencing a vague sense of the larger dimensions of existence. It is possible within our imaginations to become aware of much that is beyond our immediate experience. The sight of a mountain may be so magnificent that it sparks within us a vague sense of the mystery of all existence. It is possible to relax into the calm peace of freedom of the imagination, with an openness in which we release ourselves from our usual thoughts and directions.

The openness of an enlarged sense of awareness may give us a sense of freedom; we surrender ourselves to a freedom that lets our minds have experience without purposefully directing the thoughts into particular channels. This mental freedom is one of the characteristics of a spiritual orientation.

Al: Who bothers with that stuff anyway? We eat. We sleep. We work. We play—if that's what you would call running on a track or going to a basketball game. Who bothers with minds drifting in space?

Yes. Right. For many, the enlargement of the imagination is very remote from anything with which they are concerned. It seems foreign, something for dreamers and poets.

For some people, the larger scheme of things does come into view when facing crises. At times of grave misfortune, these individuals may become aware of and question the meaning of life and its tribulations. This questioning of the significance of life may lead to wondering about the meaning of existence in general. At these times, a person's thoughts may wander into the realm of the universal.

Of course, at these times of crisis, the universe may not seem all that grand. It may seem unfair or haphazard. In fact, chance and chaos are component qualities of the universe. We will elaborate on this in Chapter Twelve.

We have talked about the realization of the meaninglessness of existence. Now let's take a look at the disillusionment with a spiritual outlook. In this country I believe there is considerable doubt about the existence of God. It will be helpful to consider the course of the general outlook in this country since the 1940's. During World War II the mood of the country toward religion was generally traditional. I remember the popular saying, which referred to front-line troops: "There are no atheists in foxholes." Following the war I recall a shift in the public outlook toward an attitude of doubt about the existence of a deity. At least, doubt was presented in the popular press and could be inferred from a shift in the way the clergy was presented in some movies: superficial and bumbling. In the last century Nietzsche had made a statement that God is dead. As I recall, in the 1950's the "death of God" became a widespread concern in this country, a concern voiced in popular national publications. It was an alarming concept for the country—a new national problem.

However, since then, for a large segment of our nation's population, I believe that this concern with the "death of God" apparently has become immaterial. The general population seems to be less concerned with the existence of God. It doesn't matter to them. They might ask: "Why bother with that question?"

Many in our current culture do not seem to have a place for God. Many have become focussed on material consumption. Spiritual life seems foreign to them. Materialism tends to center a person on self-indulgence and self-image. Both of these are aspects of self-centeredness. With a materialistic orientation, deeper values are rarely sought or considered. Life is lived on a more superficial plane, acting and reacting to the immediacy of material wants.

For many, the general tone of life is an "I want" instead of an appreciation for what is. Let's look at a different path than "I want." An enlarged awareness has the potential for creating a positive outlook on life. The sense of enlarged awareness is a source for happiness.

Al: Let me interrupt here. I would not say that an enlarged awareness necessarily gives a person a positive outlook on life. For instance, T. S. Eliot and Leopardi did not seem to have a positive outlook. You might look again at the passages that you quoted. It appeared to me that those authors might have had an attitude of despair.

An enlarged awareness does not automatically guarantee happiness. When this enlargement of awareness is in the mode of thankfulness, we are more likely to experience happiness. The taking up of an outlook of thankfulness carries us beyond concern with our goals and desires. In this way an orientation of thankfulness enlarges our outlook. In addition, thankfulness implies a valuing of that for which we are thankful. Such valuation gives a positive tone to life. Therefore, an attitude of thankfulness is a source for happiness. We will talk about this further in an early chapter of the book.

In addition, when an enlarged awareness includes a sense of wonder and awe, this awareness may more likely become imaginative. Wonder and mystery can be experienced by a mind that has the freedom of an imaginative openness. Wonder, openness, and freedom of the mind are psychologic elements which incline us toward a positive outlook on life, a

God Unmasked; the Full Life Revealed

welcoming of that which is. This welcoming outlook is a source for appreciation and thankfulness.

Returning to our pervading cultural climate, God is indeed dead to many in our society who neither have nor want a spiritual dimension in their lives. Each day takes care of itself, more or less, until disaster strikes or till a realization develops of an emptiness, a hollowness in life. Then questioning of values may begin. And then, poor fortune and the realization of the haphazardness of life may lead to cynicism and despair.

There are many other possible outcomes to the questioning of values. Some might begin this questioning in spite of belief in God and, in fact, question that belief. Also, some conclude this questioning by directing themselves away from a sense of spirituality. Others have never had an awareness of the spiritual. Furthermore, many embark on a quest for the spiritual and founder in a ceaseless grasping for new orientations, for perpetually new sources of spirituality.

Certainly, many find relief from a materialistic orientation when they enter into the spiritual realm. Their lives may then become more meaningful. There may be more of a fullness to their lives. But there can be problems with some forms of spiritual fulfillment. Within their religious orientation, some individuals may hold ideals that are antagonistic to a fullness of life. For instance, they may be intolerant of exposure to any knowledge that might be construed as contrary to their beliefs. Furthermore, they may be intolerant of people who have different beliefs or appearances.

Various forms of religious practice have developed. In the course of history, movements of religious reformation and renewal have indeed emerged as new religions, seen by their adherents as separate from that from which they have sprung. Various sects have developed, each of which tends to see itself as "the true path".

Anthony Giddens, sociologist, has discussed the impetus toward new forms of religion:

> Not only has religion failed to disappear. We see all around us the creation of new forms of religious sensibility and spiritual endeavor. The reasons for this concern quite fundamental features of late modernity. What was due to become a social and physical universe subject to increasingly certain knowledge and control instead creates a system in which areas of relative security interlace with radical doubt and with disquieting scenarios of risk. Religion in some part generates the conviction which adherence to

the tenets of modernity must necessarily suspend: in this regard it is easy to see why religious fundamentalism has a special appeal. But this is not all. New forms of religion and spirituality represent in a most basic sense a return of the repressed, since they directly address issues of the moral meaning of existence which modern institutions so thoroughly tend to dissolve. (207)

Al: I can't disagree with you so far, that is, not that I am particularly trying to disagree with you.

And I am glad that you are agreeable, at least so far. Now let's summarize the foregoing sections. Existence does not seem to have meaning; many have expressed this. That is not to say that these were their final conclusions. For instance, Pascal found meaning in his religious beliefs. Furthermore, the emptiness associated with a lack of meaning has been a major factor in fueling the search for spirituality in its various forms. In the modern world the prevalence of an increased awareness of doubt has, at least for some, intensified the quest for a spiritual life.

DEFINITIONS

Al: I would like to say something here.

Go right ahead.

Al: We are talking about the spiritual life. According to Webster's dictionary, one definition of spirituality is "the sensitivity or attachment to religious values." Furthermore, the definition of the word "religious" is: "relating to or manifesting faithful devotion to an acknowledged ultimate reality or deity." By definition, religion is "the service and worship of God or the supernatural." And the definition of God is: "the supreme or ultimate reality," or: "the Being perfect in power, wisdom, and goodness who is worshiped as creator and ruler of the universe."

PROOF AND PROBLEMS

Al: But the actuality of God cannot be proven. I want to know if God exists: yes or no.

Let me put it this way. If the existence of God could be proven, then it would be just about another objective fact. It is in the nature of the concept of God that this concept cannot be proven.

Al: Well, that's interesting.

Armstrong points to the lack of objective knowledge about God: "We will only know our own 'God' since we cannot experience him objectively; it is impossible to know him in the same way as other people" (238).

Al: So, do you have the answer to the puzzle about the supernatural?

Do you doubt any answer?

Al: Yes. Frankly, I do.

That is the answer.

Al: What do you mean?

Well, that is part of the answer.

Al: You haven't explained what you mean.

Doubt is part of the answer. I will say at this point that there is a reason for the non-provability of God. There is an emotional content associated with the belief in God. We will enlarge upon this point later, but it can be said at this time that there must be a step of faith or at least some type of "proof" that is not accepted in a usual way that objective facts are accepted. As put by William James:

> ... the absence of definite sensible images is positively insisted on by the mystical authorities in all religions as the *sine qua non* of a successful orison, or contemplation of the higher divine truths. ... So we have the strange phenomenon, as Kant assures us, of a mind believing with all its strength in the real presence of a set of things of no one of which it can form any notion whatsoever. (59)

Al: Well, as you say, there are strongly held emotional beliefs in non-objective facts. That sounds like a formula for problems, for big troubles.

That is putting it mildly. Throughout history humans have inflicted much pain and suffering for the sake of God and religion. The fractiousness of religious belief is described by German philosopher Ernst Cassirer:

> (Religion) is fraught with theoretical antinomies and with ethical contradictions. It promises us a communion with nature,

Initial Remarks

with men, with supra-natural powers and the gods themselves. Yet its effect is the very opposite. In its concrete appearance it becomes the source of the most profound dissensions and fanatic struggles among men. Religion claims to be in possession of an absolute truth, but its history is a history of errors and heresies. (97-8)

In this vein I also quote parts of an article by James Haught in *The Oregonian* [originally in the *Charleston Gazette,* (W. Va.)]:

> Everyone knows the good face of faith. In Charleston, for instance, 'manna meals' are served at St. John's Episcopal Church to the down-and-out. Samaritan Inn provides shelter for the homeless. The Salvation Army cares for winos. The Mountain Mission gives furniture and clothes to the needy. . . . (other examples) . . . . All these things reinforce the universal belief that religion makes believers kind and caring. But what can explain the opposite result?
>
> As for the holy wars between ethnic groups, scholars and historians say the hatred isn't religious, it's cultural and political and economic.
>
> They're right—but they're wrong.
>
> It's true that many factors mingle in any human conflict; yet the chief dividing element in some horrors is faith.
>
> In Northern Ireland , how would two residents of Belfast know they're enemies if they didn't go to different churches? They look, speak, and dress alike. They live in similar houses.—Why don't their families intermarry, work together, socialize together and forget ancient grudges? Because religion keeps them alienated in hostile camps. 'Religious tribalism' is a name applied to it.
>
> In Bosnia-Herzegovina, next-door neighbors equally alike suddenly began killing each other. Why? Because they pray to different gods. Otherwise there would be no way to distinguish between the neighbors.
>
> Religion-based gore has been recurring for at least nine centuries. When Europe's Crusaders marched off to rid the Holy Land of infidels, they first paused to slaughter 'the infidel among us'—Jews living in Germany.
>
> The Holy Inquisition burned an estimated 200,000 women in the historic witch hunts.

The Reformation triggered scores of Catholic-Protestant wars, including the Thirty Years War, which killed half the population of Germany. England's Puritans and Anglicans waged ferocious combat. Anabaptists were executed by both Protestants and Catholics for the crime of double baptism. (E7)

Yes, there are immense problems with the manifestation of spirituality. The revelations of history show this time and again. But, in spite of these problems, it is true that there is within humans the need to express spirituality. Again Armstrong is quoted:

> The idea of a personal God, like one of us writ large, is fraught with difficulty. If this God is omnipotent, he could have prevented the Holocaust. If he was unable to stop it, he is impotent and useless; if he could have stopped it and chose not to, he is a monster. Jews are not the only people who believe that the Holocaust put an end to conventional theology.
>
> Yet it is also true that even in Auschwitz some Jews continued to study the Talmud and observe the traditional festivals, not because they hoped that God would rescue them but because it made sense. There is a story that one day in Auschwitz, a group of Jews put God on trial. They charged him with cruelty and betrayal. Like Job, they found no consolation in the usual answers to the problem of evil and suffering in the midst of this current obscenity. They could find no excuse for God, no extenuating circumstances, so they found him guilty and, presumably, worthy of death. The Rabbi pronounced the verdict. Then he looked up and said that the trial was over: it was time for the evening prayer. (376)

Psychologist Abraham Maslow also states this need for the expression of spirituality:

> People who might otherwise lose their "faith" will hang onto it because it gives a meaningfulness to the universe, a unity, a single philosophical explanation which makes it all hang together. Many orthodoxly religious people would be so frightened by giving up the notion that the universe has integration, unity, and, therefore, meaningfulness (which is given to it by the fact that it was all created by God or ruled by God or is God) that the only alternative for them would be to see the universe as a totally unintegrated chaos. (59-60)

PREVIEW

This book characterizes the qualities of the full life, including that aspect of life which may be said to be spiritual. Even though the spiritual aspect of life is included, there is a full commitment to the importance of doubt and truth.

Though the god concept and spirituality is explored in Part III, let's consider it first. Since I consider the god concept to be subjective, there will be no attempt to prove the existence of a supernatural consciousness in this book. But I do indicate the way in which subjective experience is valid and valuable, and I look at the interposition of subjectivity and objectivity. A correlation is made between the god concept in the subjective realm and an objective understanding of the nature of the universe. This provides one possible answer to the problem as stated by the French philosopher Gaston Bachelard: "The dramatic problem of philosophy is how to integrate scientific truths within human reality" (Imagination, *xviii*).

Many people are unaware of the effect of a scientific outlook on spirituality. To understand that effect on spirituality, first note that the scientific approach is comprehensive, encompassing all of existence. This scientific orientation to an understanding of the universe in all its aspects tends to lead to the destruction of traditional bases for spirituality. To many, the meaning of science is just an occasional interesting nature program to be watched on television. They do not appreciate that the heart of scientific progress is the ability to doubt in order to observe and hypothesize with fresh perceptiveness. And doubt is anathema to faith.

Also, some people may feel that the findings of science are just as incomprehensible as the claims of a religious belief. Therefore, they might consider that it is just as reasonable to believe one as the other.

As I previously stated, in this book I will demonstrate a reconciliation of the scientific and the spiritual. This may seem impossible. However, it is possible in a way that is not only acceptable, at least for some, but a valuable central theme for the valid fulfillment of life.

The second area of this book is an exploration of the psychological factors which predispose a person to an awareness of God.

The final topic, addressed throughout the book, is the description of basic factors in mental outlook that make possible the development of fullness of life, a wholeness of being.

Now for a more detailed review. Following the initial remarks of Part I, Part II describes those qualities of life that are intrinsic to a fullness of life. A mindfulness of these qualities is also necessary for an understanding of God as presented later in this book.

Later in Part II, in Chapter Six, I note the modern tendency toward self-absorption, and I take issue with it. In Chapter Seven I reconcile the thoughts of Nietzsche and Christ.

Al: Wait a minute here. Back up the philosophy train. That's not possible.

Let me modify what I said. I will reconcile parts of the thoughts of Nietzsche and of Christ as I interpret those parts. Incidentally, I will add that, though the words love and empathy are not synonymous, there is some similarity, and I will be using the word empathy in that chapter.

By the way, while on the subject of word usage, when using the word "cosmic," I do not refer to something hokey, just the word as defined in Webster's dictionary: "of or relating to the cosmos, the extraterrestrial vastness, or the universe in contrast to the earth alone."

Chapter Eight is concerned with social effects, and Chapter Nine integrates the entirety of Part II.

Part III elaborates on various aspects of spiritual life and bases those aspects on that which, in my point of view, is valid for personal life but not contrary to the orientation of science. The first three chapters of Part III present conceptual factors—both subjective and objective—involved in the understanding of God. These are further integrated in Chapter Fourteen. Later chapters in Part III elaborate on various aspects of spirituality.

Part IV brings together information presented in the whole book. Chapter Twenty three is a review of this information, and Chapter Twenty four presents the final and complete integration of the book.

To add to the previous summary, it seems apparent that existence has no meaning and that this belief has been widely experienced; several authors have been cited. The emptiness associated with the lack of meaning has been a major factor in fueling the search for spirituality in its various forms. In the modern world the prevalence of an increased awareness of doubt has, at least for some, intensified the quest for a spiritual life.

The openness to doubt and the inclination toward spiritual experience can be reconciled. The discerning openness of a scientific orientation does not necessarily mitigate against a valid expression of spirituality. This book reconciles the scientific and religious perspectives of life and of existence in general. Surprisingly, this reconciliation of the scientific and the religious reveals the elements of psychologic well-being.

PART II

FULL LIFE

1

Green Light

An Unimportant Conversation About Importance
Fantasia I
Fantasia II
Fantasia III
Serious Note

AN UNIMPORTANT CONVERSATION ABOUT IMPORTANCE

A: How important is your direction in life?

B: Direction? What direction? I just live. And work. And play. I'm not heartbroken because I can't play the zither.

A: But that's a real tragedy.

B: I survive.

A: Let's take the broad view.

B: I'll put on my glasses for this.

A: I hope you have surreal glasses.

(This chapter is in the realm of fantasia. Expect disconnected thoughts here. There is a reason. Do not be overly concerned about finding the reason at this point. If you are uncomfortable with a disrupted flow of words, it would be well for you to skip to Chapter Two.)

FANTASIA I

C: *Slide down the slide. Go ahead.*

D: *Right. I'll go first.*

(D slides down, and then C.)

C: *To the swings.*

D: *No. The teeter-totter. Phew. This is fun.*

Ow; that hurts. I fell off. And you got hurt, too.

In pain, we walk in the woods. The knurly trunks with scraggled limbs
    reach out to
        block our path
                and hold us in the
        pale green light
            Soft, white glow
    slightly green
           with leaves
    softly
                  rustling...

D: *Rustling? That's a hackneyed word.*

C: *Hackneyed word, you say. Why don't you suffer some more—from your fall off the teeter-totter?*

D: *You have a question mark at the end of that sentence, but you don't mean it as a question. You want me to suffer. You want me to have a painful anatomical part.*

C: *Pain again. I had hoped this wouldn't get too serious. I can still see the beautiful, green leaves. Even though I work ten hours a day, sometimes more.*

D: *And the state of your marriage is questionable. Is that a real chasm developing between you and your spouse?*

C: *All this work for nothing? Three years after your statement ten seconds ago. Time flies, and family life is down the tube. I occasionally see* the kids, who, thank God, are healthy. Will they get involved with street drugs? Are they on drugs now?

FANTASIA II

G: I say what I think.

E: Hey, wait. You're out of turn.

F: We get to speak first.

G: I have ideals. I know what's right. I stick by my principles and by the rightness of things.

E: Well spoken.

F: Well spoken.

G: Good. I commend you both. On the other hand, I condemn C and D. They did not say: "Well spoken."

C: Speech.

D: Speech.

G: That's not good enough.

(C dies, in disgrace, not having agreed to G's ideals.)

FANTASIA III

M, who looks much like C: I see a soft, green light.

Consolation.

I can relax. I just work eight hours a day now. In the evening I can rest. The day time

proceeds at a horrible pace.

Work hard

to keep up with the

competition

that works hard

Green Light

and harder
and harder
to keep up with me
and surpass me.
So I work harder
to surpass them,
to survive.
Survive?
What?
You say I will die?
When?
How long do I have to live?
Can't say?
But I can't get on the teeter-totter again?
And my heart will have to be amputated?
No, I can't survive that.
My disability is death.
I give up this life.
But I'm still talking.
How can I be dead? I still see the soft glow
the peaceful, green light
almost shimmering in the bits of yellow,
golden,
shining, glorious
substance of
space.
I live.

SERIOUS NOTE

The joy and wonder of childhood may fade in the light of subsequent knowledge. We learn about responsibility, the need for acceptance, and the various vagaries of life. We learn about work, love, marriage, deceit, pain, disease, and death.

Is there a common ground upon which the happiness of youth and the knowledge of life's contortions can both play? Is it possible for us to live a life that can be called "a full life?"

If there is a way to the full life, what is that way? How would we live to make a wholeness of life possible? An answer to this is what the next twenty three chapters are about.

Green Light

2

Doubt: the Path to Truth

Uncertainty Today
Doubt and Truth
Characteristics of Doublt
Summary

UNCERTAINTY TODAY

Let's start the main body of the text with the subject of doubt.

Al: Doubt is a downer. I don't want to start with doubt.

An access to doubt is very important. In this chapter I will go into some detail about why doubt is important. In addition, in Chapter Twenty two I will describe the process of minimizing doubt while maintaining a full openness to doubt.

Al: Chapter Twenty two? That's almost at the end of the book.

End of the book? Now it appears that we need to talk about patience. However, that is another subject, and it will also be brought up later. This chapter is centered on the topic of doubt.

There are and certainly have always been conflicting claims about knowledge. There are different points of view from which people characterize their knowledge, different points of view concerning where truth lies.

Al: You can say that, but I say that truth doesn't lie. People lie.

That's true, but we will let your comment lie, at least, let it recline.

Al: How do you let a comment recline?

With patience. Believe me: a comment lies with patience.

Al: I don't know what you mean.

I'm glad you question that. Questioning is characteristic of the path to truth. I wanted to say the word "patience" to lead into the next sentence. With patience we will explore the nature of truth.

Let's start with a particular problem in the modern era concerning the discernment of truth. The dissemination of information to the general public has accelerated with the advent of television. Also, an explosive advance of technical information has multiplied the number of ways of interpretation of this information. Differing opinions abound. We are exposed to various presentations of fact. Of course, information is not the problem. The difficulty lies not with the revelation of new information but with the ability of individuals to evaluate the validity of this information.

For instance, consider conflicting claims presented by a number of authorities concerning the health effects of foods. A kaleidoscopic sampling of opposing points of view shows: fatty foods are harmful, which fatty foods are harmful, who disagrees with that and says other fatty foods are harmful, and I have even heard it said that most fatty foods are beneficial.

There are often a variety of opinions in many realms of knowledge, including differing evaluations by those with expertise. The variations in risk assessment contribute to a climate of doubt. Truth is elusive.

In his book *Modernity and Self-identity,* sociologist Anthony Giddens talks about risk assessment and doubt. He states: ". . .in circumstances of late modernity, many forms of risk do not admit of clear assessment, because of the mutable knowledge environment which frames them; and even risk assessments within relatively closed settings are often only valid 'until further notice' " (32). He went on to say:

> The point, to repeat, is not that day-to-day life is inherently more risky than was the case in prior eras. It is rather that, in conditions of modernity, for lay actors as well as for experts in specific fields, thinking in terms of risk and risk assessment is a more or less ever-present exercise, of a partly imponderable character. It should be remembered that we are all laypeople in respect of the vast majority of the expert systems which intrude on our daily activities. The proliferation of specialisms goes together with the advance of modern institutions, and the further narrowing of specialist areas seems an inevitable upshot of technical development. The more specialisms become concentrated, the smaller the field in which any given individual can claim expertise; in other areas of life she or he will be in the same

situation as everyone else. Even in fields in which experts are in a consensus, because of the shifting and developing nature of modern knowledge, the "filter-back" effects on lay thought and practice will be ambiguous and complicated. The risk climate of modernity is thus unsettling for everyone; no one escapes. (123-4)

Yes, we live in an era of uncertainty.

Al: You say "era of uncertainty." But every generation has its uncertainties.

Some uncertainties are the same throughout history and some are different. I will cite an example of changing concerns in the health field. In the past people were fearful of getting poliomyelitis. This had been a major problem, and therefore it was an element in the panorama of doubts about future health. With the advent of effective vaccination, we no longer have this concern about polio. However, new information and new problems have developed in the health field: AIDS, increased bacterial resistance to antibiotics, increase in the scope of management of the diseases of aging, etc.

Not only have new problems developed; the general public awareness of these problems has greatly increased in tandem with the enormous development of technical information and accelerated dissemination of this information. A sense of risk accompanies this awareness; when exposed to increased information and conflicting claims, people have an enlarged realization of potential risks. Concern about increased risks and uncertainty about opposing claims regarding these risks feeds a climate of doubt.

In reaction to this climate of doubt, the sense of uncertainty fuels a need to overcome the doubt pattern with definite answers. Doubt is unsettling, and we usually have the desire to rid ourselves of doubt. We want a foundation of certainty. Over three hundred years ago Blaise Pascal, French philosopher, was referring to religious experience when he exclaimed: "Certainty, certainty, heartfelt, joy, peace" (309).

However, intolerance for uncertainty can lead to many problems. In fact, the need for certainty has often resulted in dire consequences, in both pain-provoking attitudes and destructive actions. In this regard, the certainty of religious and political dogmas has often led to the creation of pain and suffering.

DOUBT AND TRUTH

Let's look further at the effect of an attitude of uncertainty on people's lives. The need for the feeling of certainty is quite important for many. For some, the sense of certainty is more important than being limited by an objective outlook; the feeling of certainty is more important for them than objective reality. In fact, surprisingly, the understanding of actuality may be seen to be antagonistic to the sense of certainty. Eric Hoffer, longshoreman/philosopher, elaborates on this subject:

> The effectiveness of a doctrine does not come from its meaning but from its certitude. No doctrine however profound and sublime will be effective unless it is presented as the embodiment of the one and only truth. It must be the one word from which all things are and all things speak. Crude absurdities, trivial nonsense and sublime truths are equally potent in readying people for self-sacrifice if they are accepted as the sole, eternal truth.
>
> It is obvious, therefore, that in order to be effective a doctrine must not be understood, but has to be believed in. We can be absolutely certain only about things we do not understand. A doctrine that is understood is shorn of its strength. (76)

Al: You are talking about establishment of unfounded truths. When put this way, it seems ridiculous.

Yes. In his masterpiece, *Don Quixote*, Miguel de Cervantes expresses this quite well:

> "Sir Knight," he said, "we do not know who this beauteous lady is of whom you speak. Show her to us, and if she is as beautiful as you say, then we will right willingly and without any compulsion confess the truth as you have asked of us."
>
> "If I were to show her to you," replied Don Quixote, "what merit would there be in your confessing a truth so self-evident? The important thing is for you, without seeing her, to believe, confess, affirm, swear, and defend that truth." (1200)

I will point out the effect of our interests and prejudices on perception. We often guide our vision toward that which we want to see, and that may be quite different from actuality. Not infrequently, we have inadequate doubt about our perceptions. Again I quote Cervantes: "The dust clouds he had sighted were raised by two large droves of sheep coming along the road in opposite directions, which by reason of the dust were not visible until they were close at hand, but Don Quixote insisted so earnestly that they were armies that Sancho came to believe it" (1250).

Information from external sources influences our perceptions, and our own interests affect how we see things. Our view of actuality is warped by attitudes—by subjective input. Three authors are cited in this regard. British philosopher Stuart Hampshire points to the fact that a person's perception selects facts relevant to his or her concerns (309). The projection of our attitudes is described by the literary theorist Kenneth Burke: "

> … our interests shape our "perceptions" of objects. This brings us close to the "pathetic fallacy" in its purity: the tendency to find our own moods in the things outside us. And the equivalent for this, in the intellectual plane, would be the tendency to find our own patterns of thought in the texture of events outside us. (214)

Simone Weil, French philosopher, points to the occurrence of distorted perception, preconceptions, and to the need for detachment. She indicates that we project predispositions of the self into that which we would call "reality." As she says: "Attachment is a manufacturer of illusions…" (259). Weil also describes the loss of a sense of self-awareness during exploration of truth: "To empty ourselves of the world…. To reduce ourselves to the point we occupy in space and time—that is to say, to nothing…. Then we possess the truth of the world" (257).

Al: I want to say something about preconceptions here. Preconceptions are valuable; they are a mental tool that we use all the time. The word "preconception" has a pejorative tone. Let's circumvent that by using an alternate word, "belief," which has a more positive connotation. And I'll add this: it is not true that all established viewpoints are necessarily counter-productive. Many are highly valuable. When we look with favor upon such viewpoints, we are more likely to call them "beliefs," and when attitudes are destructive, we might call them preconceptions.

Well said; I see your point. And here is an example of the favorable use of a pre-established mind-set to guide me. When I plant a blueberry bush, I don't disregard my preconceptions or beliefs. I have certain preconceptions; I direct my vision in certain ways. For instance, I look for a shovel. I find the right spot to plant the blueberry bush. I am not completely open to all things in front of me. My perception is directed.

Al: Right. Inclinations and aims guide us. But it is valuable to maintain the capacity to be open to new understanding. The "right" spot may be a poor place for the blueberry bush, with inadequate sunlight and soil drainage.

Ideally, there is a mental flow between the directedness of our activities and openness to new perception. It is well to maintain an openness to the awareness of that which is new and not be entirely focussed on the direction of the self. This openness employs the availability of detachment from our preconceptions and attachments and an ability to doubt these same preconceptions and attachments.

Of course, in talking about the interweaving of openness and focus on direction, I do not mean to disregard those instances where total focus is indicated and appropriate. Some situations require total focus, for instance, when life is endangered.

There is value in having a measure of detachment regarding that toward which we may be excessively concerned. On the other hand, detachment can be overdone. Happy situations and happy relationships call for a full measure of joyful interaction. It is not valuable to conjoin detachment, doubt, and hesitancy to such joy. In these felicitous circumstances, it is well to forget about doubt and detachment.

However, if problems lurk, reality should not be denied. The inclination toward doubt and detachment is a path toward truth. Detachment affords some distance from preconceptions and provides the mental climate in which doubt can take place. And doubt opens the possibility for new understanding of reality, a new discernment of that which might be called "truth."

At this point we will dip into ancient Eastern wisdom, citing two passages from the Tao Te Ching:

> Not-knowing is true knowledge.
> Presuming to know is a disease.
> First realize that you are sick;
> then you can move toward health. (71)

A second quote from the Tao points to some of the characteristics of that uncertainty which accompanies the search for truth and also describes the outward appearance of those who have the humility to doubt:

> The path into the light seems dark,
> the path forward seems to go back,
> the direct path seems long,
> true power seems weak,
> true purity seems tarnished,

God Unmasked; the Full Life Revealed

> true steadfastness seems changeable,
> true clarity seems obscure,
> the greatest art seems unsophisticated,
> the greatest love seems indifferent,
> the greatest wisdom seems childish. (41)

The value of doubt is expressed in ancient Greek philosophy; Plato's quotation of Socrates is noted: ". . . I am better off than he is,—for he knows nothing, and thinks that he knows; I neither know nor think that I know" (436).

In the search for truth, an individual may look for an authority upon whom one can entirely depend, but there is a lack of any totally reliable authority. No person has a lock on truth.

The utilization of doubt as a tool in the search for truth does not mean that you wallow in an excess of doubt. Overindulgence in doubt can turn a person into a caricature, into someone who has an automated response. In his novel, *Lord Jim,* Joseph Conrad said: "Wherefore this craving for incertitude, this clinging to fear…" (360). William James also remarked about this: "To admit one's liability to correction is one thing, and to embark upon a sea of wanton doubt is another" (260).

Although he warned about excess doubt, James did indicate the following: "I am no lover of disorder and doubt as such. Rather do I fear to lose truth by this pretension to possess it already wholly" (261).

Of course, no one wants to flounder in a sea of doubt. A balanced view shows that it is far more satisfactory to accept truths that seem reasonable. These truths are then acted upon while holding the truths as tentative and subject to possible future modification as new information becomes available.

Furthermore, as I said, many circumstances and many interpersonal relations may be quite satisfactory and fulfilling. Recourse to doubt and detachment in such situations is not only not necessary; it may be deleterious. In Chapters Twenty one and Twenty two I discuss this and relate it to the development of trust.

CHARACTERISTICS OF DOUBT

Let's now look at the characteristics of doubt. It embodies a willingness to look at things with a fresh point of view, unencumbered by preconceptions. We can doubt our predisposed outlook on that which we see before us.

Al: That's a laugh. I interrupt again. There is not a single person who is able to be entirely free of preconceptions. Everyone carries some mental "baggage." And another thing: we have our beliefs. What may appear as mental baggage to one person is a belief to another. One person's preconception is another person's belief. I'd like to repeat something you said: not all preconceptions are bad. That mental content which we bring to situations often gives us helpful guidance. For instance, I believe excess caffeine drinks may be harmful. Therefore, I limit that indulgence. I think you mean this: we allow for those preconceptions that have been substantiated as reasonable. These are our beliefs. Beyond this allowance for beliefs, we minimize our utilization of preconceptions as much as possible in order to approach more closely to the truth.

You put words in my mouth. I certainly agree with that. And I will add a further dimension. Freedom from attachments and desires includes freedom from the distortion that can occur if the search for truth is pursued in an unproductive manner. In certain instances, the concern for learning truth might not be worthwhile. Some questions have no answers, or the answers may be impossible to find at the time, requiring patience for later information. Patience and acceptance are utilized when a person has some measure of tolerance for uncertainty and doubt.

We should realize that uncertainty is a characteristic of the nature of life. We are not sure we will have life in the next hour. We are not sure that excess rain won't destroy the vegetable crop. We are …

Al: Enough. I get the point.

Well, I do want to add this: uncertainty extends not only to the future. We are not sure of the present and of the past. We have limited information and at least partially limited understanding. The capacity for uncertainty and doubt is a welcome capability; this capacity for uncertainty and doubt can provide us with an openness to new comprehension of what is and what has been.

Truth is not a golden goal. Truth is a tentative revelation, a partial view of actuality. The availability of the inclination to doubt is a valid component of all truth.

Doubt helps us to release ourselves from preconceptions. Any certainties should be considered temporary and subject to possible future change. It is well to have an openness to new information and be free to doubt all. We should welcome the doubt component of truth and know that a complete revelation of truth is not possible. To quote Conrad: "... truth, which, like Beauty itself, floats elusive, obscure, half submerged, in the silent still waters of mystery" (248).

We not only welcome doubt as an adjunct to truth. In addition, we recognize doubt as a prime component of the modern outlook. Anthony Giddens describes the pervasiveness of doubt in our current era:

> Doubt, a pervasive feature of modern critical reason, permeates into everyday life as well as philosophical consciousness, and forms a general existential dimension of the contemporary social world. Modernity institutionalizes the principle of radical doubt and insists that all knowledge takes the form of hypotheses: claims which may very well be true, but which are in principle always open to revision and may have at some point to be abandoned (3).

Now let's consider the subject of confidence in doubt.

Al: That doesn't sound right. Doubt means uncertainty, a wavering. Doubt seems to be the opposite of the assurance of certainty.

Confidence in doubt is confidence in method, that is, in the method of learning that degree of truth which is ascertainable at the time while recognizing such truth as tentative. A person develops confidence in openness, in freedom to scan for any hindering perceptions and attitudes—confidence in having the capacity for doubt of attitudes and perceptions. This confidence arises from the realization that doubt provides the freedom to see things with fresh vision. Doubt allows a closer approach to truth, and this is the welcome result for those who would doubt.

The capacity for doubt, then, is one of the factors that leads to a sense of wholeness, a sense of fullness of life. Doubt is a part of the full life because, with an openness to doubt, you will know that your outlook is based on that amount of truth which is most possible to be obtained at that time.

In spite of its value, some people are highly intolerant of doubt. The acceptance of doubt by some and intolerance for it by others is described by James:

> If we claim only reasonable probability, it will be as much as men who love the truth can ever at any given moment hope to have within their grasp. Pretty surely it will be more than we could have had if we were unconscious of our liability to err.

Doubt: the Path to Truth

Nevertheless, dogmatism will doubtless continue to condemn us for this confession. The mere outward form of inalterable certainty is so precious to some minds that to renounce it explicitly is for them out of the question. They will claim it even where the facts most patently pronounce its folly.... When larger ranges of truth open, it is surely best to be able to open ourselves to the reception, unfettered by our previous pretensions. (260)

It is my opinion that, aside from theological questioning, a religious outlook usually tends to discourage doubt and find certainty in faith. On the other hand, theologian Leslie DeWart describes the impetus toward doubt in the process of seeking truth and sees this tendency to doubt as a possible manifestation of his faith, a possible component of Christianity. I quote from his book, *The Future of Belief*: " ... there may be something in the nature of man, in the nature of experience, in the nature of truth, and possibly even in the nature of the Christian faith, that impels man to look ever deeper into the truth and indeed, to be dissatisfied with the very truth of what he holds to be true" (89). We will further discuss doubt and religious practice in a later chapter.

Let's take a look now at the nature of science. Doubt is at the heart of scientific inquiry. Development of knowledge in the realm of science depends upon the utilization of doubt, which facilitates an openness to new truths. The realization that truths are tentative and subject to doubt can create a confidence in this method because openness to a new understanding of truth often leads to new discoveries. Ideally, in scientific pursuit, that which is thought to be true is held as just tentative truth. Bachelard indicates: "Science educates itself through the continuous and collective process of error correction and is by nature in a state of constant pedagogy" (Imagination *xxv*). As stated by Giddens: "Science depends, not on the inductive accumulation of proofs, but on the methodological principle of doubt. No matter how cherished, and apparently well established, a given scientific tenet might be, it is open to revision—or might have to be discarded altogether—in the light of new ideas or findings" (21).

SUMMARY

It's time for a summary. The climate of doubt and uncertainty has increased in the modern era of mass communication and technical specialization. In reaction to uncertainty, the certainty of religious and political dogmas and slogans can have and often has had disastrous consequences for human well-being.

Inadequate doubt, preconceptions, and excessive psychological attachments can lead to warped perception. In utilizing doubt as a method to learn truth, however, ideally a person should not hesitate to act when the situation calls for action, even though it is known that the truth of information acted upon is only tentatively valid. Excess soul-searching can be debilitating, leading to inaction at a time when action is reasonable.

Doubt involves detachment from preconceptions and psychological attachments, and the utilization of doubt can lead to tentative truth. It is true that all truth is tentative and open to doubt. This is so in personal life and in the larger social realms. The utilization of doubt and the realization of the tentativeness of truth is also at the heart of scientific inquiry.

Confidence is the natural accompaniment of the utilization of doubt as a means to learning tentative truths. We experience confidence because we know that the truths we believe in do not entail denial of the test of questioning and because we do not fear further questioning. We remain open to new understanding of truth.

This confidence in the efficacy of doubt is important as one of the major components in the fulfillment of life.

3

Wonder, Thankfulness

Look at that sky. Streaks of clouds
    lifting into white, soft
        strands . . . almost like
            cotton wisps, lifting into the
                sunlit breeze of
                    early summer
                        air.

Al: Wait a second. We just finished a chapter about doubt and truth, about detached perception. Now you've got poetry—or something like poetry. You're going in an opposite direction. What's going on here?

Yes. Let's get back down to earth. With doubt and detachment, reality can be more clearly perceived. With clear perception, we can have a fresh look at things. That which had previously been seen as familiar becomes fresh and novel; it becomes new to us and a potential source for wonder.

In considering the topics of novelty and wonder, we are led to a concern about the nature of subjectivity and its converse, objectivity. Let's look at a certain interrelationship between objectivity and subjectivity. Objectivity involves the inclination toward finding that which can be called "truth" and acknowledges the tentative nature of truth. With objectivity, we can observe the world as clearly as possible. However, we include the subjective aspect of perception when there is a degree of wonder. Furthermore, subjective input affects the objectivity of perception. The same perceptive experience contains elements of both objectivity and subjectivity. We perceive a degree of objective input of sensory perception while, regarding the subjective aspect, we emotionally guide and interpret this perception. For example, when I look at a rose, I see certain color patterns—in an objective sense—and this meshes with the subjective aspect: wonder for the beauty of these color patterns which so impress me.

Particularly, the subjective element of wonder has special value. Consider how often things are taken for granted. A sense of wonder adds new insight to perception of the objective world. The understanding of actuality becomes enhanced when a sense of wonder accompanies perception. To quote author Joseph Conrad:

> "It's extraordinary how we go through life with eyes half shut, with dull ears, with dormant thoughts.—there can be but few of us who had never known one of these rare moments of awakening when we see, hear, understand ever so much—everything—in a flash—before we fall back again into our agreeable somnolence." (164)

The impulse to wonder can become deadened when there is conscious effort towards attaining a sense of wonder. I will elaborate on this point: instead of a preconceived directedness toward wonder, receiving the gift of wonder is made possible by a relaxation into an appreciation of the sensations of the moment. It is true that the desire for wonder can set the stage for an openness to experience wonder. However, too conscious an effort to experience wonder can make that experience impossible to attain. When a person releases himself or herself from directedness and becomes open to the freshness of present experience, the realization of wonder is nurtured.

The French philsospher Albert Camus describes the loss of the facility for wonder: "A day comes when, thanks to rigidity, nothing causes wonder any more, everything is known ..." (Sisyphus 141).

Al: That happens. No sense of wonder; things taken for granted. It's not uncommon.

But now consider the contentment of wonder:

Without words

the sun brilliance

flows

into clouds

and to streaks;

dulled yellow,

losing, fading,

softly,

>   *to the night;*
> *to the blue*
>   *of sky,*
>   *of ocean—*
> *the hush and whisper,*
>   *speaking*
>   *without words.*

The joy of wonder is expressed by the French author Jean-Jacques Rousseau:

> The sound of the bells, which always singularly affects me, the song of the birds, the beauty of the daylight, the enchanting landscape, the scattered country dwellings in which my fancy placed our common home—all these produced upon me an impression so vivid, tender, melancholy and touching, that I saw myself transported, as it were, in ecstasy, into that happy time and place, wherein my heart, possessing all the happiness it could desire, tasted it with inexpressible rapture, without even a thought of sensual pleasure. I never remember to have plunged into the future with greater force and illusion than on that occasion ....
> (1634)

Al: I agree with you in that things can often be too easily taken for granted. I realize that, if perception is enhanced by wonder, familiar experiences can become joyful.

Yes. You see what I mean. Now let's go on to a special consideration—a consideration of prime importance. While you are reading this book, you are alive. You and I have life. And look beyond our lives: that tree exists; the grass and bees exist. Yes, we exist; we are still alive. At the very least, I am alive as long as I am writing this book. And I would like to point out that it is wondrous that we have existence.

The wonder of existence is described by John Hick:

> ... the odds against one's own present existence are truly prodigious. To take just one link fairly close to hand in the vast chain of improbabilities: in order for me now to exist my parents had to meet and conceive me. That these two particular individuals, out of all their contemporaries in the same social milieu, should have married is statistically highly improbable. But

when they conceived me that improbability was thereby multiplied many million-fold. For the male contribution to conception consists of some three to six hundred million sperm—say, on average, four hundred million—each of which is unique in the genetic code that it carries. (88)

Hick then discusses chromosome arrangements and randomness and goes on to summarize:

> The antecedent improbability of an individual being conceived who is precisely *me* is thus already quite staggering. But a comparable calculation applies to each of my parents, and then to each of their parents and grandparents and great grandparents, and so on back through all the generations of human life, with the odds against my own present existence multiplying at each stage. The resulting improbability of my now existing, on the basis of this one factor of genetic inheritance alone, is accordingly truly astronomical. But it still has to be multiplied by the improbability of all the innumerable other conditions required at each successive moment for distinctively human history to have occurred, and before that for the wider evolution of life on this earth, and before that for the formation of galaxies and our solar system, and before that for the whole cosmic evolution of the universe back to the big bang. As a result the antecedent improbability that the unique individual who is *me* should now exist is inconceivably great. To say that I am lucky to be alive is a monumental understatement! (89)

He adds that the same kind of calculation applies to everyone and everything else in the universe.

A brief quote from Zen master Shunryu Suzuki expresses a similar sentiment: "…whatever we do is unusual, because our life itself is so unusual" (53).

I will relate a personal note that will help you to know one of the reasons why I have a sense of awe and wonder toward life. In 1946, shortly after my seventeenth birthday, I joined the Army for an eighteen month stint. My Army time included one year of service in Korea. At the end of my tour of duty, I received a discharge from the Army at Ft. Lawton in Seattle. At that time I decided to locate some of my blood-line relatives in Spokane, Washington. I should inform you that, at age twelve, my mother had told me about my adoption and also about the deaths of my natural parents in Spokane when I was an infant.

I remember the long bus ride through that night in November, 1947, from Seattle to Spokane. I slept in short stretches and every so often would waken to see small town bus stops and the wide, rolling, sparsely vegetated stretches of the central Washington landscape. The night was clear and dim starlight was its brightness. In that distance of time I don't recall moonlight.

In the morning it only took two phone calls to locate my aunt and uncle. I found their pawn shop and met them. They were surprised in more ways than one. In their calculations they had thought that at that time I would have been an eighteen year old high school student. Instead, what they saw was a Staff Sergeant in uniform, just back from service in Korea.

I met more in the family and learned more about the circumstances of the death of my parents. As I indicated earlier in this book, my mother had died five weeks after I was born. She had had a post-partum complication: a blood clot (embolism) that traveled to the lungs. Three week later my father committed suicide.

Al: Now that's a commitment a person sticks with.

This is no time for jokes. Of course, I'm not still in mourning. That was a long time ago. Many things can happen in a person's life, and there are plenty of events that can be seen to justify carrying a sense of regret, pain, and misery through life. Also, for me, there is another aspect of my view of life which few others have. If I had never had life, my parents would both probably have lived many years longer. My very existence could be seen as a source of guilt for the death of my parents.

There is, then, this question: how do I view my existence? What is to be the general underpinning of my outlook on life? What will be my orientation to life?

Enough has happened, including events of subsequent years, to justify remaining in a state of misery, regret, and guilt. But as to the events of my infancy, I obviously had no intent to cause any problem, such as someone's death. By centering on intent rather than the bare facts, I could accept life as it comes.

In looking further, the circumstances surrounding the beginning of my existence have made me more aware of the fact of existence. Life is not something I take for granted. Existence, for me, is something wondrous. The fact of life fills me with wonder.

Most matter in the universe is elemental: random atoms and whatever else the physicists tell us is in the cosmic stew. Most of existence has no

Wonder, Thankfulness

sight and no consciousness. But, instead of scattered bits of matter blindly circling in the universe, my being is real, a stupendously intricate array of chemicals that provides me with the capacity to move, the capacity to see and hear, and the capacity to enjoy that bounty which life presents. I am in awe and wonder for the fact of my existence.

Enough about me. Let's carry on the discussion. There is a particular technique which can be helpful for appreciating a wonder for things. It involves mental projection into a future time when you will not exist. You then visualize that which will likely continue to exist. The freeways are still full of cars. World news is still being reported at 6PM. Your grandson has just become a grandfather. All things evolve into a newness of each moment. When seen from this point of view, the presence of all that exists in each moment can be seen with new wonder—new wonder of the past, now, and the future.

A realization of the time beyond the period of existence of the self may afford a release from an excess centeredness on the self and toward a more comprehensive understanding of existence. Also, when your awareness is in the projected realm of the future, you can visualize back to the time of present life and thereby gain a new perspective on current life. Everything in the present can take on a slightly different appearance. Things may not look quite the same as before, and, with this new perception, we are presented with the possibility of a deeper understanding of that which exists.

The essence of this reverie of future vision can be carried forward into everyday life. While you would not expect such an awareness to be continuous, it could nevertheless be quite worthwhile at times.

I can mention another technique, but I will warn that it may seem inconceivable to some. Picture the converse. We look at the past with hindsight, knowing that humanity will appear in a later part of the course of evolution. But humanity need not have necessarily appeared. In the great expanse of limitless time and limitless space, or space and time limited to inconceivably vast dimensions, human consciousness and awareness might never have developed. The universe—the vastness of empty space populated by unthinking and unseeing masses of seething atomic events—might never have included the human ability to search into, and wonder at, the secrets of existence. If we can set aside the preoccupation with our own agendas, we may realize that we, and all of life, might never have existed. The completely wondrous fact of our existence is something about which we can surely marvel and give profound gratitude.

Al: I want to say something here. It is great to have a sense of wonder, but most of us are wrapped up in the problems of the present. It is not all that easy to maintain a sense of wonder when there are specific, major problems to be solved and failings to be corrected.

Yes. A lot can go wrong. However, it is true that some of the difficulties are not as problematic as they might seem. It is possible that many of the events and situations of life are perceived and interpreted in too negative a light. The circumstances may not be all that bad. Of course, there are real problems, as we all know.

Let's take a look at some of life's problems, particularly the primary problems that all of us face. Disability or disastrous fortune may be part of our lives. Certainly, we all face the ultimate fact of death.

Basic beliefs may help us in how we perceive difficulties, but these beliefs are sometimes brought into question. In this regard, Conrad describes the loss of reliance on basic beliefs:

> When your ship fails you, your whole world seems to fail you; the world that made you, restrained you, has taken care of you. It is as if the souls of men floating on an abyss and in touch with immensity had been set free for any excess of heroism, absurdity, or abomination. Of course, as with belief, thought, love, hate, conviction, or even the visual aspect of material things, there are as many shipwrecks as there are men…. (139-40)

In Charles Wallraff's book, which reviews the thought of German philosopher Karl Jaspers and quotes from his work, we find the following note about the insolubility of some difficulties:

> Unlike the problematic situations that we can easily manage, especially with the professional assistance of lawyers, pastors, counselors, and the like, these situations present insoluble problems that can be dealt with only in superficial and, in the end, futile ways. 'There are situations which remain essentially the same even if their momentary aspect changes and their shattering force is obscured: I must die, I must suffer, I must struggle, I am subject to chance, I involve myself inexorably in guilt.' One can take out life insurance, learn to say that there is no death, employ anesthetics, acquire first-rate weapons, and so on, but he can no more banish death, agony, or combat than he can avoid the fortuitous or live without sin and guilt. (142)

William James notes the difficult times in life: "The normal process of life contains moments as bad as any of those which insane melancholy is filled with" (138). He further states:

> In the healthiest and most prosperous existence, how many links of illness, danger, and disaster are always interposed? Unsuspectedly from the bottom of every fountain of pleasure, as the old poet said, something bitter rises up: a touch of nausea, a falling dead of the delight, a whiff of melancholy, things that sound a knell, for fugitive as they may be, they bring a feeling of coming from a deeper region and often have an appalling convincingness. The buzz of life ceases at their touch as a piano-string stops sounding when the damper falls upon it.
>
> Of course the music can commence again;—and again and again,—at intervals. But with this the healthy-minded consciousness is left with an irremediable sense of precariousness. It is a bell with a crack; it draws its breath on sufferance and by an accident. (118)

The fleeting nature of life is described in the Old Testament:

> For the living know that they shall die: but the dead know not any thing, neither have they any more a reward; for the memory of them is forgotten.
>
> Also their love, and their hatred, and their envy, is now perished; neither have they any more a portion for ever in any thing that is done under the sun (Eccl. 9: 5-6).

The realization of life's vulnerability can present more than just a negative connotation. The sense of vulnerability may have not only a negative side; the awareness of vulnerability can also carry with it an affirming quality. This realization of vulnerability presents the possibility for an enlarged sense of awareness of life and its place in the universal nature of things. It becomes possible to have the awareness of life's precariousness lead to an enhanced comprehension of and appreciation for life.

I will describe a parallel regarding appreciation for that which is realized as temporary. In areas that have harsh winters, the fall weather, with its mild days, is likely to be more appreciated because of the realization that it is coming to an end. The anticipated finish of pleasant weather tends to enhance the appreciation of that weather. Likewise, in becoming more aware of the temporary nature of life, we may be better able to appreciate the magnificent gift of existence which nature has provided us.

The awareness of vulnerability can be a source for a sense of thankfulness, for gratefulness for that which we, in fact, do have. The recognition of good fortune, health, and life as temporary—this recognition of impermanence—can fuel a sense of thankfulness for those gifts which we have. The realization of the fleeting nature of life can be a source for appreciation. We can have gratitude for life and that amount of good fortune and good health with which we are blessed by the fortunes of existence.

Consider the following perspective on death. This is a universe of occasional clumps of atoms and fragments of matter immersed in huge expanses of empty space. There are infinitesimal odds against development of life forms—and then of humanity with its consciousness and awareness. And further, as previously indicated, it is against unbelievably huge odds that we have existence. Each of us is a product of the union of one particular egg and sperm, an end process of similar previous repetitions from time immemorial, each a single event against huge odds. We have this fantastic gift of life. Would it not seem ungrateful toward that which gave us life and health to bury our outlook with the negatives of life?

To emphasize this last point social psychologist David Myers is quoted: "Facing the terror of our mortality, being aware of life's impermanence, also adds value to our present moments" (202). And to quote from Hick: "The consciousness of our chancy and insecure place in the scheme of things can nevertheless induce a swirling intellectual vertigo. It can also elicit a sense of gratitude and responsibility in face of the extraordinary fact of our existence" (90).

An outlook of thankfulness can carry with it an attitude of acceptance of that which must be accepted, living in harmony with that which cannot be changed. Thankfulness also can create a positive mental outlook. With thankfulness, there is a "positive feeling toward" life in general rather than a "feeling against" the vagaries of life. An outlook of gratitude may allow the replacement of a feeling of frustrated struggle or despair with a sense of thankfulness. In place of darkness you can have a "light touch," a joy of life. Realization of the wonderful gifts of life can bring joy.

Al: "Light touch" means pickpocket to me.

You reveal your Chicago roots. We live in a world beyond the city now. We live in the world of the mind as we explore it. Think about trees

Wonder, Thankfulness

and sunshine as we continue. In fact, you can think about your last good meal. You or your partner bought the food and cooked the meal—while sitting in some type of shelter for which you pay rent or mortgage payments. And you probably had clothes on. You paid money for the food, shelter, and clothing. You earned that money. It was by your effort that food, shelter, and clothing were available. But it was by an impressive confluence of circumstances that you had the health and good fortune to be able to work to earn money—good fortune in having a job, in living within a social structure that is adequately conducive to individual well-being, good fortune in having no crippling disability and in having life itself. There are many things for which to be thankful. Your own effort is but one segment in the full picture of the much larger mesh of a multitude of factors. An excess of pride in your own effort might diminish the awareness of a sense of gratitude for the many circumstances beyond your control.

It's time for concluding remarks on this chapter. When we have an outlook of thankfulness for, and wonder of, that which exists, we are more likely to have a positive orientation to life. With a welcoming of life, happiness is more likely to accompany us.

Wonder toward existence can be a source for joy. We can realize the precariousness of our existence and the enormous odds against our ever having received the gift of existence. And we give thanks.

Al: Thanks to whom?

I appreciate your question.

Al: But you don't answer it.

Have patience. All will become clear in the ensuing chapters and be brought together in the final chapter. But I will advise you not to read the final chapter now. There is groundwork to be done first.

4

The Swamp of Anguish; the Flow of Openness

Overview of the Chapter

Anguish

Control

Engaged Detachment

Freedom

Openness

The Cleared Mind

Word-symbols

Imagination

Summary

OVERVIEW OF THE CHAPTER

We begin with anguish.

Al: Hold it right there. Some of this could be painful. We just talked about thankfulness, and now you want to discuss anguish. I feel like skipping to the next chapter.

Everything in its time. Joy comes after darkness. And take heart; we will not be spending a large amount of time discussing anguish. Also, we will talk about the control of anguish.

Al: Fine. I like to control things that might cause anguish.

Right. But, is there too much desire for control at times? Life tends to become less full when there is a compulsion toward control. There are ways to find relief from the bonds of an excessive desire for control.

The impetus toward an excessively controlling outlook may become mitigated by the development of an orientation of openness. This release from excessive control can benefit individuals. In this regard, several aspects of openness are considered.

Sections concerning detachment and freedom lead to the subject of openness. The value of openness is discussed and then supplemented by descriptions of the cleared mind. Also, the discussion about openness includes concern about the significant effects of language.

Finally, we will look into one particular mode of openness, the realm of imagination. This is an area that has been extensively explored by French philosopher Gaston Bachelard, and I quote from him liberally.

ANGUISH

Let's start with a look at what we mean by the word "anguish." It involves intense negative emotion. Anguish is different from feelings that are intense but welcomed as a positive experience. For most people, anguish is not welcomed; it is not a preferred state. Nevertheless, some individuals relieve boredom by precipitating anguishing situations. Also, some welcome anguish as a challenge. However, in the context of a satisfactory life, the impulse toward anguish is moderated by a natural tendency to avoid pain or to keep pain to a minimum. Gaston Bachelard said: "For anguish is factitious: we are made to breathe easy" (Reverie 25).

However, in opposition to these statements, I must say that there are various ways in which someone may accept, or even seek, anguish.

Some lives appear to be set upon a course of anguish; some are engaged in a habituated role of anguish, and they actively search for sources of discomfort. Whenever peace approaches, these souls cast about for some type of anguish, such as excess doubt, or guilt, or undue concern for possible wrong decisions. Peace may seem boring when there is no anguish: peace may seem too tame for those who are in a habit of ruminating endlessly on problems. For these individuals, there is a boredom in the pace of a peaceful life, and this boredom can be suffocating for those accustomed to participation in painful experiences. However, a life geared to pain will eventually take its toll in the form of significant problems both for those who create pain and for the victims of the painful acts. People who want drama to an excessive degree are most likely at some point to be overwhelmed by pain. Such people may ultimately realize the damage to themselves and also to others caused by efforts to create anguish—to inflict pain and to incite the reaction of others. At that point, hopefully, for those who inflict anguish, the development of empathy and integrity will guide them to a different course, a course less painful for themselves and others.

Al: That's easy for you to say, but how do you create empathy and integrity?

We will discuss these soon.

Al: Are you sure we will?

You can trust me.

Al: How do I know?

Because you have empathy.

Al: We are almost back to the first question.

This is a good time to ask who is on first.

Al: Not if you haven't seen old Abbott and Costello movies.

Enough jesting. Let's look at one aspect of the subject of anguish that is more welcome.

Al: That sounds odd. I can't imagine anguish as ever being welcome.

If you'd rather, instead of "anguish" you could use the word "pain"—or, maybe, "discomfort" or "distress."

To continue, pain or discomfort can be appreciated as a fullness of experience, as a mental focus that obliterates extraneous thoughts. When consequences of this anguish are not destructive and when there is a choice to experience intense feeling, the occurrence of anguish may be welcomed.

Here is an example of anguish that can be anticipated in a positive sense. It's true that, in this example, the words "mild pain" may fit the case better than the word "anguish." When I ski, I hurt. It's a little uncomfortable to herringbone up a hill. When I careen off a steep mogul, I welcome the mild fear of a possible loss of balance. That anguish is part of the exhilaration. There is simultaneous experience of both the pain and a degree of detachment from this experience of pain in order to maintain the skiing activity. There has been a freedom to choose the activity of skiing and freedom to choose a particular mogul to negotiate. This freedom affords an ability to detach from the pain and thereby allows a welcoming of the intense feeling. With freedom to choose, the skier can become an observer of his or her pain; he or she is both participant and observer. A parallel to this is....

Al: Excuse me. You are talking about parallels. You must mean parallel skiing when you refer to skiing.

And you are trying to make a pun.

Al: A pun is fun—for someone.

That is really anguishing! Now we have the anguish of simple rhyming.

Let's look at a more profound manifestation of anguish as a chosen experience that is welcomed. Consider the performance of tragic drama. Audience, actors, and actresses all take part in the awareness of anguish, and this is welcomed as a focussed expression that cleanses random concerns from the mind.

Also in the aesthetic mode, anguish is at the heart of creativity. The anguish that a tortured soul feels becomes the source for creative expression. There are many well-known examples of this. I can cite a few: the writings of Edgar Allan Poe, Ernest Hemingway, and F. Scott Fitzgerald, and the music of Beethoven.

The German philosopher Friedrich Nietzsche gives a vivid presentation of the desire for an experience of anguish:

> For the soul which hath the longest ladder, and can go deepest down: how could there fail to be most parasites upon it?...
>
> The most comprehensive soul, which can run and stray and rove furthest in itself; the most necessary soul, which out of joy flingeth itself into chance: ...
>
> The soul in Being, which plungeth into Becoming; the possessing soul, which seeketh to attain desire and longing:...
>
> The soul fleeing from itself, which overtaketh itself in the widest circuit; the wisest soul, unto which folly speaketh most sweetly:.... (461)

There is a more subtle cause of anguish that, in addition to not being chosen, may be unexpected and unwelcome. A person is often blessed with joy when working toward a goal. Nietzsche describes a joy of approaching fulfillment: "His step betrayeth whether a person already walketh on his own path: Just see me walk! He, however, who cometh nigh to his goal danceth" (496). For many, however, the completed accomplishment of a goal can leave a sense of emptiness. Anguish can occur after goals are met and because those goals were met. This contrasts with that joy which is experienced in the act of working toward goals. The struggle is ended, the goal is attained, and now the experience may be a feeling of loss. Fulfillment was in the effort, not in achieving the goal.

It may be helpful to anticipate some degree of letdown following the completion of a goal, realizing that you may be left with anguish due to a loss of the activity of striving for a goal.

Much of life can be seen as cycles of yearning and fulfillment. These cycles occur often in everyday life. Work can be characterized as striving for some goal that will become completed, and, when finished, if not worked out of a job, new goals present themselves. Completion of these is followed by additional goals. This example illustrates the recurring cycles of yearning for completion of goals and the attainment of those goals. Such cycles of yearning and fulfillment are common in life.

The yearning and fulfillment pattern is operative in many fields. In sports there is no enjoyment if there is no striving and no striving without goals, unless it is totally within the realm of play. The pattern of yearning and fulfillment in literary works is described by Kenneth Burke: "... an arousing and fulfillment of desires.... one part of it leads a reader to anticipate another part, to be gratified by the sequence" (*xxv*).

To summarize, the word "anguish" signifies the intense feeling of distress. When this feeling is freely chosen and the circumstances of the anguish are not significantly harmful to self or others, anguish may be a welcome experience. However, if the source of anguish is not of our choosing or there are painful consequences, anguish is a mood that we usually try to avoid. Furthermore, an inclination toward habituated anguish is an unpleasant way to live, and those that live that way usually seek relief.

CONTROL

We move on now to one of the prime sources of anguish: the fear of loss of control. This fear, this concern about loss of control, is often realistic and appropriate for real threats. However, anxiety about a possible loss of control is also frequently overemphasized and exaggerated. We have goals and ways to achieve them, but they narrow our outlook if they dominate us. The impetus toward control can have damaging consequences. When a desire for control is excessive, the mind may become focussed too much on a particular course of action. The fear of loss of control may narrow the mind, causing a possible exclusion of broader perception.

It is helpful to be open to the fact that, in the course of events, things can often become out of control. As the Scottish poet Robert Burns says:

> The best-laid schemes o' mice and men
> Gang aft a-gley ... (41)

I do not want to deny the aspect of control that incorporates an understanding of realistic needs, such as for security and safety. However, when there is a realization that the concern for control is excessive, a development of freedom from the excess concern will allow a person to consider such needs as security and safety with a more balanced perspective.

Certainly there are ultimate aspects of life over which we have no control or limited control—the vagaries of fortune and health, and, finally, death. In a sense, the natural world itself is "transcendental," that is, the events of the world—and even processes within the self—transcend one's abilities and knowledge in regard to the capacity for control, aside from whatever extent control is possible. For examples of limited control, I can mention heart attacks, cancer development, plane crashes ...

Al: Stop. I get the picture. You said it before.

I won't elaborate except to quote the Tao:

> ... the universe
> is forever out of control,
> and that trying to dominate events
> goes against the current of the Tao (30).

I will say this: don't worry excessively about control. Employ that amount of control that is reasonable and possible, and accept that which cannot be controlled. Accept vulnerability. Accept limits. Life is not for painful anguish in yearning for that which cannot be.

Although some anguish is unavoidable, accept it, but don't anguish over being anguished, and release yourself from the anguish of desire for unreasonable control. Have some degree of detachment from the worldly things that would destroy our equanimity.

This release from anguish is not to deny the details of life that make up the content of our everyday world, but these worldly concerns are best held as secondary to the broad aspects of life. Work loads and responsibilities can be more efficiently handled when there is a primary orientation to the fundamentals of life: appreciation for life and fortune, and the other fundamentals which I will be describing.

Let's look at another aspect of the orientation toward excessive control. The desire for control can be destructive of relationships. Control, in the guise of security in relationships, can be damaging to those very relationships. Psychologist Janette Rainwater discusses this:

> People who fear the future attempt to 'secure' themselves—with money, property, health insurance, personal relationships, marriage contracts. Parents attempt to bind their children to them. Some fearful children are reluctant to leave the home nest. Husbands and wives try to guarantee the continuance of the Other's life and services.... This clutching at security can be very discouraging to interpersonal relationships, and will impede your own self-growth. (56)

Response to vulnerability is only one of the factors that evokes the desire for control. Another source that may lead to a controlling outlook is the commitment to some form of idealism. Control may be manifested in the manner in which idealism is expressed. In an idealistic march of self-righteousness, the banner of a focussed ideal often guides people into a pattern of exclusiveness, rigidity, and control. The certitude and righteousness of a noble notion often leads to controlling actions that are destructive of human dignity and even of life. More attention is paid to this subject later in the book.

Al: I want to ask a question here. Surely you do not advocate total relinquishing of control, do you?

How could I brush my teeth or write this book without some measure of control? I need to discipline myself to perform these tasks. I certainly do not advocate a total loss of control. But there should be that amount which is appropriate for the situation.

A sense of control is important in life. We want to be able to have a say in what we do and in what happens to us. What work do we do? Are we able to modify the work if we want to make it more productive or more fulfilling? Can we live where we want to live? Can we have the sort of life we want? We want to be able to have some say, some control, in handling these questions.

But the desire for control can be overdone. It is valuable to have strong personal interrelationships, but these relationships cannot be guaranteed. Also, some aspects of life cannot be modified. Some illness cannot be cured. Some misfortunes cannot be reversed. And, in the end, death is unavoidable. When the desire for control is unrealistic, it is frustrating and disruptive to one's peace of mind.

There is another way in which the desire for control can be particularly damaging in the realm of interpersonal relationships. Control may be employed to express dominance. Some people want to have control of others—by expressing authority or by manipulation. I suspect that the control of others is the very source of life's fulfillment for some people. However, this control not only enslaves others; it also restricts the outlook of those who do the controlling. The desire for control limits both the victim and the perpetrator.

Al: I agree with you. But not entirely. Kids need to be controlled until they have some understanding of the consequences of their actions and have some ability to control themselves.

I was going to say that.

Al: You don't want kids putting fingers into electric sockets.

I certainly agree. You want to maintain the life and health of the child and of the family. The child must respond with blind acceptance to authority and control; he or she must not put a finger in an electric socket and not test it for himself or herself. However, during child training it is well to include the transmission of a sense of esteem and value along with the expression of authority and control. Later, when the blind acceptance of authority becomes internalized as discipline, control as dominance becomes control as discipline. This discipline is utilized in a way that is maximally beneficial when it is balanced with reasoned doubt and with appreciation for the value of others and value of self.

ENGAGED DETACHMENT

Now let's center our attention on an outlook which is quite different from control, and, at times, quite the opposite. Detachment may afford some release from an excessively controlling orientation.

Detachment can also give some release from desires which might be too focussed. When attachments to goods, conditions, and interpersonal relationships become excessive, perception can become distorted. We do not then see things as clearly as might be possible. Our perceptiveness becomes decreased. With distorted perception, we become more susceptible to following unproductive or counter-productive paths. Exaggerated thoughts and fears can propel us into a wide assortment of unsatisfactory directions. For instance, a narrowed vision may render us more susceptible to manipulation by others. It was Sixteenth Century political writer Niccolo Machiavelli who said: "Men are so simple and so subject to present needs that he who deceives in this way will always find those who will let themselves be deceived" (1067-8). On the other hand, some measure of detachment is likely to facilitate a more lucid perception. We may then be able to have a more full understanding of situations.

Distortion of perception also occurs in the process of avoidance. Psychotherapist David Reynolds refers to avoidance when he states: "Many people work hard to avoid noticing what needs to be done because when they notice the requirements of reality they are confronted with the necessity of doing something about them. What they don't notice, they think they aren't responsible for" (67-8).

Al: Wouldn't you say that if someone avoids noticing something, it is easier to have detachment from it?

Well, there is quite a difference between the value of detachment and the narrowing effect of avoidance. For instance, an argument may be avoided by changing the subject or leaving the room. However, you can employ detachment while maintaining attention to the situation. Engagement in the contentious subject may continue if detached judgment indicates that it is right to remain engaged in it. Then, with engaged detachment, a fuller perception of the situation becomes available. In fact, some measure of detachment may create the possibility for greater engagement in the situation or relationship. This is because detachment can allow a more accurate perception of actuality—a greater understanding of what is. With greater understanding, a person may become more involved.

The Swamp of Anguish; the Flow of Openness

This is a good time to state that the employment of detachment is not recommended when the situation does not call for it. In happy times and with enjoyable relationships there is no need for recourse to detachment. In fact, at these times detachment can be harmful. It is better to enjoy the happiness rather than to establish a degree of mental separateness.

However, when circumstances indicate a need for clarity of perception—a need for greater perceptiveness—then an engaged detachment may be helpful.

When you employ some measure of detachment, it may become more possible to have empathy for the situation and to be less hindered by preconceptions. Although it is a stretch of the imagination, empathy with detachment could be implied in a statement by Camus: "Everything begins with lucid indifference" (Sisyphus 70). I appreciate Camus' words, but the word "indifference" could easily be construed as being isolated from involvement. Engaged detachment involves both a release from involvement and a maintenance of involvement. In the stream of mental consciousness, there is a flow that encompasses both involvement and non-involvement. A person remains actively engaged but employs a measure of detachment from his or her aims, goals, and desires. Aims and goals are not denied but viewed as by an interested observer, allowing release from a narrowed vision in order to be open to deeper insight and more comprehensive perceptiveness. This increased perceptiveness may open the path to greater understanding of the self and insight into the character of others. Such deepened insight is the foundation for empathy with others. Empathy may then become more valid, rather than just a projection of one's own thoughts or some preconceived sympathy. I will cite an example. With some measure of compassion, I am able to learn about a stranger's problems. This compassion may be made more comprehensive when it includes some amount of detachment. The detachment is a means to maintain an openness to truth—to full perceptiveness.

The ability to have some measure of detachment from established mental patterns is liberating for the mind. Stuart Hampshire describes this realization when he indicates that a person considers himself or herself more free when, through the utilization of detachment, his or her current patterns of thought can be seen with a fresh point of view (309).

A similar realization was voiced many centuries ago in the Tao Te Ching:

The mark of a moderate man
is freedom from his own ideas. (59)

The Tao further states:

> Can you step back from your own mind
> and thus understand all things?
> Giving birth and nourishing,
> having without possessing,
> acting with no expectations,
> leading and not trying to control:
> this is the supreme virtue. (10)

The Tao even refers to a detachment from the orientation to a sense of self:

> If you want to become whole,
> let yourself be partial,
> If you want to become straight,
> let yourself be crooked.
> If you want to become full,
> let yourself be empty.
> If you want to be reborn,
> let yourself die.
> If you want to be given everything,
> give everything up. (22)

With the use of engaged detachment, you give yourself a measure of freedom from the struggle for goals. I don't mean that you do not act or that someone else performs the action. Mentally, you step part way back from the struggle, even while your action proceeds toward goal fulfillment. This engaged detachment releases you from excess drive toward a goal, a drive so focussed that it could miss the realization of that which might reasonably demand an alteration of action.

Furthermore, the utilization of detachment does not exclude attachments and wants. Desire is an integral part of life. However, the ability to employ detachment furnishes a person with the capacity to examine his or her attachments when necessary. Attachments and desires may be held up to the light if or when there is a right time for them to be examined.

Let's look at another aspect of detachment. Detachment can be considered a self-surrender in order to clear the mind—to release oneself from preconceptions, such as established attitudes and desires, to the extent possible. This detachment from preconceptions allows surrender into openness—to full reception of the experience of the moment at hand. You become actively receptive to the experiencing of that which is before you

The Swamp of Anguish; the Flow of Openness

in the present moment. You engage in a state of openness to the experience of the immediate time.

Al: Wait a minute, here. I really rebel against talk about self-surrender. We should always be able to protect ourselves and to question authority. Surrender leaves us defenseless. We should be able to look out for our interests.

I certainly don't deny that. However, as I said before, although detachment with self-surrender leads into a state of openness, this does not necessitate either self-denial or an abandonment of the availability of doubt and discernment. For example, self-surrender to the pulse of the music when dancing does not mean that you cannot stop dancing. Immersion into activities and outlooks need not eliminate the possibility for recourse to examination and evaluation of those activities and outlooks. Indiscriminate self-surrender can be enslaving. I believe the Spanish philosopher Jose Ortega y Gasset had indiscriminate self-surrender in mind when he described the superstitious outlook: "The superstitious mind is, in effect, a dog in search of a master…. (Men) feel an incredible anxiety to be slaves. Slavery is their highest ambition: slavery to other men, to an emperor, to a sorcerer or to an idol. Anything rather than feel the terror of facing singlehanded, in their own persons, the ferocious assaults of existence" (134).

New perception that is attuned to actualities of the present may confirm a sense of self and of self-protection and boundaries. The self-surrender that accompanies detachment can allow a more accurate view of self-interest by providing a release from the narrowness of a mind set upon old pathways. Surrender into an understanding of the immediate situation can strengthen our protective position by providing us with more complete perception. With greater understanding, our options for action are multiplied. We become better equipped to handle that with which we are dealing. Surrender to full perceptiveness does not mean surrender of action. However, the action we do take will be more appropriate for the situation when there is more comprehensive perception.

Al: I see what you mean. But I have another difficulty.

Two difficulties in a row?! I'm glad you bring them up. I will have some answer for anything. And, if you take the answers with a grain of salt, I will appreciate the fact that you follow my advice in Chapter Two about doubt and truth.

Al: My point is this: I have to tell you that I find the idea of detachment difficult. Detachment may help me to see things more clearly, but it is hard to get beyond preconceptions. It is difficult to get beyond the impressions and attitudes that program our minds into set patterns of narrowed perceptiveness.

Yes. Perhaps it may seem impossible, but you can accept the realization that a total detachment is not possible and also accept that degree of detachment which is possible. In fact, this brings to mind another point. If there is an active striving for detachment, the attainment of detachment is difficult. The effort of striving may narrow the mind, putting it in a state of activity rather than receptivity. You attain detachment and self-surrender when it is easy, when you relax and allow it. Bachelard discusses receptivity and self-surrender when he quotes from Andre Saulnier, who quotes from Madame Guyon: "When I had been reflecting, it would be taken from me and I would enter into intolerable pain; but as soon as I abandoned myself, I would find inside myself a candor, an innocence, a child's simplicity and something divine" (Reverie 131).

T. S. Eliot illuminates the process of self-surrender when he tells of listening to music:

. . . music heard so deeply
That it is not heard at all, but you are the music
While the music lasts. (44)

Detachment with self-surrender is discussed by Cassirer in the perception of works of art: "In art we are absorbed in (the immediate appearance of phenomena), and we enjoy this appearance to the fullest extent in all its richness and variety" (216).

Al: I am sure I would not want to live a life of self-surrender and detachment. I enjoy doing things. I go skiing. I hike in the mountains. I talk with friends. I do a lot of things.

And you surrender yourself into these activities, enjoying them more fully by not cogitating about them while doing them. Detachment and self-surrender do not require passiveness in a lethargic sense. Initiative and action are certainly part of the full life.

At this time let's reconsider the subject of doubt. Doubt and truth were discussed in Chapter Two. We can now see that doubt and detachment are two aspects of the same process.

Al: I don't see much connection.

Let me explain further. Doubt and detachment both involve a standing apart from preconceptions. In this application of the word "doubt," I am not referring to doubt as connoting a sense of insecurity. In fact, the word doubt is used with a sense of confidence because it stands me in good stead for leading to whatever truth I am able to know at the time, that is, to tentative truth, as discussed previously. Also, detachment, in this context, is not accompanied by disengagement and isolation. Detachment, as described, includes engagement with circumstances, this engagement being separated from preconceptions as much as possible. Engaged detachment means the release from a narrowed understanding while maintaining involvement with the situation.

Doubt and detachment, then, are two aspects of the same process, the holding of self apart from a narrowed outlook. With doubt, one can view the world with an openness to new dimensions of truth. Detachment may release the mind from that narrowness which would inhibit perceptiveness and understanding.

FREEDOM

The process of detachment frees the mind. Detachment opens the outlook to the possibility for new insights and potentialities. With freedom we venture into the new experience of each moment. T. S. Eliot speaks of the freedom provided by a detachment from desire. Eliot shows that this freedom may enlarge the experience of love rather than diminishing it:

> For liberation—not less of love but expanding
> Of love beyond desire, and so liberation
> From the future as well as the past. (55)

The inclination toward this sense of freedom is a characteristic of human nature, a characteristic held by each of us. The impetus toward freedom of the mind is one of the great propensities of humanity. There is an urge within men and women for freedom, even at times to the point of destructiveness. Editorial comment on the Russian author Fyodor Dostoevsky's *Notes From Underground* illustrates this:

> Man wills the irrational and evil because he does not want to become an organ-stop, a piano key, because he wants to be left with the freedom to choose between good and evil. This freedom of choice, even at the expense of chaos and destruction, is what makes him man.... This freedom is, of course, not political freedom but freedom of choice, indeterminism, even caprice and willfulness, in the paradoxical formulation of the Underground man. (1850-1)

However, it should be kept in mind that freedom which is capricious can itself become a preconception, a narrowed orientation. A person may push the concept of freedom to the point of caricature, becoming a pose rather than an expression of openness. In its more extreme manifestation, a person may become obsessed with reaching for freedom and may be compulsive about the longing for freedom even when the constraints on his or her freedom are feeble or non-existent.

It should be understood that the freedom to which I refer is primarily in the mental realm. Freedom in overt action should be modified by empathy and by respect for others and for self. The need for a balanced outlook that includes social responsibility and civility is real. This will be discussed further in Chapter Eight.

The expression of freedom includes a measure of detachment from anticipated outcomes. Camus expresses this: "The final effort for these related minds, creator or conqueror, is to manage to free themselves also from their undertakings: succeed in granting that the very work, whether it be conquest, love, or creation, may well not be; consummate thus the utter futility of any individual life. Indeed, that gives them more freedom in the realization of that work … " (Sisyphus 86-7).

I do have to express a certain measure of disagreement with the statement by Camus in that I do not totally deny the value of goals and directions in life. But, with freedom, a person can be released from a narrow-mindedness toward those goals and directions. In addition, a realization of freedom can enhance the expression of initiative in finding goals and directions. The mind is not just an agent of response to the vagaries and opportunities of life. The free mind also initiates direction in life out of the wellspring of its freedom.

At this point I will indicate a relationship between an awareness of life's limitations and the experience of freedom. A consciousness of life's limitations may lead to a realization of the value of acceptance. This awareness of limitations includes the limits intrinsic to existence: disease, misfortune, death. Acceptance of the fact of dispersion of self-worth—which is non-being, non-existence, death—acceptance of this fact may be seen to be valuable. When acceptance of the ultimate unavoidable takes place, a person may realize a peace of mind. You may become released from the struggle against insurmountables. When you are released from contention with those ultimate facts of life that are unavoidable, a sense of peace is likely to follow, and a relaxation tends to take place. Life's activities and goals become measured against the ultimate issues of life; daily concerns are put in balance. Do you feel this calm and peace when you read these words from the Old Testament?

> To every thing there is a season, and a time to every purpose under the heaven: A time to be born, and a time to die; a time to plant, and a time to pluck up that which is planted ... (Eccl. 3:1-2)

With relaxation regarding the ultimate concerns of life, the mental outlook may be allowed to become free and open, receptive to the experience of the moment. A mind that is settled in regard to the ultimate questions of existence is also a mind that is likely to be free and spontaneous.

Al: That is not necessarily so. Someone who has a warped religious view of the ultimate concerns may have a very narrowed, bigoted mind, a mind that is not free and spontaneous at all.

You are right. We must always be able to doubt that which we believe and always be open to new truth. The capacity for doubt is a necessary part of a person's mental outlook. We have said quite a bit about the value of doubt and will be saying more later concerning that topic.

Al: I will appreciate that.

Suffer the joy.

Al: What did you say?

I said, "Suffer the joy."

Al: Where does that come from?

Ah! A preposition. You ended the sentence with a preposition. You were telling me not to do that, but you did it.

Al: I wouldn't worry a lot about that. More to the point: how can you say, "Suffer the joy?" What do you mean? And how does that fit in here? It does not seem to follow anything.

Ah—discongruity. Discontinuity. Disjointedness. Let's celebrate disjointedness.

Al: Fine. I'd like to tell a joke, but I can't think of one right now.

That's a shame. Then we are back to seriousness.

Al: I don't follow.

Right. And this disruption may seem foreign to a mind accustomed to continuous discipline. But is there another dimension to life? Duty and discipline are very important, but is there more to life? Production. Get things done. Keep the goals in mind. And our goal right now is to point out a parallel between the management of productivity and the handling of fears and anxieties. These are two quite disparate aspects of life, but the management of both is facilitated by the utilization of an orientation which releases a person from a narrowed focus on concerns. This release is afforded by the orientation of openness.

Al: Don't you want that as a new section heading?

Oh, yes. Here it is:

OPENNESS

In both the course of productivity as well as in the course of facing fears, the attitude of openness serves a person well. The outlook of openness affords the possibility for someone to perceive the situation at hand with an enlarged awareness. Perceptiveness is facilitated by the outlook of openness to present experience. With openness, a person has the opportunity to realize alternate pathways of action and alternate attitudes in communication. His or her outlook is less narrowed by pre-arranged content.

The outlook of openness to an enlarged awareness does not require denial of concerns; it does not bypass needs. But it eases the perception of concerns, thereby allowing a more open and free perceptiveness for greater understanding and possible solutions.

When there is an absence of openness, a person's vision is narrowed. Some of the present experience is not seen; it is excluded. Such narrowing of perception is described by Camus: "…nothing is true that forces one to exclude. Isolated beauty ends up simpering; solitary justice ends up oppressing" (Sisyphus 141). Regarding openness to the experience of the present moment, Shunryu Suzuki states: "We should find the reality in each moment, and in each phenomenon" (119).

When you are immersed fully into the experience of the present time, you are more likely to also experience wonder and appreciation. Furthermore, with openness to present experience, perceptiveness is enhanced, and there is enlargement of awareness of the number of paths for freedom of action. Adequate plans for the future are maintained, but these are always tentative and not absolutely binding. Tentative plans are definitely important, but consideration of such plans is balanced by an awareness of the present. The decision for a course of action includes future needs and present experience. However, the present is not held hostage to the future. Present sacrifice may be necessary for future goals, but this depends on particulars of the situation. Plans may modify present action in order to reconcile that action with whatever is appropriate for future concerns. But the future is not an absolutely fixed plan; the future consists of tentative goals. Here I will again quote the Tao:

> A good traveler has no fixed plans
>
> and is not intent upon arriving.
>
> A good artist lets his intuition
>
> lead him wherever it wants.
>
> A good scientist has freed himself of concepts
>
> and keeps his mind open to what is. (27)

Openness is a state of receptivity, a welcoming of the moment, a releasing of oneself into the fullness of the immediate. If there is disruption of a thought process, the disruption is welcomed and addressed. If an anguished person fears the source of anguish, an open outlook allows a receptivity to perceptiveness that affords more possibilities for solutions to the problem. Even further, an anguished person may have a fear of an anticipated sense of emptiness if the anguish were to become resolved. A degree of openness can allow a more facile acceptance of the state of peace and rest, which, when experienced, may become a state that is welcomed. An example is a marriage toward which someone feels pain and misery. There may be fear that a resolution of the anguish would entail dissolution of the marriage. In this situation, an outlook of openness could ease the acceptance of a possible anticipated divorce state. I hesitate to have cited this example because, in the current state of family life in this country, marriage is increasingly a temporary arrangement, and divorce can be sought on trivial grounds.

When you live in a state of openness, you welcome the experience of the moment. In this state of openness there is a positive inclination toward that which is happening or about to happen. You are drawn to the present moment of unfolding, evolving existence, and, possibly, anticipation of the moment may even carry with it an eagerness and joy.

Al: I take issue with your statement. Not all moments are joyful. Sometimes there is pain and misery.

You are right, certainly. And an anticipation of pain can be enervating. In that situation a sense of enlarged awareness is helpful. Disease may strike. Accidents occur. And finally we all know that death, in fact, is the promise of birth. All who are born will die. Death cannot be denied. The point to be made here is not that there is death, disease, and misfortune, but that there is life and that amount of health and good fortune which we have and have had. For this we are grateful. The attitude of thankfulness implies value because experience is more likely to be welcomed as valuable when there is gratefulness. The grateful outlook inclines a person toward a positive state of mind that welcomes openness to perception and understanding. Even pain may be experienced with less stress when a person has an enlarged awareness of the gift of life and thankfulness for it. His or her life is seen as part of the huge unfolding of all the forces and events of the universe. Life is part of the immense workings of existence. We express thankfulness for that amount of time in which we have consciousness and awareness. This thankfulness feeds our openness to experience.

What takes place then is. . .

Al: Wait a minute. I hate to be picky, but that's an awkward beginning for a sentence.

Ah, disruption. You are right. How is this: there can then be a balance—no, a flow—a flow between an outlook of openness to disruption in one stream of mental activity, and, in the other stream, the management of productivity and the handling of fear and anxiety. These streams can flow together. When the mind becomes too focussed on production or efforts or fears, a disruptive release into openness frees the outlook. The disruptive liberation of outlook provides not only a greater potential for productivity through an enlarged awareness of possible solutions; it also can facilitate a more comprehensive perceptiveness of the situation. The interaction between disruptive release and an orientation toward effort may not only alternate as separate streams of outlook; they may flow forward together in a harmony that carries with it the possibility for joy in the moment, a fulfillment of life in the immediate.

Al: And when you said "Suffer the joy" three pages back, you meant…?

Exactly.

Al: Exactly what?

The discomfort that may accompany the anticipation of effort or anticipation of the fearful becomes a current in the stream of openness. The problems become a part of the solution; they become a fluid element in the course of life's fulfillment.

Al: This openness you talk about: it seems vague.

It is vague. That is its nature. When you have an open outlook, you are released from a narrowed vision. The orientation toward openness welcomes perceptiveness of that of which it had not previously been aware. It is a move into the uncharted, the unknown—a release into freedom, welcoming the discovery of that which had not been known.

Although the quality of openness is vague, it does not shut out planned specifics. The open outlook does not require denial of those actions and plans which are needed for future directions. Tentative plans and courses of action are initiated and maintained, but maintained with an openness to modification. Plans are not absolute.

THE CLEARED MIND

Openness implies an emptiness of the mind in being receptive to that which is, receptive to that which exists in the present experience. An open outlook is facilitated by the presence of a cleared mind, a mind released from encroaching thoughts. Necessary and appropriate concerns are maintained but with an engaged detachment that allows release to fresh perception. For example, I take precautions when I walk through the woods. I do not want to touch poison oak because the skin reaction to poison oak is painful and lasts several days. Therefore my perception remains engaged in scanning for poison oak while walking. But I do have a degree of detachment regarding this perception, this scanning. It does not override my general state of mind, which is an enjoyment of the walk. Engaged detachment allows continuing concerns to be maintained but within an orientation of openness that welcomes the complete experience of the present moment. This receptivity arises from a blankness of mind, a cleared mind. There can be a flow of mental awareness that incorporates both the stream of engaged detachment for concerns and the stream of freedom of a cleared mind. Valid needs are addressed as they arise, but they are addressed within the flow of a mind receptive to the present by way of its openness, its emptiness.

In similar fashion there is a welcome flow of the mental stream of awareness when there is a merging of freedom of the cleared mind with the needs for discipline and self-control. The disciplined outlook is not incompatible with freedom. With total acceptance of that amount of discipline which is appropriate for the situation, a person frees himself or herself from hassling about the discipline and simply accepts it. This allows discipline to be expressed within the freedom of action. Discipline and freedom then merge in the flow of action.

I want to point to a negative aspect of the cleared mind. The cleared mind may be a factor for some who resist exposure to new circumstances. For these, the comfort of a routine, circumscribed life allows a mental relaxation, not disturbed by challenges. Novel situations are too unsettling for some; they may find comfort in an outlook attuned to that for which there is an established pattern of life.

I should add that an outlook too settled into routine may lead to an excessive need for control. Such a life may become narrowed into a controlling pattern. For these individuals, the desire for the relaxation of a cleared mind results in a mind centered on concern and control. In such circumstance, a cleared mind is not attained, although such individuals may find comfort in the self-righteousness that often accompanies a controlling attitude.

Let's return to the discussion of the positive aspects of the cleared mind. The topic has been addressed by several writers. The emptiness of mind is discussed by S. Suzuki when he describes a certain type of Buddhist practice, zazen (meditation while in a sitting posture):

> People who know, even if only intuitively, the state of emptiness always have open the possibility of accepting things as they are.... To understand reality as a direct experience is the reason we practice zazen, and the reason we study Buddhism.... it is necessary to clear your mind of these various distortions. A mind full of preconceived ideas, subjective intentions, or habits is not open to things as they are. That is why we practice zazen; to clear our mind of what is related to something else. (86-8)

In regard to openness and blankness of mind it is worth while to quote other passages from Suzuki's work: "Moment after moment, everyone comes out from nothingness. This is the true joy of life.... It is rather difficult to explain, but naturalness is, I think, some feeling of being independent from everything, or some activity which is based on nothingness" (107-8). Further on he says: "If it comes out of nothingness, whatever you do is natural, and that is true activity.... To have nothing in your mind is naturalness" (109). Later he continues: "So to have a firm conviction in the original emptiness of your mind is the most important thing..." (128).

In the same vein I quote from the Tao Te Ching: "Stop thinking, and end your problems. . . . I am like an idiot, my mind is so empty" (20). And from the Eleventh Verse of Tao:

> We shape clay into a pot,
> but it is the emptiness inside
> that holds whatever we want.
> We hammer wood for a house,
> but it is the inner space
> that makes it livable.
> We work with being,
> but non-being is what we use. (11)

Camus expresses a release from mental stress and the relief of a cleared mind: " 'Oh, to be nothing!' For thousands of years this great cry has roused millions of men to revolt against desire and pain" (Sisyphus 131-2). The same author points to the value of "...attention to something that has no importance. The mind profits from such recurrences. In a sense this is its hygiene..." (Sisyphus 128).

The cleared mind releases itself from knowledge, and this release is operative in the expression of creativity. The realm of aesthetics exemplifies this creativity. Bachelard quotes Jean Lescure, who refers to the painting of Charles Lapicque: "Knowing must therefore be accompanied by an equal capacity to forget knowing. Non-knowing is not a form of ignorance but a difficult transcendence of knowledge. This is the price that must be paid for an oeuvre (a work) to be, at all times, a sort of pure beginning, which makes its creation an exercise in freedom" (Space *xxviii-xxix*).

T. S. Eliot also describes the blank openness of the mind when he refers to the sounds of a hidden waterfall and children playing:

> . . . half-heard, in the stillness
> Between two waves of the sea.
> Quick now, here, now, always—
> A condition of complete simplicity.... (59)

When your mind is cleared and open, you can have a receptiveness to and a positive anticipation of the experience of each moment. It is true that all in the universe is on the brink of that which it will be like in the next moment. With open receptivity that the cleared mind provides, you can feel wonder in anticipation of the next moment. States Nietzsche: "Every moment beginneth existence, around every 'Here' rolleth the ball 'There.' The middle is everywhere. Crooked is the path of eternity" (469).

At times anticipation of the immediate may be in a negative context. As previously stated, when anticipation is painful, it is helpful to maintain some degree of detached engagement in the situation in order to see actuality more clearly and also to be aware of those positive aspects for which one might be able to be thankful.

Regarding anticipation in the positive sense, when you have openness of mind, a freedom is created which can allow an anticipation of the moment joyfully and with eagerness. There is a flow that finds fulfillment in the moment. In fact, anticipation becomes the fulfillment. As psychotherapist David K. Reynolds states: "We trust the appropriateness of merging ourselves with our circumstances and situation. The opposite approach brings disharmony and unnecessary struggle and suffering. When we adapt ourselves to the needs of this moment, we become part of the moment itself. There is no resistance through wishing life were otherwise, no longing for the ideal or for what ought to be" (68).

WORD-SYMBOLS

One of the aspects of a narrowed mental outlook involves the use of language. Words can restrict the mind. Indeed, the utilization of language, the utilization of words, commonly has a restricting effect. Of course words are highly valuable tools for communication. But there is a negative aspect to the use of language. Words often move the word-user one step apart from his or her perception of reality. Each thing seen may be mentally fitted into some linguistic pattern. When that happens, words become a handy substitute for the awareness of reality, and the actuality is often not so likely to be as clearly seen as when there is no word available for it. When the usage of words lessens the experience of the immediate, perception is no longer fresh and new.

Let's look at an illustration of this point. This phenomenon—awareness as word-symbols which, to some extent, substitute for the realization of reality— is manifested in the difficulty with which an adult learns a foreign language. By comparison, children usually learn languages much more easily. The difference between adults and children is probably related—at least to some extent—to the pervasiveness of speech activity in adult minds. The stream of words in the native language tends to overshadow fresh experience which may be correlated with words of a new language. Cassirer gives a good description of this process:

> We can still when learning a foreign language subject ourselves to an experience similar to that of the child. Here it is not sufficient to acquire a new vocabulary or to acquaint ourselves with a system of abstract grammatical rules. All this is necessary but it is only the first and less important step. If we do not learn to think in the new language all our efforts remain fruitless. In most cases we find it extremely difficult to fulfill this requirement. Linguists and psychologists have often raised the question as to how it is possible for a child by his own efforts to accomplish a task that no adult can ever perform in the same way or as well. We can perhaps answer this puzzling question by looking back at our former analysis. In a later and more advanced state of our conscious life we can never repeat the process which led to our first entrance into the world of human speech. In the freshness, in the agility and elasticity of early childhood this process had a quite different meaning. Paradoxically enough the real difficulty consists much less in the learning of the new language than in the forgetting of a former one. We are no longer in the mental condition of the child who for the first time approaches a conception of the objective world. To the adult the objective world already has a definite shape as a result of speech activity, which has in a sense molded all our other activities. Our perceptions, intuitions, and concepts have coalesced with the terms and speech forms of our mother tongue. Great efforts are required to release the bond between words and things. (171-2)

An appreciation of many things requires an openness to experience them. No amount of words or explanation can begin to transmit as much information about the experience as having the experience. An openness to experience can be much more informative than relying on word-symbols about the experience. An example is to feel the experience of swimming, which is quite different from knowing only the mechanisms of that activity.

Much of our mental life is a stream of words. We experience things directly; we see the roses and sometimes even smell them. But direct experience is commonly encroached upon by a stream of conversation that our minds hold with ourselves when not conversing with others. This sea of words is often so pervasive that direct experience very often becomes muted and quite incidental.

The outlook of openness provides a receptivity to direct experience, a perceptiveness of the actuality before us. We become attuned to seeing the reality which the present moment brings. The flood of words that usually inundates our minds is released into a backwater upon which we remain able to draw. However, with openness to the present moment, the pool of words in the backwater does not drown the vision of direct experience. Words become tools that we use instead of preoccupations that engulf us.

When understanding is narrowed by preconceptions that are wrapped in words, perceptiveness is inhibited. However, I will say, as an aside, that the role of words may at times be quite different from the usual role, which is objective representation. In this different role words become part of the direct experience, relaying experience by their subjective, expressive quality as distinct from objective actuality.

Al: I don't know what you mean by that. What do you mean by words as subjective experience separate from objectivity?

I have a good example for you, the first verse of the poem "Jabberwocky" by Lewis Carroll. It might call forth visual images, but the experience is primarily a subjective awareness.

'Twas brillig, and the slithy toves
Did gyre and gimble in the wabe;
All mimsy were the borogoves,
And the mome raths outgrabe. (267)

Words can be used to create an awareness that is primarily subjective, as just illustrated. However, let's note the inadequacy of words in describing subjective experience. In this realm, the inadequacy of words for the description of subjective mental content is considered by Armstrong when she discusses non-verbal aesthetic experience. She refers to the work of the Early Middle Age Greek monk Nicephoras, who correlated visual experience with the effect of music: "When describing the effect of these religious paintings, Nicephoras could only compare it to the effect of music, the most ineffable of the arts and possibly the most direct. Emotion and experience are conveyed by music in a way that bypasses words and concepts" (223).

IMAGINATION

The consideration of poetry and music has brought us to the subject of the imagination. To begin this section, let's first look at the relationship between imagination and aesthetics. A characteristic of the aesthetic realm is artistic expression that draws a person into an awareness of immediate experience. This awareness of present experience may be enhanced by imagination because imagination can provide the mental freedom to be open to perceptiveness. An understanding of the imagination is valuable for gaining a greater insight into the nature of freedom and openness.

Cassirer discusses the effect of aesthetic experience in the broadening of perceptiveness: "Our aesthetic perception exhibits a much greater variety and belongs to a much more complex order than our ordinary sense perception. In sense perception we are content with apprehending the common and constant features of the objects of our surroundings. Aesthetic experience is incomparably richer. It is pregnant with infinite possibilities which remain unrealized in ordinary sense experience" (185-6).

He goes on to say: "One of the greatest triumphs of art is to make us see commonplace things in their real shape and in their true light" (200). Cassirer enlarges on this theme: "The plastic arts make us see the sensible world in all its richness and multifariousness... The infinite potentialities of which we had but a dim and obscure presentiment are brought to light by the lyric poet, by the novelist, and by the dramatist. Such art is in no sense mere counterfeit or facsimile, but a genuine manifestation of our inner life" (215).

The observer is not passive during aesthetic experience. He or she is actively receptive to the experience. As an active recipient, the spectator of an aesthetic presentation becomes also a participant. Cassirer refers to this activity of the observer: "The artistic eye is not a passive eye that receives and registers the impression of things. It is a constructive eye, and it is only by constructive acts that we can discover the beauty of natural things. The sense of beauty is the susceptibility to the dynamic life of forms, and this life cannot be apprehended except by a corresponding dynamic process in ourselves" (193).

Knowledge about the effect of imagination in the various areas of aesthetics — the plastic arts, literature, and music—helps to elucidate the psychologic processes of imagination. The expression of aesthetic works bears witness to the processes of imagination. Receptiveness to aesthetic experience demonstrates how imagination favors the manifestation of freedom, spontaneity, and openness. Words do not confirm this; the experience does. Bachelard refers to the manifestation of freedom associated with the imagination (using the term "reverie" in referring to the dynamics of imagination): "It is striking that the most favorable field for receiving the consciousness of freedom is none other than reverie.... Psychologically speaking, it is in reverie that we are free beings" (Reverie 101). The expression of the imagination carries with it an expression of freedom.

This freedom afforded by imagination can give a lighthearted touch to the direction in which we are going and activities we are pursuing when we include a capacity for the imagination in everyday life. Imaginative freedom can ease attachments and desires. A lighthearted outlook may release a person from an excessive focus on his or her direction, allowing greater appreciation for the ongoing experience of the immediate moment. This can provide a flowing course of fulfillment in that experience which is occurring at the time.

This is not to deny future needs. Attention to these remains adequate to the situation. Responsibility for the future is maintained, but maintained with an engaged detachment. This detachment welcomes the primacy of the moment, not in denial of responsibility but as detachment that opens a person to a receptiveness to the immediacy of experience. Living in the moment is valuable, but not when there is denial of future needs or valid concerns.

Imagination can provide the freedom that allows insight into previously unrealized shades of meaning and understanding of what is now, of what may be in the future, and a more clear idea of the actuality of the past.

Let's look at a comprehensive view of the nature of the imagination. Of course, the imagination is active when experiencing fantasies and wondrous images, but, as I alluded to above, it is more than just that. Certainly imagination is a vehicle to the world of fantasy, but, in addition, imagination is an active and important part of everyday life. Imagination provides a person with a "feel for things;" it is a vehicle for perceptiveness and appreciative wonder. A person can realize an added dimension of awareness by the use of imagination. With imagination, the personality of another individual can become more fully realized; the awareness of another individual's character takes on added depth. Also, with imagination, the visualization of potentialities for future actions and interactions are often multiplied. Imagination is a vehicle for both greater awareness of the present and for future potentialities. In addition, the freedom of the imagination may allow a clearer idea of the actuality of the past.

At this point, let's look at the role of imagination in relation to initiative. Much of life is usually greatly affected by the expression of initiative. The choice of goals and attitudes are determined not only by objective circumstances but also by subjective tendencies. An active initiative typically has a large influence on these choices. Furthermore, the imagination is active in the capacity to visualize potentialities and is therefore a significant factor in the creation of initiative. It is not surprising, then, that the imagination is a major component of life. It is true that the imagination is subjective. However, the realm of subjectivity should not be disregarded because it is non-objective, non-factual. The imagination is highly important; it is a very significant part of the full life. The role of initiative attests to the value of subjectivity and the imagination.

Take another look at the role of the imagination in the facilitation of perceptiveness. Imagination frees the mind; imagination affords a receptivity to insight into that which had previously been only partly seen or understood. In place of an understanding completed by the short-cuts of language and preconceived habits of perception, a person can become more open to the immediate, allowing a fuller knowledge of the present actuality. Often the experiences of life are taken for granted. However, in place of a mundane—and possibly bored—outlook, imagination affords freedom for a more authentic perceptiveness. Such freedom of the imagination is similar to the outlook during childhood, that time of life when there is freshness of vision and openness to new experiences. Such openness contrasts with the vision of a world that is mentally cluttered by word-symbols and preconceptions. The view of the world that adults have is often a view which is distorted by the persistence of prior experience and preconceptions. Bachelard alludes to this phenomenon: "Opening onto the objective World, entering into the objective World or constituting a World we hold to be objective are long processes that can only be described by positive psychology. But these steps taken to constitute a stable world after a thousand readjustments make us forget the brilliance of the first openings" (Reverie 13).

Imagination frees the mind into an openness, a receptivity into expansiveness that welcomes experience. Bachelard describes this: "In the human psyche, (imagination) is the very experience of opening and newness. More than any other power, it determines the human psyche" (Imagination 19). He elaborates upon this receptiveness: "The I no longer opposes itself to the world. In reverie there is no more non-I. In reverie, the 'no' no longer has any function: everything is welcome" (Reverie 167).

This welcoming quality of openness has the sense of entering upon a newness of experience. Bachelard refers to this sense of newness in poetic reverie: "The poetic reverie is always new before the object to which it attaches itself" (Reverie 156). He then correlates poetic experience with a general view of psychological life: "Undoubtedly, the imaginary lays down images during its prodigious life, but it always appears to exist beyond its images; it is always a little more than its images. The poem is essentially an aspiration to new images. It corresponds to this essential need for newness that characterizes the human psyche" (Imagination 20).

Imagination is active in the welcoming anticipation of experience. There is fulfillment in both the experience itself and in the anticipation of that experience. When I reach for an ice cream cone, the pleasure comes with both the enjoyment of the cone and the anticipation of that enjoyment.

Imagination allows ambiguous correlations, including dipping into the seemingly unrelated and into the more profound or universal. New perspectives come to the attention. One becomes aware of new potentialities. Again to quote Bachelard: "... images reveal different ways to live human time and to interiorize objects and distances" (Imagination *lviii*).

Openness of imagination to awareness of the unfolding experience includes more than experience of that which is objective and concrete. With imagination we are also open to ambiguity, to the wide range of possibilities that are not guided in some particular direction but are free to be carried into uncharted perspectives and concepts. Furthermore, such non-directed experience can be correlated with the facts, with objectivity, with logical thought. The synthesis of the non-directed experience of imagination with that which is more objective carries the potentiality for enlarging a person's outlook. This synthesis of the subjective with the objective is a source for novelty in practical applications. It is also a source for wonder, for joyful awareness. Bachelard refers to the correlation of the real with the imaginary:

> Indeed, our manner of escaping reality points unmistakably to our inner reality. A man deprived of the *function of unreality* is just as neurotic as the man deprived of the *function of reality*. One can say that a disturbance of the function of unreality has repercussions on the function of reality. If the function of *opening out*, which is precisely the function of imagination, is badly

performed, perception itself remains obtuse. We must therefore find a regular connection from the real to the imaginary. (Imagination 37)

A further delineation of the function of unreality is described by Bachelard, and in this note he points to a release from the automatism of language: "With poetry, the imagination takes its place on the margin, exactly where the function of unreality comes to charm or to disturb—always to awaken—the sleeping being lost in its automatisms. The most insidious of these automatisms, the automatism of language, ceases to function when we enter into the domain of pure sublimation" (Space *xxxi*).

I will restate that a receptivity to perceptiveness is enhanced by freedom of the imagination. Furthermore, this freedom is facilitated by two mental processes that have been previously discussed: doubt and detachment. When preconceptions dominate one's view of things, a person's vision becomes narrowed. However, when a person has some measure of doubt of and detachment from preconceptions, he or she is more likely to be free to be open and perceptive, more free to engage the imagination for fullness of insight and understanding. Both doubt and detachment facilitate the freedom described.

Al: Excuse me. You said that imagination frees the mind. Then you said freedom facilitates the imagination. That sounds circular.

It does because it is. Imagination provides a ground for freedom, and freedom can open the way to the imagination. Imagination and freedom are companion psychological processes.

Imagination welcomes openness to insights that go beyond that which had been previously known. The activity of imagination encompasses an enlarged sense of awareness. Furthermore, it is often a spontaneous happenstance that the enlargement of awareness is accompanied by a feeling of happiness and well-being. That view which is more encompassing tends to bring a sense of well-being with it. Bachelard alludes to this phenomenon by using the word "sing" to signify happiness and well-being: "Imagination is not, as its etymology would suggest, the faculty of forming images of reality; it is rather the faculty of forming images which go beyond reality, which sing reality" (Imagination 15).

Caution is indicated for one particular tendency: the inclination of the imagination to unify diverse experiences into common categories. There is a natural tendency for the mind to unify the disparate appearance of experiences, a tendency to abstract common themes in order to get a circumscribed perspective. Abstractions ease our handling of the multitude of perceptions that we encounter. This abstracting tendency has much value. For instance, witness the enormous value of inductive reasoning for the realm of science. Advances in scientific understanding and technology are made possible by the inclination to unify the input of diverse observations. However, the tendency to unify experience can be overdone in many realms: in scientific conclusions that are premature, and in the course of everyday life and other non-scientific realms. There are pitfalls. The translator of Bachelard's *On Poetic Imagination and Reverie*, Colette Gaudin, characterizes this:

> We must always bear in mind Bachelard's vigorous warnings against the temptation to unify and reduce to identicals, which he saw as one of the most important 'epistemological obstacles.' Instead of immobilizing the intuition by a too rapid unification, as in prescientific theories, living thought should be dominated by its 'shifting character,' which is an ability to shake off intellectual habits, to accept the lessons of an evolving science. For Bachelard this is the *sine qua non* of the modern educator. He rejects the role of the scholar who shares the fruit of his learning in the form of established truths, and invites us to experience with him 'the essential mobility of concepts.' (She adds a footnote:) This is a central notion of Bachelard's philosophy. It designates not a superficial mobility which replaces one concept with another, but an internal dialectic which does not need to change denominations. Modern science has progressively 'rectified' ancient concepts, such as that of the atom, by detaching them from a fixed content. This mobility is equally essential to imagination. Reverie shatters frozen meanings and restores to old words ambivalence and freedom. (*xxxiii-xxxiv*)

We have discussed that aspect of imagination which gives a greater awareness of the present and in fact leads to an enhanced perceptiveness of the past, the present, and potentialities for the future. In later chapters we will further explore the elements of ambiguity and opposition in the workings of imagination.

I have one final note for this section, a quote by Bachelard regarding the significance of imagination: "Psychically, we are created by our reverie, for it is reverie that delineates the furthest confines of our mind" (Imagination 33).

The Swamp of Anguish; the Flow of Openness

SUMMARY

It's time for a review of the chapter. We talked about anguish. Much of the time in which anguish is present, it is burdensome, and we usually want to avoid this anguish by resolving it or denying it. However, when anguish is freely chosen and causes no great difficulties, it may be welcomed.

One of the ways in which anguish is handled is to seek control.

Al: Fine. I like to control anguish.

Right. But, is there too much control at times? A balance in dealing with the issues of control is valuable for the full life. Though a reasonable amount of control is important in everyday life, difficulties can be associated with an excessive drive for control. Overemphasis on control can decrease a person's perceptiveness and it can be destructive of interpersonal relationships. In addition, at those times when only a limited amount of control is possible, an acceptance of that limit can mitigate anguish.

In contradistinction to a controlled attitude, the outlook of openness is free and spontaneous. Openness implies a cleared mind that is receptive to an awareness of the immediate experience. A full life includes the merging of control—control as that amount of discipline and responsibility appropriate for the situation—with the flow of openness and spontaneity. Both control and openness are part of the full llife.

In looking further at the nature of openness, the importance of detachment and freedom was emphasized, and reference was made to the effect of language on openness.

The utilization of detachment can provide a release from excessively focussed desires and goals. With detachment, freedom is gained, allowing an openness which can give relief from possibly distorted perceptions and beliefs.

However, I do not recommend a detachment that is total; the term "engaged detachment" provides for the retention of those beliefs and goals which are appropriate for the situation.

At times, detachment involves self-surrender, a giving of oneself to the experience at hand. An example is a surrender to the mood of music. By self-surrender I do not mean to imply either self-denial or the relinquishment of an access to doubt and examination. The use of the term "engaged detachment" signifies that, if such detachment is manifested in a state of self-surrender, the capacity to release oneself from that state is retained.

Finally, we talked about the characteristics of imagination as a manifestation of openness, and we explored the role of the imagination in aesthetic experience. Imagination plays a role in the experience of wonder, in the perceptiveness of actuality, and in an awareness of potentiality. To quote Bachelard: "... one can also understand the great value in establishing a phenomenology of the imaginary where the imagination is restored to its proper all-important place as the principle of direct stimulation of psychic becoming" (Reverie 8).

5

Review and the Realms of Being and Becoming

Al: Chapter Four covered a lot of territory. I'd like to take a break. Could we walk outside and see what you have planted around the house?

Sure. Through this door. This is a big bush with little leaves. And this is a little bush with little leaves. And this is quite a tree. Then there's this one. And this one.

Al: I'm glad you didn't tell me the names of the trees and bushes. I don't want to come across much new information in this chapter. It's break time.

Would you like to hear a brief overview during this break?

Al: That would be good.

Fine. Let's start with Chapter One. This was a stylized presentation meant to convey an understanding of the value of the information being presented in this book.

In Chapter Two doubt and the nature of truth were discussed, including a concern about the traps of self-righteousness that may accompany a faith in absolute truths. Truths can be recognized as tentative while maintaining an openness that can doubt all. Furthermore, the capacity to be open and to doubt can inspire a confidence that tends to avoid self-righteousness.

In Chapter Three an outlook was described that is axiomatic, having no objective base upon which to justify it except its useful outcome. This outlook is the attitude of thankfulness. There are a multitude of possible mind-sets toward the existence of the self and the universe. A person could say that all is evil, corrupt, self-serving, and without value. The universe can be seen to have any number of negative characteristics. At the opposite pole is the attitude of thankfulness for life, health, and good fortune. This has the salutary effect of generating a welcoming outlook toward that which we experience.

Openness and freedom were discussed in Chapter Four. This discussion included descriptions of many facets of openness: freedom, the cleared mind, anticipation of the immediate experience, the sense of enlarged awareness, ambiguity, and the imagination.

We can now consider the characteristics described in the context of "being" and "becoming." Thankfulness is an attitude toward existence, toward being. Openness takes place in the realm of becoming. Thankfulness is an outlook toward that which exists now and that which has led to the current state of existence. Openness, freedom, and the imagination are operative in the ongoing realm of the present and extend into possibilities for the future. This does not deny the place of imagination in visualizing the past, but, as related to the qualities of openness and freedom, the role of the imagination in the present and future is particularly emphasized.

6

Self-absorption

Absorption With Self
A Commercial
Many Paths
Out of the Pit

ABSORPTION WITH SELF

"When the images of earth cling too tightly to memory, when the call of happiness becomes too insistent, it happens that melancholy rises in man's heart… " (Camus, Sisyphus 90).

Al: I appreciate the quote by Camus. But I will say that I want to be happy.

Well said. Most people want to be happy. And many feel they are not treating themselves well enough to be happy. This brings to mind a non-poem:

I'm Not Thinking Enough About Myself

Am I doing enough for myself?
I'm not thinking enough about
myself. I'm not treating
myself well enough.
I should become a machine
geared to my own
gratification.
Then I'll be happy.
Well—maybe not happy.
But at least I'll be thinking about
     being happy.

For many people, life is centered on looking for happiness in a way that is characterized by excessive focus on the satisfaction of their physical and emotional needs. Their life is lived in the pit of self-absorption. When people are totally wrapped up in thoughts about their personal circumstances, they are self-absorbed.

Al: Is self-absorption wrong? Shouldn't we indulge ourselves? Shouldn't we keep eating till we are full and satisfied—and maybe even somewhat bloated?

You don't have to limit your question to eating. You could ask the same about any indulgence. Should we stuff our homes with goods? Should we stuff our pride with a continual search for affirmation by others?

Look at what others have to say about the excess desire for that with which we would indulge ourselves. In his masterpiece, *The Divine Comedy*, the medieval Italian author Dante puts it this way: "Now may you see the fleeting vanity of the goods of Fortune for which men tear down all that they are, to build a mockery" (*Inferno* VII, lines 61-3).

Dissatisfaction with the goals of our desires is described in the Old Testament: "He that loveth silver shall not be satisfied with silver; nor he that loveth abundance with increase: this is also vanity" (Eccl. 5:10). Also, in the Old Testament: "... ye shall eat, and not be satisfied" (Lev. 26:26). Dissatisfaction may manifest itself in wrath, as described by St. Paul in the New Testament: "Among whom also we all had our conversation in times past in the lusts of our flesh, fulfilling the desires of the flesh and of the mind; and were by nature the children of wrath, even as others" (Eph. 2:3).

A compulsion toward any desire can lead to pain. Tolstoy describes an obsession with finding peace in his story of *The Death of Ivan Ilyich*: "... he said that he needed peace, and he watched for everything that might disturb it and became irritable at the slightest infringement of it" (1965).

I want to say something about what is called the "me generation." the awareness of a me generation began quite some time after World War II. The orientation of individuals in the me generation is self-centeredness, as opposed to concern about others. This orientation seems to be more than just a passing phase; the attitude of a centeredness on the self appears to be a continuing norm for many. I believe the thought of concern about and service to others seems strange and unnatural to a large number of people. For this me generation, the focussing of attention on activities is apparently satisfactory only when safeguards are in place that constantly survey these activities so that the self is indulged. With this amount of self-centeredness, the needs and desires of others tend to be excluded.

God Unmasked; the Full Life Revealed

In the next two chapters we will consider more extensively the subjects of empathy and the interaction with others. In the present chapter I take issue with that outlook which is excessively self-centered.

Self-centeredness is an outlook that is more an "in-look." Instead of the freedom and spontaneity of openness, the experiences of life are constricted into a mode of judgment and evaluation. When there is excessive self-centeredness, experiences are continually weighed in a balance that favors the self.

In arguing against self-centeredness, I do not mean to imply a denial of the needs and concerns of the self. The protection and fulfillment of the self require attention, but the attention should not exclude that freedom and spontaneity which can accompany a full measure of openness to the experience at hand. If such openness includes an appreciation of others, this need not be avoided by a self-absorbed individual on the grounds that it is not self-serving. Self-centeredness should not inhibit the joy of experiencing that which is occurring in the immediate moment. It is valuable to have a wholehearted receptivity to ongoing experiences.

Neither openness nor self-centeredness need to be exclusive of each other. As stated above, self-centeredness should not inhibit an openness to the joy of the moment. On the other hand, the free flow of openness and activity should not entail a negation of the needs of the self. For example, if I am skipping rope, that activity includes some watchfulness to minimize the chance of tripping on the rope. If I enjoy hiking on a mountain trail, the experience can be a wholehearted enjoyment without excluding a watchfulness that I don't slip off the path and into some deep ravine.

I will break in to mention something parenthetically here about an aspect of self-centeredness: the topic of indulgence. The subject of indulgence brings up a point concerning the larger social realm. Is it right for one segment of society to have the means for gross over-indulgence while another group goes hungry? How much inequality in the distribution of economic goods is justified? These are questions about fairness in the distribution of goods. I won't address those technical aspects of social and economic structure in this book. The characteristic of self-indulgence that we do take up is that which may negate the sense of wholeness and fulfillment of our lives. Can it be all that satisfying to center our lives on the endless piling in of that which pleases us?

The desire for things is certainly promoted by mass media. The heart of our economic system is the creation and maintenance of a demand for goods. Advertising enhances this demand.

The desire for goods is often open-ended, ready to ask for more in spite of that which has already been fulfilled.

Al: Yes. When I pick raspberries, I am looking for the next one while I'm eating the one I had just picked.

I do the same. I am not promoting a denial of life's pleasures. Instead, I recommend a moderation that releases a person from an imprisonment in a state of constant desire. It is constricting for psychologic well-being to remain in a state of desire that excludes a more complete outlook on life.

There is a "me-centeredness" that accompanies excess self-indulgence. Furthermore, the increased exposure to advertising in the modern era can lead to an attitude of self-centeredness. This self-centered orientation often sets one's outlook into a pattern of comparison. A person may habitually compare his or her state to what might have been, obsessively regretting that which has been lost or was never obtained.

It is common for a person overly concerned with comparisons to be excessively aware of the material state of others. A continuing orientation of comparison with others constricts life into a state of constant envy. Such a constricted life of envy makes someone less likely to find contentment and happiness.

A COMMERCIAL

Let's pause for some relief from these thoughts about self-absorption. Here is a surrealistic television commercial:

(Scene 1; setting: television studio)

(Cast of characters, alphabetically: A, B, C, D)

A: I'm choosy. I value my ability to doubt. I want to discern what is best.

B: Cut. Don't use the word "discern" in a television commercial.

A: O. K. I want to find out what is best. Some brands look good but lack quality.

B: You can say that about people, too.

A: That doesn't belong in the commercial. We are not selling people. We are selling a product.

B: But this is more than a commercial. It's a way of life.

A: Production stops while you philosophize.

B: We are still in production. We are looking for value in people. Some are worthy, and some we avoid.

A: So you judge quality.

B: We both do, and judge quality in ourselves, too. There is a state of perfection, an ideal. What are the needs for this ideal? How does reality measure up? Our lives are in a state of judgment.

A: Do you smear this judgment with something obnoxious?

B: What do you mean?

A: Do you corrupt this judgment and throw it into destruction?

B: I have values. I don't destroy values.

(Scene 2; setting: sunny outdoors)

C: The light. The warmth of reality. I see a face. I see a mountain. The leaf has become yellow, now dropped, withered,

       lost,

              unable to know the new bud, the new leaf,

new, green and warm in

        the sun. The life. . . and

   death. I hear groaning. . . pain. . . and joy.

       Pit of dying. Magic of life.

(Second observer takes drink of orange pop.)

D: That's a nice reverie you have.

C: In judgment . . .

D: Yes?

C: is destruction.

D: Tell me an easier riddle.

C: That's not a riddle. Do you want to know a secret?

D: I want to know what you are getting at.

C: But you have to be lost.

Self-absorption

D: *I know where I am.*

C: *That's the problem*

D: *I asked for an easy riddle.*

C: *This is extremely easy. If it's hard, you can't solve it. The way to the solution is the solution. The way is easy.*

D: *And you mean what?*

C: *You have a need to know what I mean.*

D: *Yes.*

C: *And you have a need to value your experiences. What is the best product? What fills your needs?*

But life is not a commercial. You are more than a mechanism of need. You need bread. You need water. You need a two-door sedan with anti-lock brakes and airbags. You need a partner that meets your needs.

D: *Is there a limit on how many times we use the word "need?"*

C: *That's the point. We can get beyond the "n" word. We can hold our needs in abeyance so that they are not denied but handled in due time. We can surrender our thoughts and fill our minds with wonder and thankfulness. We can surrender to the experience itself, in thankfulness and wonder. We can live in the experience before us, open to the vibrance of the person, the tree, the air and the clouds. In joy we fill the cup of experience, renewing it with each new perception.*

D: *Excuse me, but no way does this sound like any sort of television commercial, and it hasn't for most of this bit that you call a commercial.*

C: *That's true. Maybe you could call it an anti-commercial. And let's wrap up this anti-commercial with these qualifying words: The release from excess need and judgmentalism need not entail a denial of beliefs, values, and responsibilities. Needs, values, judgments, beliefs, responsibilities—these are all maintained and in balance with the joys of openness and freedom. In addition, it is well to have the openness to be able to examine needs and values and maintain the ones that should be maintained.*

We do not deny that which is valid for our lives. However, we can free ourselves from judgmentalism and release ourselves from an excess concern about needs. Any value can be doubted, re-examined, and maintained when valid. The open outlook allows new doubt, new perceptiveness, and the possibility to become aware of new potentialities. Openness is the path to wonder, thankfulness, and joy.

In the New Testament St. Paul talks about a release from excess desire. Though the religious basis for his statements is different from that presented in this book, it is worthwhile to hear his words: "Not that I speak in respect of want: for I have learned, in whatsoever state I am, therewith to be content. I know both how to be abased, and I know how to abound: every where and in all things I am instructed both to be full and to be hungry, both to abound and to suffer need" (Phil. 4:11-12).

The view of the good life as presented by advertising is, of course, far different from that of St. Paul. Advertising presents the concept that a fulfilled life is equated with the consumption of goods or with an image that the use of those goods presents to others. This advertised image can become a projected view of what the self should be like. In *Legislators and Interpreters,* social scientist Zygmunt Bauman describes the presentation of image in the promotion of goods. In this passage he points to the tendency of marketing forces to promote frustration in order to increase sales:

> Individual needs of personal autonomy, self-definition, authentic life or personal perfection are all translated into the need to possess, and consume, market-offered goods. This translation, however, pertains to the appearance of use value of such goods, rather than to the use value itself; ... The market feeds on the unhappiness it generates: the fears, anxieties and the sufferings of personal inadequacy it induces release the consumer behavior indispensable to its continuation. (189)

MANY PATHS

Let's move on to the next topic; excess self-indulgence is but one form of self-absorption. There are many forms that self-centeredness may take. Some people are stuck in repetitive patterns of self-examination. They are inclined to mull over their problems endlessly in a compulsive pattern of self-observation. As Nicolas Berdyaev, Russian philosopher of religion, says: "...boundless self-affirmation, which admits nothing save itself, brings about man's immediate ruin" (137).

We have previously talked about the value of a positive outlook afforded by a sense of thankfulness. Not only does an endless state of

Self-absorption

self-examination inhibit the likelihood for that positive experience created by the outlook of thankfulness; continual self-examination can also detract from an openness toward awareness of the actuality of the present moment. The narrowing of vision that is associated with excess self-examination can be better comprehended by noting an example that is similar. This does not involve self-examination, but it does point to a problem associated with being in a constant process of evaluating. I refer to a particular difficulty when watching a pair of excellent figure skaters on television. The announcer's running commentary, evaluating the performance, detracts from enjoying the beauty of the experience.

Self-centeredness may take the form of narcissism. A person may be so centered on his or her own state and own needs that they have no realization of the needs or states of anyone else. Others are seen as merely agents available for the use of such narcissistic individuals. Giddens comments on this subject:

> Narcissism relates outside events to the needs and desires of the self, asking only 'what this means to me'. Narcissism presumes a constant search for self-identity, but this is a search which remains frustrated, because the restless pursuit of 'who I am' is an expression of narcissistic absorption rather than a realizable quest. . . . The horizons of the person's activity seem bleak and unappealing in spite of, or rather because of the chronic search for gratification. At the same time, any sense of personal dignity or civic duty tends to evaporate. Authenticity substitutes for dignity: what makes an action good is that it is authentic to the individual's desires, and can be displayed to others as such…. The narcissistic personality has only a shadowy understanding of the needs of others, and feelings of grandiosity jostle with sentiments of emptiness and inauthenticity. Lacking full engagement with others, the narcissist depends on continual infusion of admiration and approval to bolster an uncertain sense of self-worth. (170-2)

Self-destructiveness is another area of self-centeredness. The German writer Goethe noted in his work *Faust*: "How men torment themselves, that's all I see" (1644).

Some self-destructiveness is probably intentional in that some people may want to experience pain. In this book I won't conjecture about possible psychologic mechanisms involved in self-destructiveness. I am just pointing to self-destructiveness as one of the areas of self-centeredness.

The well of self-centeredness may leave a person with a cynical view of life. Many authors have described this effect in people and may themselves have this view of life. To quote the ancient Greek poet Homer: "Such is the way the gods spun life for unfortunate mortals, that we live in unhappiness ... " (*The Iliad: XXIV*, lines 525-6).

Another manifestation of self-centeredness is the state of excess want for want, the need for "angst," the excess drive toward being in the state of striving. Fulfillment may just lead to more striving. This additional striving may fill the need to avoid a sense of emptiness. Maslow describes the feeling of emptiness that may accompany the fulfillment of desires: ". . . affluence itself throws into the clearest, coldest light the spiritual, ethical philosophical hunger of mankind. (This is so because striving for something one lacks inevitably makes one feel that life has a meaning and that life is worthwhile. But when one lacks nothing, and has nothing to strive for, then…?)" (38)

It is often the case that the desire to be in a state of desire and striving takes the form of desire for perfection. This drive for perfection aims beyond any possibility for achievement; therefore, it is a potential source of misery. Psychiatrist Fritz Perls makes a statement about the excess of perfectionism: "Leave this to the human—to try to be something he is not—to have ideals that cannot be reached, to be cursed with perfectionism so as to be safe from criticism, and to open the road to unending mental torture" (8).

The impact of perfectionism can, indeed, be quite upsetting, particularly when the impossibility of perfection is realized. It is a revelation to most of us when we learn about personal imperfections which are difficult or impossible to correct. Such can be alarming discoveries. I quote from Conrad: "I tell you my friend, it is not good for you to find you cannot make your dream come true, for the reason that you not strong enough are, or not clever enough. *Ja!*—And all the time you are such a fine fellow, too! *Wie? Was? Gott in Himmel*! How can that be? Ha! ha! ha!" (245).

I will say that physical or personality deficiencies are not something about which to remain in a state of denial. They are not to be ignored unless they have no significance. Instead of denial, the acknowledgement of a deficiency can lead to an acceptance of that deficiency. In addition, the openness to realization of that which can be considered an imperfection carries with it the potential for a modification of perception of the deficiency and the possibility for constructive change of this perception. Regarding the outlook on imperfection, Shunryu Suzuki states: "In your very imperfections you will find the basis for your firm, way-seeking mind" (38). He further says: "... there is no certain way that exists permanently. There is no way set up for us. Moment after moment we have to find our own way. Some idea of perfection, or some perfect way which is set up by someone else, is not the true way for us" (111). And later: "In constantly seeking to actualize your ideal, you will have no time for composure" (116).

An acceptance of imperfection does not necessitate passiveness. A person can have an active role in the process of acceptance. In that process there is a mental shifting, a reorientation, that occurs. A new sense of awareness develops concerning that which had been understood in the old way. As Reynolds states:

> ... the usefulness of accepting reality, both that part of it we can change and that part we can't. We may see acceptance as a sort of giving up, a last resort. In fact, acceptance of the way things are is always the first step in changing things. Denial of reality, resistance to reality, fantasies, and even elaborate plans don't accomplish change. ... we must distinguish between positive acceptance and negative passivity. (35)

He further states: "When we accept the reality of what is and what is not possible, we stop pressuring ourselves to achieve the unachievable" (78).

I will mention a problem with an outlook that is opposite to the desire to have desire. The desire to not desire: that is also desire.

Al: I lost track, and I couldn't say that three times fast.

It's more than a tongue-twister. Let me explain. Some who have an orientation toward Eastern religion strive for that enlightenment which is manifested by the achievement of having no goal, having no striving. The ones who strive for this are still goal-oriented, albeit toward the end of having no goal. On the other hand enlightenment becomes more closely approximated by losing that goal of having no goal.

Al: You mean: "Don't sweat it?"

You have the picture. Now let's pull some of this information together. Fear, excess mental ruminations, perfectionism, excess indulgence—there are many pathways to self-absorption, to self-centeredness. It is even possible to hear religious services that pander to self-centeredness by proclaiming the message: "You can be great! You can be that wonderful person inside of you." If this sort of statement is overdone, the centeredness on the self can become excessive; self-image can become excessively indulged.

OUT OF THE PIT

Let's climb out of the pit of self-centeredness. Let's welcome a fullness of life.

That climb from the depth of excess self-absorption does not entail self-denial. Certainly, pleasures are a part of the full life. The release from self-absorption does not require a denial of that which we would enjoy, so long as the search for or indulgence in pleasure does not consume the individual. A passage in the Old Testament discusses this: "There is nothing better for a man, than that he should eat and drink, and that he should make his soul enjoy good in his labour. This also I saw, that it was from the hand of God" (Eccl. 2:24). The prime fact of life is existence—the presence of life itself—and the primary values are thankfulness for existence and the openness and freedom of a cleared mind. A commitment to these prime values does not require a denial of worldly pleasures. A grounding in fundamental values may, in fact, enhance the experience of pleasure. These values can facilitate a degree of detachment which allows pleasures to be indulged in without the compulsion of excess neediness. With an open, free outlook, it is easier for us to have a freedom from excess desires.

In place of self-denial, a detached view of self can allow a more valid sense of self to emerge. Detachment makes possible that amount of self-awareness that is needed and appropriate for self-maintenance, direction, and a sense of identity without being absorbed into a pit of excess self-concern. In this perspective, self-awareness is incidental to the life of self-surrender and secondary to the life of full engagement. A healthy degree of self awareness is a part of the full life.

Some people are not attuned to openness, to freedom, to the value of self-surrender and the sense of enlarged awareness. Such a person could say: "I don't want to be free. I want to be imprisoned by my own desires, by my own image. Things should be in their arranged order and under control. Life is to be circumscribed by order and prepackaged knowledge. All is to be in arrangement."

Al: Hold on, there. I get suspicious when I hear the term self-surrender. Too many people blindly follow authority. It is too easy to give up your mind, to give up your sense of what is reasonable, to a person or a slogan or an institution or whatever. It is not right to blindly surrender to anyone or anything.

I am glad you know the lesson of doubt. I am glad I put in that chapter about doubt early. And I did discuss self-surrender in Chapter Four. Do you remember the example of the music? A self-surrender to the rhythm of the music does not mean that you cannot stop dancing. By self-surrender, I do not mean that the availability of doubt and discernment should be avoided.

Let's say just a bit more in finishing this chapter. I want to repeat my point about the value of obtaining relief from the constricted outlook of self-centeredness. Release from self-centeredness can enlarge a person's view; this release can allow an openness to an enhanced awareness and understanding of surroundings. Life is enriched by this outlook of enlarged awareness. As Hick states:

> ...by ending or suspending this self-centered discriminative activity we can at last experience the world as it is. By renouncing the ego point of view we can become part of the dynamic movement which is reality itself in its pure "suchness," with its own ineffable fullness and richness. ... When one is empty of the discriminative self-concerned ego, then the world is empty of all that human thought had projected upon it; and it is now just what it is, full of its own being.... (289)

7

Empathy, Anti-empathy, and Action

Overview of the Chapter

Definition of Empathy and Predisposing Factors

Love

Action and Anti-Empathy

Factors That Limit Empathy

Self-negation

The Interplay and Flow of Empathy and Action

OVERVIEW OF THE CHAPTER

An overview of this chapter will be helpful. We start with the definition of empathy and the factors that predispose toward empathy, followed by a short discussion about love.

A shift to the subject of physical action includes a consideration of characteristic modes of action. One of the possible attitudes that can be associated with action is an opposition to empathy. An attitude of anti-empathy is a significant force in human interaction, and its value and drawbacks are discussed. Other paths to an anti-empathy orientation include: withdrawal from interpersonal contact, rebellion, and impatience.

Also, there are many factors that may not exclude empathy but tend to limit it. These factors that tend to decrease the inclination toward empathy are pre-programmed attitudes. Such attitudes include judgmentalism, undiscerning sympathy or love, an excessive desire for action or for desire itself, rigid expectations and orientations, misguided suspicion, fear, and excess pride.

Next is a note about self-negation, pointing out that the inclination toward feeling empathy need not entail an outlook of self-denial.

In the last section we take up the interplay of empathy and action. A feeling of ease and peace can accompany the expression of action when the course of action flows in a mode of openness, a mode of receptivity to the inflow of experience.

DEFINITION OF EMPATHY AND PREDISPOSING FACTORS

We talked about the rigidity of self-centeredness in the last chapter. With some relief, we are returning to an aspect of life that is a manifestation of the flow of openness. Openness is one of the factors that can predispose a person toward empathy. Openness implies a receptivity to experience. When someone is receptive to experience, he or she is likely to be empathetic, that is, to be sensitive to the thoughts and feelings of another. An outlook of openness welcomes a perceptiveness of another's personality and outlook, and it gives fresh insight into his or her situation. Therefore, openness can lead a person to empathy, and, just as openness is one of the components of the full life, the ability to empathize, likewise, is a part of the full life.

Here is the dictionary definition of empathy: "the action of understanding, being aware of, being sensitive to, and vicariously experiencing the feelings, thoughts, and experience of another of either the past or present without having the feelings, thoughts, and experience fully communicated in an objectively explicit manner" (378).

The potential for empathy is enhanced when there is a degree of freedom from preconceptions. In this vein S. Suzuki states: "When you listen to someone, you should give up all your preconceived ideas and your subjective opinions; you should just listen to him, just observe what his way is" (87). In further elaboration he says: "The important thing in our understanding is to have a smooth, free-thinking way of observation. We have to think and to observe things without stagnation. We should accept things as they are without difficulty. Our mind should be soft and open enough to understand things as they are" (115).

This description of empathy by Reynolds is informative. However, in contrast to his statement, I would say that realization of similarity is helpful but it is not totally necessary as a condition for empathy:

As we listen with full attention to what others tell us, we begin to notice the similarities between their reality and our own. Their anxiety looks more and more like ours, their struggles resemble ours. With training, we almost seem to become them for periods of time. In other words, they become part of the situation with which we merge. This merging is rather like what is called empathy, though it is broader, encompassing objects and other phenomena as well as people. (68)

The psychologic merging to which Reynolds refers can take place without the necessity for a concept of similarity of problems or outlook. I am more open when I detach from my own situation and become fully receptive to the understanding of the other person. Engaged detachment involves a "distance from" that allows a "closeness to." The detachment is a separation from my own agenda. Empathy, then, need not imply a realization of an alikeness of self with the other.

Openness is one factor predisposing a person toward feeling empathy. Another factor is thankfulness. As I elaborated in Chapter Three, thankfulness provides us with a positive outlook, a welcoming of the experiences of life. This welcome is in the context of a general outlook on the totality of life, and thankfulness also can provide a positive orientation toward the particulars of everyday life. A feeling of thankfulness, then, can incline a person toward openness—toward a receptivity to experience —and openness predisposes that individual toward empathy. You develop a positive anticipation toward a comprehension of what others are like and what their concerns are. Also, consideration and respect for others tends to accompany this experience of empathy. Thankfulness and openness are both operative in the development of an outlook that welcomes the experience of empathy.

LOVE

And now, since we know about empathy, we know about love.

Al: No, we don't. That is, I have experienced love, but you haven't talked about any definition or predisposing factors for love. You like to talk about predisposing factors. Can you tell me a predisposing factor for love? But before you do, I can guess that you will say empathy is one of those factors.

Empathy, Anti-empathy, and Action

Right. When someone is in love, that person has a feeling for and a sensitivity to another. In other words, empathy is involved in the experience of love. In addition, the object of love is highly valued. According to psychology consultant Geoffrey Hamilton:

> Words such as "like," "enjoy," "fondness," "appreciate," etc. represent lesser intensities of emotional value. I suggest that we reserve the word "love" exclusively for the things in our experience that we value the most: for things that have the most importance to us. I recommend that we utilize all the other words at our disposal to represent anything less than what we love. Let "love" define that to which we assign our highest value. (38)

I should point out that we will discuss values in Chapter Twelve and Chapter Twenty-four.

ACTION AND ANTI-EMPATHY

Al: Fine. I can wait for that discussion. Also, I agree with you that empathy, openness, and thankfulness are valuable. These are all valuable qualities, but they are all outlooks, attitudes, orientations. Life is more than mental orientation. Life is also action—doing things. Do you include any comments about action in your concept of the full life?

I certainly do. Obviously, action is a major dimension of life. Except for times of sleep and particular states, such as quiet meditation, action takes place all the time. Furthermore, the will to action is innate. As Cassirer states: "Man cannot live his life without constant efforts to express it" (233). And Nietzsche expresses the joy of action:

> Many heavy things are there for the spirit, the strong loadbearing spirit in which reverence dwelleth: for the heavy and the heaviest longeth for its strength.
>
> What is heavy? So asketh the load-bearing spirit; then kneeleth it down like the camel, and wanteth to be well laden.
>
> What is the heaviest thing, ye heroes? Asketh the load-bearing spirit, that I may take it upon me and rejoice in my strength. (442)

Caution. Keep this in mind: there are reservations about a blind will to action. Action without perceptiveness can be destructive. When openness to new understanding is lacking, the results of actions can be painful.

For some people, a favored recourse to characteristic modes of action may have destructive consequences. Kenneth Burke refers to this problem when he states:

> In a world where one has at his disposal a million ways in which to be inferior, one must necessarily be selective—and one's gifts guide the selection. The trouble seems to arise from the fact that certain superiorities do not reward us or prosper us, so that in the very act of succeeding we may fail. Our abilities may prove obstructive, forcing us either to renounce our best capacities and to concentrate upon more serviceable ones, or to persevere in our ways at the risk of disaster. Usually, in the normal social texture the vocational is marked by a balance of favorable and unfavorable factors. A Beethoven somehow managed to live by the same habits of mind that on occasion gravely endangered him. The difficulty generally arises from the fact that one tries to solve too much by the devices of his gift. In the business of means-selecting, instead of choosing the means with respect to the nature of the problem to be solved, one tends to *state the problem in such a way that his particular aptitude becomes the "solution" for it.* Thus, the young pugilist will so ethicize his fists that he tends to simplify a great diversity of human relationships by considering them capable of treatment in terms of an actual or threatened rap on the chin. And an earnest musician might spontaneously turn to his violin as a cure for disorders which might better be solved by political expedients. Conversely, radical agitators become so engrossed in their political preoccupations that they begin to look upon any other mode of action as evasive. (242-3)

As implied in the above quote, the accustomed mode of action may be instrumental in predisposing someone toward a characteristic mental outlook. In this regard, a relationship can occur between action and mental state that is a reversal of what is considered usual. In Myers' words, our attitudes can be consequent to and be formed by our behavior:

> If social psychologists have proven anything during the last thirty years they have proven that the actions we elect leave a residue inside us. Every time we act, we amplify the underlying idea or tendency. Most people presume the reverse: that our traits and attitudes affect our behavior. That is true (though less so than is commonly supposed). But it's also true that our traits and attitudes *follow* our behavior. We are as likely to *act ourselves into*

a new way of thinking as to think ourselves into a new way of acting. (123)

Al: Let's consider something here. Since empathy implies openness, empathy may involve a willingness to accept a new attitude. This would be a break in the pattern of attitudes. Right?

Yes.

Al: Well, then, if patterns of attitudes and action are so closely interwoven, empathy would seem to be excluded. Empathy would involve a break in that pattern because empathy signifies an openness to the possibility of a fresh and new perceptiveness of another person or situation.

That's true. The openness to empathy implies the potential for a break in the pattern. However, there also is a certain degree of value in the opposite orientation, action without empathy, action without openness to insight and understanding. However, I would not give a blanket defense of this point of view. I will explain what I mean by first quoting Nietzsche: "Thus demandeth my great love to the remotest ones: *be not considerate of thy neighbor!* Man is something that must be surpassed" (453). I expect this passage is surprising to most of us, but it can be taken many ways.

Al: It is a cruel statement. Nietzsche is really saying: "Arise. Dominate. Fight for the Master Race."

You express one interpretation, in fact, an interpretation of major historical significance, as those who lived through the events of the 1930's and 1940's certainly know (i. e., the rise of Nazi power in Germany). But there are other ways of viewing Nietzsche's quotation, not all of which are necessarily warlike or destructive. This quote does illustrate one of Nietzsche's themes: action without empathy, in fact, action that is anti-empathy. Nietzsche sees the expression of the individual as, indeed, so superior to the needs of interpersonal relationships and society in general that the pragmatic workings of society seem unimportant to him, at least, the workings of any society in which relationships are not based on power. Not only that; Nietzsche denigrates empathy with others. He is antagonistic to sympathy and understanding of others.

In spite of this, Nietzsche does express a valid point. He implies the value, even the exuberance, of blind action, movement without conscious thought. There can be a fulfillment when the mind is blanked out in mindless action, in activity that is not inhibited by anything that could be regarded as an analysis of the social situation. One could be picking peaches or washing dishes, running or marching in a parade, playing baseball or swimming. In many pursuits the joy is in physical activity without conscious thought.

Al: I do not think of washing dishes as being joyful or as being a fulfillment.

Many actions may be done only with a sense of duty. Conversely, it is possible for the activity to be pursued in a spirit of fulfillment. The performance of duties need not preclude a sense of fulfillment. Wholeheartedness and joy can be realized when the conscious mind is relaxed into a full focus on and acceptance of the activity at hand.

Al: Ah! For instance, keep running, even if there is a wall in front of you!

Of course, I don't mean that. Keep looking while you are doing. Don't close your eyes and your mind. By blank mind I don't mean to imply an avoidance of perceptual input. During an activity, openness can be maintained toward the unfolding experience of the present, and action can be modified when the situation warrants change.

Al: When I blank out conscious thoughts, I really like to blank out. At that time, I don't want to be thinking about someone else's feelings, just my own. I just plunge ahead and do things. When I am chopping wood, I do not want to feel a closeness with the squirrel in the tree or the spider on the woodpile.

Fine. Enjoy your wood-chopping. But realize that some people are engrossed in physical or mental activity at least partly as a means to blank out empathy with others, that is, as a mode of separation, of distancing. This distancing is different from the type of detachment in which engagement is maintained. Engaged detachment employs that detached quality of perception which affords some amount of objectivity. On the other hand, for those who are in a mode of separateness from others, activity is an aspect of self-centeredness that indulges the self to the exclusion of others. This exclusion is necessary for all of us at those times when we need rest or respite from situations and when it is appropriate for the situation to do so. However, for some, the distancing is a manifestation of self-absorption. They are in a mode of anti-empathy; their behavioral orientation centers on an immersion into the self.

Let's look at another manifestation of anti-empathy. For some individuals the expression of freedom is manifested as an energizing opposition. The inclination toward being antagonistic may present as an expression of anti-empathy or anti-value. Empathy may be downgraded as a hindrance to action. Evidence of this mind-set is manifested in the stage attitudes and lyrics of many popular singing groups.

An outlook of anti-empathy and anti-value can impede the access to openness to whole ranges of actions and attitudes. This narrowed outlook is an impingement even on freedom itself in that a restricted orientation does not allow a free openness to express a wide range of possible modes for interaction. And an attitude that manifests antagonism to empathy can damage interpersonal relationships.

For those with the restricted outlook of antagonism, a fuller realization of the needs of self and society may eventually lead to a release from the pose of anti-value and anti-empathy.

I have described how the mood of anti-empathy can find expression when there are inclinations toward separateness and toward antagonism. Impatience is another possible source for anti-empathy. An example would be the impatience that can occur with driving a car behind a slow driver when there is no opportunity to pass that car. The absence of a visual contact with the driver ahead increases the likelihood for an absence of empathy. At times the driver ahead is an elderly person who is being extra cautious, and this caution is understandable. But exasperation—with the slow pace of movement plus the press of time for tasks to be done—may lead a person to impatience and a mood of anti-empathy toward the slow driver ahead.

This example is exaggerated because there is no visual contact with the other person. However, in the general run of life, impatience often can lead to a mood of anti-empathy.

FACTORS THAT LIMIT EMPATHY

When a person is self-absorbed, the view of others can often be short-circuited into pre-judged categories. It is a frequent tendency of some self-absorbed individuals to resort to judgmental views of others. They have a tendency toward prepackaged opinions. This judgmentalism is the opposite of a perceptiveness that seeks understanding.

The awareness of limitations may have the effect of releasing a person from a self-centered orientation and toward an openness to empathy. In this regard, there is an instructive quote that refers to two qualities: love and justice. Empathy is involved in both. Clear perception is a pre-condition for empathy, and empathy, as I said earlier, is a facet of that human state which we call "love." In the passage I would like to quote, Simone Weil discusses the subjection to force and an ability to transend the narrowed outlook that such subjection would tend to impose. She says this ability is a pre-condition for love and justice. Weil speaks an awareness of limitations, including those limits imposed by being subjected to force. (On an opposite tack regarding the subject of force, I believe that some individuals who are callous do not begin to have some understanding of others until they become limited by a realization of some form of superior force.) I quote from her book:

> … the sense of human misery is a pre-condition of justice and love. He who does not realize to what extent shifting fortune and necessity hold in subjection every human spirit, cannot regard as fellow-creatures nor love as he loves himself those whom chance separated from him by an abyss. The variety of constraints pressing upon man give rise to the illusion of several distinct species that cannot communicate. Only he who has measured the dominion of force, and knows how not to respect it, is capable of love and justice." (192)

For some who develop a realization of the limits of will and the limits of abilities, tolerance for a release from the agenda of the self may develop. These individuals may discover a capacity for detachment from aspirations, goals, and outlooks that may have been rigid or unrealistic. Such is a path to openness—for a receptiveness toward new information. This is a path which can lead to empathy with others.

Regarding judgmentalism, at times you may witness unethical acts, and intolerance for these acts may, indeed, be justified. But often intolerance is a manifestation of prejudice. Openness allows a fresh perceptiveness of the other person, which may counteract prejudice. When intolerance is not justified, openness and perceptiveness create the possibility for the development of tolerance, a receptiveness toward accepting the other's endeavors and idiosyncrasies.

There are caveats, things to be concerned about, in the manifestation of empathy. At times the inclination toward empathy becomes a mind-set of sympathy. Empathy can become rigid in the form of a mind-set of programmed sympathy that is expressed without regard to an appropriateness for the immediate situation. For the person with such outlook, reflex attitudes are not attuned to the varying aspects of people and events. This narrowed mental orientation of pre-programmed compassion runs counter to a free and spontaneous openness. It inhibits that openness which could lead to clearer and more valid perceptiveness, and, therefore, a more valid empathy. The pre-programming of an attitude can be considered to be a manifestation of a self-centered agenda, a mind-set that is not in tune with reality.

In this regard Hick says: "...we must be prepared to recognize that the compassion released by negating natural self-centeredness involves an objectivity and lucidity of vision which is sometimes as tough as it is tender" (338). Armstrong expresses the same sentiment: "Compassion is a particularly difficult virtue. It demands that we go beyond the limitations of our egotism, insecurity, and inherited prejudice" (391).

Let's look at another example of exaggerated compassion. It is my opinion that some group support meetings degenerate into "sympathy circles", "pity parties", where everyone is in a mode of programmed sympathy. When appropriate, sympathy is helpful, but excess sympathy can feed group confirmation of self-centeredness and self-absorption.

I should mention a side-point here. Although the words compassion and empathy are to an extent interchangeable, in this chapter I use the word "compassion" when there is an exaggerated tendency toward empathy.

A broader look at the subject of the restriction of empathy can be pursued. As previously stated, anti-empathy may be expressed as the manifestation of a variety of factors: the desire for separateness, antagonism, and impatience. Also, there are many factors which can cause the capacity for empathy to be limited. These include judgmentalism and pre-programmed sympathy, which have just been discussed. In the ensuing pages, several other factors that may limit empathy will be noted: unconditional love, the desire for desire, an excessive impulse toward activity, a rigid agenda of expectations, rigid orientations, misguided suspicion, fear—including the fear of a modification of identity, and excess pride.

Regarding an inhibition of openness by pre-set attitudes and concepts, the centering of the mind on such words as "love", "unity", and the like tends to place preconceptions in the mind. This may lead to a variety of problematic mental outlooks. Such preconceptions can funnel a person's mind into states of self-righteousness, insincerity, or possibly even insipidness. The self-righteousness of exaggerated compassion tends to block true empathy—true understanding of the other. For example, exaggerated compassion may occur in the process known as co-dependence. In a co-dependent situation, there can be a counter-productive increase in the enabling allowances made for the problems of another person. A narrowed view of both the actual and the potential states of that other person can contribute to the co-dependency of the relationship.

In looking at co-dependence on a larger scale, another example of the problem of an exaggerated compassion is that aspect of Public Welfare programs which, for some people, tends to sap initiative. For these, the provision of assistance can debilitate incentive and prolong dependency.

For some individuals, an unconditional love may distort perception of problem areas to the extent that problems are aggravated. Unconditional love may carry with it a denial of reality. Preconceptions may play a role in idealized love; an idealized view of the other person can limit the awareness of his or her actual personality. This idealized but narrowed perception tends to decrease the degree of fulfillment in the relationship. There is a narrowing of the range of potential interactions when the relationship is based on distorted understanding. Such narrowing of interaction may possibly lead to resentment or manipulation.

As a general outlook, such words as "love" and "unity" may be helpful in that they may increase the tendency toward openness and they imply value. However, a predisposition toward the experience of value may have some constricting effect on the clear vision of openness.

Al: You didn't seem to worry about the constriction of openness by pre-set value when you talked about the value of thankfulness. A thankfulness for the existence of self and surroundings implies value. In fact, you said the same.

Right—but there is a difference between the value experienced for what is and the value projected for that which is about to be—that in which you are an active participant. Consider this example. You may feel thankful for the opportunity to experience the awesomeness, beauty, and power of a charging rhinoceros. But the value of this thankfulness for that which is does not include a value (such as might be implied in "love" or "unity") for what will occur in the moments ahead and in which you have an active part.

Al: That's for sure. But, instead of protecting myself by shooting a charging rhino, I would not expect to be hunting in Africa. Or maybe I would, but with a camera. And I would carry the means of self-protection with me. Thankfulness and respect for other life forms would not preclude self-protection.

I can say that this is a theoretical example to point out the difference between the value felt toward what exists at the moment—a value implied by thankfulness—and the potentially constricting effect of possible values imparted to what will be. The sense of value felt toward that which is should not narrow an outlook of openness, that openness which can lead to a fuller appreciation for what can be if the perception is not restricted by a pre-set orientation.

Let's turn our attention to the desire for desire. Our minds tend to be geared into ongoing activity. A continuous pattern of words floats across our minds. Regarding the mental stream of words, a recurring theme often embodies a desire to be in a state of desire; the mental content is geared into continually expressing the desire for some goal, in contradistinction to the actual attaining of the goal. A person may want the longing for something rather than actually having it. The aim for some people is to be in a state of desire. Fulfillment of desire may then be disappointing since fulfillment negates the actual aim, which is to be in a state of desire and unfulfillment. In this regard, Armstrong describes a jaundiced view of love: "Love is essentially a yearning for something that remains absent; that is why so much of our human love remains disappointing" (235).

The disturbing aspect of a desire for continuous physical or mental activity draws a cynical comment from Camus: "Something must happen—and that explains most human commitments. Something must happen, even loveless slavery, even war or death. Hurray then for funerals!" (Fall 37) An endless desire for activity, then, can be destructive. In a different direction, openness implies an ability to step back from activity, an ability to relax with a cleared mind, a mind which has been released from pre-set patterns.

When I refer to the excessive impulse to activity, I refer to those times when a release from activity would be more appropriate. An example is prolonged activity when the physical body cries for rest.

Of course, the set-point for the balance of activity and rest varies between individuals.

Al: That's for sure. A three-year-old can run circles around me. By the way, some of this information seems obvious to me.

That's right. To some, this may seem superfluous. They don't need to hear the obvious. But, for others, this information may be quite valuable. And, for some individuals, the pointing out of known facts may help to emphasize and reinforce a movement away from problem areas and toward a more satisfactory life. I discuss many aspects, many topics, and often

God Unmasked; the Full Life Revealed

what is important for one can be well-known and seem relatively inconsequential for another.

Another potential source for mental activity-without-end is a rigid agenda of expectations. An unending search for infractions of any pattern of rules or goals can fill the mind with disquiet. This unrest can limit the capacity for openness to empathy, an openness which might require some release from or modification of the agenda.

Let's consider another example of recurrent mental activity that can have negative consequences; this is the mind-set of "if only". When a persistent mental pattern is in the form of "if only", a person is stuck in the mental groove of distress due to lack of some improved state "if only" such and such were the situation. The "if only" is seen to stand in the way of fulfillment, and if that "if only" were to become solved, the pre-set mind tends to replace it with another "if only". The point here is that the need for mental activity is fulfilled by on-going "if only"s. The result of such outlook is a lingering sense of frustration.

When a person has a continuous need to be in an active mental state, the lingering frustration does fill that need. If someone is inclined toward a particular continuing predisposition concerning his or her surroundings, that predisposition, such as "if only," fills that need. However, instead of living in the happiness of openness to fresh experience, they are stuck in the frustration of "if only." The focus on a narrowed orientation of "if only" is likely to decrease the access to an openness of empathy. Instead of the joy of an open, cleared mind, they live in dissatisfaction.

"Just when"s are similar: something causes upset "just when" everything was fine. Living in a state of "just when" also fills the need for continuous mental activity but at the expense of frustration and regret over what has happened

Let's talk about suspicion in relation to the limitation of the capacity for empathy. First, consider the situation of an inadequate suspicion. An exaggerated and unrealistic tendency toward empathy can open a person to vulnerability to opportunism. When someone sympathizes too much, he or she may become a victim of the machinations of another, responding in a compassionate way to false claims.

Of course, the opposite may apply. A person may be overly suspicious of appeals for compassion and understanding. At times, the sense of being subject to opportunistic machinations of another person may be incorrect. Furthermore, in response to misdirected suspicion, resentment tends to develop. When the intentions of another are falsely construed, this preconception can be quite damaging to interpersonal relationships, and, in some situations, resentment may fester for years.

Other factors can narrow perceptiveness and circumvent empathy and understanding. A person may be subject to threats that inhibit perceptiveness. It is true that fear may heighten perceptiveness, but also fear can distort the perception of reality. For instance, a sudden awareness of a rattlesnake on one side of you might make you less aware of a ledge drop-off on the other side. Jumping away from the snake in the wrong direction could result in a bad fall.

On a more subtle level, there may be fear of a loss of the accepted image of self if empathy were to lead one to a new view of identity. As an example, for most white Americans in 1935, the view of what it was to be an American involved an exclusion of empathy with black people.

Excess pride may involve either identity or the attainment of a goal. An exaggerated pride can constrict the mind into conceit. When the joy of either identity or goal attainment is warped by conceit, the flow of openness becomes narrowed, and the potential for harmful consequences increases. Excess pride can be destructive of human relationships. S. Suzuki refers to this excess pride as a form of selfishness: "So if you attach to the idea of what you have done, you are involved in selfish ideas" (63).

SELF-NEGATION

Al: I have to take issue with you about a particular point. Empathy with others can become all-encompassing to the point of self-denial, a negation of one's own being and identity. While this may be the way some people want to live, it's not for me.

I know what you mean. A healthy view of the self is important. Full attention in empathy need not entail denial of self. Each of us has a personal role in life. One's own self is a part of reality. An outlook of engaged detachment includes the openness to have an understanding of the nature of one's own self.

Al: Do you mean "empathy with self"?

In effect that is what I am saying; with an outlook of empathy, a person can include the development of an understanding of his or her own particular nature, at least as much as possible. Instead of self-denial, empathy includes the understanding of self.

God Unmasked; the Full Life Revealed

There is an additional reason to avoid self-denial. Others need to see you as a separate self. It is uncomfortable for people to be in the presence of someone who has submerged his or her aims and attitudes into a oneness with them. More satisfactory relationships are possible when individual freedom and individual identity are maintained while allowing an easy flow between the currents of individual life and the needs and fulfillments of the relationship.

Caring for the needs of another person may entail a temporary degree of self-denial in the fulfillment of responsibilities that have been accepted. The give-and-take of interpersonal interactions requires some meshing of activities and desires if the relationship is to be maintained. However, this self-denial need not be all-encompassing; the sense of individuality can be maintained.

In addition, I want to remind those who worship at the altar of individual freedom that the experience of empathy is usually pleasant and at times joyful. Furthermore, the realization of empathy tends to be enhanced in the course of service to others. Therefore, there can be a joy in the giving of oneself in service for others.

THE INTERPLAY AND FLOW OF EMPATHY AND ACTION

Al: Well, I agree with you. But, of course, there are many times when we act out of our individual initiative and direction. At times empathy should be held at least partly in abeyance. There are times when we must move; we must act.

Certainly. There is a time for decisiveness—for wholehearted action. Reynolds discusses the problem of indecisiveness when he states:

> (People with a tendency for indecisiveness) must act anyway, without confidence, without assurance, without a clear view of all possible outcomes. We don't need to know everything about everything before putting our bodies in motion. Careful consideration is worth our time and attention, but straddling the fence waiting for everything to become absolutely clear offers only saddle sores. If you are in pain, take the constructive step into the unknown and discover what reality has in store for you in the next moment. (71)

The Bible makes a statement about decisiveness in the face of the unknown future: "In the morning sow thy seed, and in the evening withhold not thine hand: for thou knowest not whether shall prosper, either this or that, or whether they both shall be alike good" (Eccl 11:6).

Often it might seem that the expression of activity and the open receptivity to empathy are mutually exclusive, each not allowing the manifestation of the other. Some might be inclined toward blind action and others toward hesitant speculation. However, an openness to empathy need not exclude decisiveness and action. Also, a concentrated effort toward some form of activity might seem more efficient when the distraction of perceptiveness is excluded. But a narrowed drive toward some goal may bypass realistic information that would lead to a realization that the goal or the means to the goal should be modified.

There is a mode of expressing action which minimizes the potentially harmful consequences of a narrowed concentration on activity. This involves an openness to empathy during activity, allowing an ongoing, fresh perceptiveness. Openness can provide the means to maximize avoidance of those aspects of the particular activity which may be harmful. In addition, the availability of openness also allows a recognition of the limits of direction and abilities.

However, there is also a delineating characteristic for openness to empathy during activity. Ideally, the outlook of openness should be easily entered into and easily released, always available but lightly held. There is full attention to such aspects of openness as the realization of empathy or of limitations, but this attention is easily released in the flow of activity. The currents of activity and openness merge, giving easy access to the refreshing discoveries of openness while continuing in the course of activity.

Access to openness during activity need not entail a hesitancy in the course of action. The easy flow of that pursuit of activity which includes openness can be contrasted with activity that is hesitant due to mental inhibitions. When there is easy flow of activity with openness, the action is not swamped into pools of excess mental reflection. Shunryu Suzuki gives a description of these two opposite modes of action: "These traces and notions make our minds very complicated. When we do something with a quite simple, clear mind, we have no notion or shadows, and our activity is strong and straightforward. But when we do something with a complicated mind, in relation to other things or people, or society, our activity becomes very complex" (62).

Regardless of the intensity of physical exertion, if the mind is in a calm state, there is a fuller expression of the self. This happens when the mind is cleared for receptivity of the moment. Quotes again from S. Suzuki express this: "There is harmony in our activity, and where there is harmony there is calmness" (105). And: "When you do something, you should be completely involved in it. You should devote yourself to it completely. Then you have nothing. So if there is no true emptiness in your activity, it is not natural" (109). Then: "So in activity there should be calmness, and in calmness there should be activity. Calmness and activity are not different" (119).

Reynolds also describes the openness and receptivity of a cleared mind during activity, his example being the tea ceremony:

> It is said that a certain frame of mind is developed during the tea ceremony. It is not that the participant necessarily brings this frame of mind to the ceremony. More often it is the participation in the ceremony that creates receptivity to the aesthetic of the moment. Once again, the principle of action preceding attitude or emotion applies.... Anxious, rattled feelings fade before the systematic, measured movements of the body (65-6).

When there is openness of mind into a state of receptivity, a person releases himself or herself from controlling attitudes. He or she flows with the action. In this regard, Reynolds refers to works of Morita and Stanislavski and includes a parallel reference to professional acting:

> The goal of acting, on stage and in life, is not perfect control of one's surroundings, not direct control of one's feelings, not inspiration or transcendent experience. The goal is simply learning to do what one can, leaving "nature" to bring about some results from the action. One gives up one's self in the doing and accepts the consequences as data for determining the next doing. On these points both Morita and Stanislavski agree. Two great thinkers with a common insight. (91-2)

This view of activity is also expressed by Myers: "To be in flow is to be unself-consciously absorbed ... It's exhilarating to flow with an activity that fully engages our skills. Flow experiences boost our sense of self-esteem, competence, and well-being" (132-3). Also: "Rather than vegetating in self-focused idleness, lose yourself in the flow of active work and play" (138).

And the Tao describes the surrender into the flow of action:

Empathy, Anti-empathy, and Action

Be like the forces of nature:
When it blows, there is only wind;
When it rains, there is only rain.... (23)

8

Self and Society

The Value of Social Organization
Emotion and Freedom
Television and "Emotion Junkies"
Social Control and Excess Idealism
A Balance

THE VALUE OF SOCIAL ORGANIZATION

We now turn our attention to the relationships of the self with society. In this age of relative peace and plenty, we hear much about blaming society for personal problems. We hear that a sick society makes sick individuals. Furthermore, our social, political, and economic organization is widely faulted as unjust and inadequate.

In this chapter we will not discuss particular, technical aspects of social, economic, and political problems. The subject matter of this chapter is the relationship of the individual to society. This involves an elaboration of the characteristics of a healthy interaction between the individual and his or her social milieu.

Let's start our discussion of self and society by calling to mind the subject matter of Chapter Three. For the well-being of the self, thankfulness is central; it is the fundamental source for a positive outlook on life. Gratitude for existence provides us with a sense of affirmation. An outlook of thankfulness carries with it a sense of value; appreciation creates a positive outlook, which is a source of value. This attitude of thankfulness is therefore valuable for the way we behold our lives and existence in general.

Al: Are you sure you want to start there? How can you have an attitude of thankfulness when much of our current cultural climate is aimed toward suspicion and cynicism?

I'm glad you asked.

Al: And before you answer, let me extend the question. For many, the workings of society seem repressive. There are certainly real victims. There is real injustice. However, beyond the area of specific cases of injustice, a general mood of victimization pervades the country. People feel they are at the mercy of events over which they have no control. For many of these people, the structures and arrangements of society are seen to be oppressive. Isn't a cynicism toward society valid?

Well, it is true that many conditions exist which are unfair. There often is gross injustice. It is also true that, at least some of the time, there is either no control or very limited control of social problems by individuals.

But the sense of loss of control is often exaggerated. Options for relief are not visualized. Many are blind to constructive paths for the resolution of problems. The immensity of the problems is often daunting. Complexity of problems, resistance to change, size of the population affected, the difficulties of working with established practices—these are factors in the realization of the limitation of possibility for amelioration and control of problems.

Of course, the solutions to many problems are difficult. In fact, the development of solutions can be viewed as the essence of the nature of the course of history. The distribution of political and economic power and of economic goods fuels the evolution of various forms of groups and is one of the sources of the contentious struggles of mankind.

As stated above, I will not discuss technical arrangement for distribution of power and goods. But I will point out certain factors in the interaction between individuals and society. In these interactions it must be initially understood that there will always be injustices. When some inequities are solved, others appear; this is characteristic of the complexity of social organization.

The salient point is not to carp about injustice but to have a mind-set that predisposes toward the resolution of problems. A person could easily wallow in feelings of victimization and self-pity. Even when victimization is completely true, it is more valuable for an individual's well-being to have a positive orientation toward the situation and toward possible solutions. Even with no solution in sight, a positive attitude is helpful in accepting that which, at least temporarily, must be accepted.

In noting the injustices and evils of society, some people have the feeling that the very existence of society is wrong. They glorify individual freedom to such an extent that life is visualized as ideal when there are no social arrangements and controls. Also, some of these idealists believe that all individuals are so wholesome that, in the absence of some sort of governing arrangement, everyone will automatically live in a state of bliss and cooperation.

In answer to that point of view I present a mini-scene:

Reverse Fantasia

I took an airplane flight to Guatemala to get a banana for my breakfast cereal. The trip was great. And when I got there, it only took five days to find an old, abandoned plantation where I could pick a banana without fear of someone objecting.

Alice: You must have had a great breakfast.

When I got back, I couldn't find the breakfast cereal, so I had to plow a field and grow my own wheat.

Alice: You would need a marsh to grow rice for Rice Krispies.

No such luck. I abandoned any desire for Rice Krispies. But then I looked forward to having Shredded Wheat. Except I didn't have a plow, and the tractor wouldn't run. Things looked dismal. The corner store used to have Shredded Wheat. But the corner store had been burned out in the revolution. In honesty, I couldn't get the banana anyway. All planes were grounded. And if I had been able to grow wheat, the rebels would have stolen it.

I try to survive on roots and berries. Everyone knows where the good food sources are. So we fight to stay alive. Who gets to the food first? Who is strongest? Form a group to gain strength; fight the other tribal groups. Who needs society when we have anarchy? Society is evil. Let's become savages.

The very strong, the very resourceful, and the very manipulative might survive in the absence of social arrangements, but survival would be difficult or impossible for most of us. Unless one is in favor of world depopulation and of physical power as the basis for social organization, anarchy is not a valid consideration.

Some idealistic individuals conjecture that an absence of the moderating effects of government would result in a society in which everyone is a "good person," living in peace with neighbors. It is far more likely that the absence of a centralized political structure would lead to the development of a multitude of armed bands. We would see a replay of history, with all the wars and suffering that, one thinks, might have deterred us from taking such a course.

Therefore, we are left with the realization of the need for society and for its maintenance and improvement. In the social, political, and economic realms, the development of justice and fairness becomes more likely when there is a positive outlook on the part of those involved. In the interactions among individuals, respect and value are the underpinnings of a positive outlook. When a person has respect toward others, that individual has more willingness to understand other points of view. Let's recall that the affirming sense of thankfulness brings with it the feeling of respect and value. Appreciation feeds a sense of respect. Also, thankfulness facilitates an openness to a perceptiveness of present and future potentialities. New understanding of the present and of the possible future becomes more likely when there is an openness that is fed by an attitude of gratefulness. This thankful attitude can release a person from being blinded by narrowed vision.

EMOTION AND FREEDOM

Al: I agree that it is valuable to have an attitude of thankfulness. A positive outlook certainly has value. But let's consider the negative outlook a bit further. Many seem to value the expression of emotion regardless of the subject matter of the emotion. At times, all of us may favor a negative experiential content because it carries much emotional impact. However, for a significant number of viewers, I believe that an exposure to negative extremes such as the suffering in war may be just exciting words and images to some whose minds are immersed in television.

Yes. For some people, everything becomes a passing scene with varying degrees of emotional appeal. This emotionalism implies that immediate sensation is favored, without regard to, and at times in defiance of, ultimate consequences. Furthermore, excess attunement to emotionalism often manifests as an exaggeration of the call for freedom. This demand for freedom is excessive when it is beyond the needs that called forth the rebellion.

In this country, the cry for individual freedom from perceived constraints has become more exaggerated in recent years. When this cry for freedom is beyond a reasonable limit, it has a deleterious effect on a sense of mutual understanding, appreciation, and respect. The result of a loss of respect and appreciation is a decrease in the sense of interpersonal value.

The re-establishment of a sense of value is a primary aim of many groups that have a spiritual orientation. Even though a variety of spiritual groups has developed, in part to provide a basis for the expression of value between people, the expression of this value seems contrived when it is limited to the specific times and places of group interaction. Also, the sense of mutual appreciation often tends to fade in the press of activity in the everyday world.

As I stated above, many have become too quick to interpret situations as limiting self-expression. It should be further stated that misplaced or excess demands for freedom threaten to destroy social continuity. The value of interdependence is contested when there is an absence of some concept of the catastrophe that would occur with the loss of social fabric. An article in the *International Herald Tribune* by William Pfaff cites the work of Philippe Grasset: "...the United States now is gripped by a solipsistic individualism in society and economy which is deeply subversive of America's own social and economic stability, while threatening others.... America's own moral community has been torn apart by institutionalization of an ethic of anarchic individual self-interest, destructive of family, moral codes, 'elite values,' corporate social obligation and the notion of community interest" (8). This excess centering on individual freedom is fertile ground for a mood of distrust and suspicion and for a ready tendency to develop a "victim" attitude.

An exaggerated orientation toward freedom and individualism often takes the form of disbelief of and action contrary to those sources of authority which either are, or appear to be, generally accepted. This disbelief of authority can extend to the sphere of technical information. I will note an example in the realm of health and medical care. The manifestation of individualism for a significant number of people appears as a tendency to believe only those authorities whose orientations are contrary to any of the sources of information which they may understand to be generally accepted.

Of a more ominous nature for the fabric of society, a similar antagonistic stance occurs in a reaction to the economic and political structure. In this realm some individuals rebel against anything which is established, regardless of merit. They ignore the delineation of value of that which is believed to be generally accepted; they opt in favor of an attitude of rebellion.

There are many factors in the development of an excess call for individual freedom. At this point I mention one particular factor that is easily overlooked. With the development of a massive number of labor-saving devices, the amount of physical activity performed by a large part of the population is far less than in prior years. The basic human need for physical exertion is partly fulfilled by sports and exercise programs, but many people do not have initiative in that direction. I can speculate that frustration due to a lack of action may, for some, take the form of rebellion that would seem to fulfill the need to express action; the professed target of the action may be somewhat incidental.

A pattern of physical inactivity associated with frustration due to inactivity can have deleterious consequences. Hoffer offers an interesting description of frustration of the strong impulse to action as manifested by some individuals in mass movements:

> A mass movement's call for action evokes an eager response in the frustrated. For the frustrated see in action a cure for all that ails them. It brings self-forgetting and it gives them a sense of purpose and worth. Indeed it seems that frustration stems chiefly from an inability to act, and that the most poignantly frustrated are those whose talents and temperament equip them ideally for a life of action but are condemned by circumstances to rust away in idleness. (112)

The social effects of the exaggerated cry for freedom find their counterpart in the aesthetic realm. As indicated above, emotional intensity often finds expression in a cry for freedom. Much of current, popular music presents a psychologic diet of emotional intensity, often manifested as anger. The message of much of modern music is: intensity is what life is all about. In this realm of music there is no room for more moderate expression or relaxed happiness.

There is an additional characteristic attributable to some current, popular music which may be noted; this also is a manifestation of the pervasiveness of a compulsion toward freedom. Some modern expressions of music are without that traditional structure which gives rise to and then fulfills emotional expectations. Such music becomes a blur of individual, disconnected bits of sound.

Likewise some modern painting styles present a sense of disconnectedness by expressing a random form which alienates—as distinct from that random form or other forms which draw a person's attention and empathy into it.

Al: Each to his or her own taste.

Fine. I am just pointing out some of the effects of a mind-set for total freedom.

There are many factors in the development of a sense of alienation and cynicism. Some of these factors are less significant or quite incidental. The effect of music is pervasive, but I believe the plastic arts—painting, sculpture—have much less impact. Economic, political, and social problems have a huge impact, but I do not discuss technical aspects in this book. However, particular attention will be paid to the effects of television.

TELEVISION AND "EMOTION JUNKIES"

Television has made and is making a huge impact on modern mentality. It is my opinion that the advent of television has caused enormous changes in the cultural climate. There are positive aspects of television, but note will be made here about some of its catastrophic consequences. It is important for us to realize some of the negative effects of television which impede our movement toward fullness of life.

First, we will consider television advertisements in relation to self-indulgence. In previous chapters we discussed problems with the pervasiveness of consumerism. The promotion of consumerism has intensified with the advent of television.

This consumerism has led to a glorification of indulgence which feeds self-centeredness and self-absorption. Self-absorption is at the opposite pole of that thankfulness which brings a person into an outlook of appreciation. Self-concern is the orientation that is opposite to a sense of affirmation—opposite to the welcoming of that which is.

Self-centeredness is also enhanced by the tendency for television programs to emphasize individual expression which, at times I believe, comes at the expense of understanding and empathy. Also, when a call to empathy is presented, it is often on such an emotional basis that there is a very limited balance of detached understanding.

The emotional outlook which is frequent in television programs often is not balanced by a presentation to viewers of some depiction of a healthy degree of discipline and the need for clear, calm perception. The high intensity of action and emotion is seen to be necessary for television programming in order to maintain viewer interest and to complete the programs in the allotted time slots. The consequence of excess intensity is a downgrading of patience—that ability needed in actual situations to withhold immediate response, to delay action until perspective is regained.

Al: Let me interject. For many people there is an empty space, a need for more emotion in their lives, a need for something beyond their daily routine.

I won't deny the value of entertainment. However, there is a problem when there is excess desire to be a spectator of emotional intensity. This is so particularly when a continuing impulse toward emotion colors the general outlook. Some television viewers are "emotion junkies," addicted to emotional intensity. For them television fills an empty space that has, at least partly, been created by habituation to television itself.

Television is far more readily available to the spectator than movie houses, stage-play theaters, and many other forms of entertainment. The easy access to television tends to result in prolonged television viewing by many. The emotional effect of watching television for extended periods of time can be compounded by the prolonged physical inactivity of sitting while watching. The attunement of television's appeal to the emotions may, for some, combine with dissatisfaction due to a lack of fulfillment which might have been afforded by physical activity; this combination may create an explosive temperament. Of course, for many, television will have a soporific effect. However, I will speculate that, for some individuals, prolonged television viewing is one of the factors that can stimulate an agonized, rebellious outlook.

I will mention another aspect of the effect of television on the individual's view of society. Opposition is more interesting than concurrence. Opposition draws more attention. It is therefore not surprising that television programs favor the depiction of opposition and of conflicting situations. Such program content draws more viewers than a presentation of that which is pleasant.

The pervasiveness of a content of opposition and conflict on television—and, of course, in other visual media such as movies and computer games—has the effect of promoting a general mood of distrust and cynicism. The social culture becomes "counter-culture." There is a social climate of "against" which then appropriates subjects to be against.

Robert D. Putnam, director of the Center for International Affairs at Harvard University, discusses the change in social climate noted in younger Americans. He correlates this with the growth in television viewing:

Americans rarely have been grumpier about their public institutions.... Americans born in the first four decades of the century continue to display remarkably high levels of civic engagement and social trust. Their children and grandchildren raised in the 1950s, 1960s and 1970s, however, have been struck by a mysterious "anti-civic" X-ray .... This generational pattern offers strong circumstantial evidence that television must be a prime suspect in the epidemic of civic disengagement. The timing fits: the onset began precisely with the first television-reared generation in the 1950s, and the malady has deepened in step with the growth in television watching (E5).

There is a point also to be made about television filming technique. Television filming practices tend to stimulate emotion in other ways besides the content of programs and advertisements. Camera techniques that juggle the viewer's sense of stability appear designed to arouse emotion. When demonstrating the need for a product, advertisements often utilize various techniques to spur emotion: close-ups that are uncomfortably close, fast action, at times with jerky stop-action, also nauseating camera motion.

The next point about television is: "What's next?"

Al: Well, then, what's next?

Next is next.

Al: I'm glad you are being lucid.

Clarity is next to something. And to clarify this, next is change, and change is next.

Al: You call that "clarification?"

Let me be more lucid. Without change there is no story line. Without change there is no purpose for advertisements to promote the switch to their products. The impulse in favor of change permeates television. This general mood of change tends to fixate minds on the freedom to change. It is not a difficult step from there to the exaggerated cry for freedom.

Al: This is just speculation.

Yes, but it is the only place in the book that is speculative.

Al: Right. I couldn't agree with you less some times.

But you probably will agree with me about the prevalence of the depiction of violence on television. This much-discussed subject is another

Self and Society

factor in creating habituation to emotional intensity. I quote from an article in *The Oregonian* by Marilyn Gardner: "…the high threshold it takes to keep Americans from yawning, revealing an American appetite for perpetually stimulating and sensational pictures on the television screen…. 'Entertain me' has become the insistent demand of restless Americans, who add, 'and while you're at it throw in a little violence.' " (A10)

Al: You have made several points about the effects of television on a person's mind. Are you saying that television is to the mind what cigarettes are to the lungs—a devastating poison?

No. That would certainly be an overstatement. When used in moderation and with judgment as to the selection of programs, television viewing can be entertaining, informative, and without significant negative effects. But I believe much of television watching has quite destructive effects, particularly leading many young lives toward becoming "emotion junkies."

We have discussed several aspects of the effect of television on the public mentality: self-centeredness, excess indulgence, the impulse toward exaggerated freedom and exaggerated emotions, the downgrading of empathy and patience. Implications regarding physical action and violence have been mentioned. These all tend to decrease the sense of social cohesion and foster a mood of cynicism. Bob Campbell voices the same sentiment when he comments on the movie "Quiz Show", directed by Robert Redford: "The film continues Redford's compulsive investigation, begun as an actor in 'The Candidate' and 'Electric Cowboy,' into the ways in which American reality has been corrupted by the power of manufactured images and drugged by entertainment" (D5).

Societal effects of the excess cry for freedom...

Al: Just a second here. You use the word "excess" and at other times the word "exaggerated." Where do you draw the line? How do you tell when there is an excess and when not enough?

That is a good question. To go on, we...

Al: Are you going to ignore that question?

I don't ignore questions. In fact, I was purposely avoiding it. You probably have partly surmised the answer, and I can tell you now that I will elaborate more later in this chapter. All in good time. We do have to spend some time first with an entirely different orientation.

God Unmasked; the Full Life Revealed

SOCIAL CONTROL AND EXCESS IDEALISM

I refer to that which is opposite to the excess compulsion toward freedom. The excess cry for individual freedom is at one end of a spectrum. The other end of the spectrum is an exaggerated group control of individual freedom. Control can take the form of exaggerated societal idealism and its partner, self-righteousness. Idealism and self-righteousness are also aspects of an individual's behavior and attitudes, but, for the purpose of the discussion in this chapter, we are considering idealism and self-righteousness at the group level in relation to iindividual freedom.

When some theme of the supposedly ideal life is held in common by a segment of society, this idealism favors social cohesion. However, idealism at the group level may either be congruent with or arrayed against the needs of particular individuals.

Idealism is often fixated by social pressure and not responsive to ongoing input. When group idealism is excessively rigid, there can be a repression of variation from the "ideal" by individuals.

Let's look at a more subtle level of social pressure in the context of idealism. The pressure toward idealized appearance is manifested in commercial consumerism. Giddens describes the tendency for fixation on idealized appearances by the process of consumerism:

> ...the pervasiveness of consumerism, which is a 'society dominated by appearances'. Consumption addresses the alienated qualities of modern social life and claims to be their solution: it promises the very things the narcissist desires — attractiveness, beauty and personal popularity — through the consumption of the 'right' kinds of goods and services. Hence all of us, in modern social conditions, live as though surrounded by mirrors; in these we search for appearance of an unblemished, socially valued self. (172)

A response to this outlook about social appearance can be found in the Tao, over 2,000 years ago. In fact, this quote refers to social pressure in general:

Care about people's approval

And you will be their prisoner. (9)

To me, the response of the Tao does not mean that others should be ignored; instead, a more reasonable understanding of the passage is the depiction of a challenge against a too-readily accepted imprisonment by

Self and Society

commonly held attitudes. The socially accepted: this is not necessarily wrong, but it is well to question societal attitudes and to form one's own beliefs. In his inimitable, extreme way Nietzsche expresses this:

> To be true—that can few be! And he who can, will not! Least of all however, can the good be true.
>
> Oh, those good ones! Good men never speak the truth. For the spirit, thus to be good, is a malady.
>
> They yield, those good ones, they submit themselves; their heart repeateth, their soul obeyeth: he, however, who obeyeth doth not listen to himself!
>
> All that is called evil by the good must come together in order that one truth may be born. O my brethren, are ye also evil enough for this truth? (454)

There is, then, an individual responsibility to discern truth. The individual must be able to doubt.

Idealism is often manifested as self-righteousness. Let's look into the effects of an idealism which has degenerated into self-righteousness and prejudice. At the group level, self-righteousness can be a source for innumerable injustices. I quote from *Living in Sin?* by Episcopalian Bishop John Shelby Spong: "Prejudice always defines its victims negatively, blanketing them with stereotypes that hide from view their individual humanity" (80).

In an *Oregonian* article Tom Bates describes the effects of idealism manifested as self-righteousness and prejudice:

> Pursued too zealously, almost any good idea corrupts the believer, Free trade, for example, allowed the rise of a middle class and the creation of our modern, industrial democracies. But what was the first application of this great principle? To justify the unrestrained traffic in African slaves. In the name of free trade, the Irish were allowed to starve during the Potato Famine of the mid-19th century.
>
> Saving souls is another, distinctively human, notion. In the interest of saving souls, 16th-century Spanish priests converted thousands of uninstructed Caribbean natives to Christianity in mass baptisms. Those who didn't go along were hung upside down and roasted over slow fires—twelve at a time.

Peace is one of humanity's great dreams. In the '60s, a lot of people fought for it, in the all-too-literal sense. In the year 1970, according to one estimate, more than a million Americans committed acts of violence in the course of anti-war protests....

The central paradox of terrorism—that it is motivated by righteousness—is true of all rationalized violence in all times and places. It is true of the Christian-inspired Hung Rebellion in 19th-century China, in which 33 million died; it is true of all the anti-Semitic rampages since the diaspora of the Jews. As humans, we like our wars holy....

Violence always has its reasons but is rarely reasonable. Theoretical violence, Christian or otherwise, only encourages those in whom the dark urge is strongest (E1).

A BALANCE

As previously stated, when idealism and self-righteousness occur in large segments of the population, the freedom of individuals may become restricted. Calls for freedom may be seen as dangerous to order and control, threatening the maintenance of social cohesion. However, in spite of the difficulties of society, the extreme alternative, that is, anarchy, is unacceptable. We discussed this earlier in the chapter.

A more valid course for the fulfillment of human needs is an outlook that balances the needs of the group and the needs of the individual. The vehicle for this balance is openness. It is possible for the mode of group affirmation to incorporate a sense of rightness that includes an open orientation, remaining open and receptive to new information. This is different from a self-righteousness that is narrowed and unresponsive. Furthermore, an openness of the group can be complemented by openness of the individual in realizing the value of identity within the group and an understanding the value of group-held ideals.

In addition, there is a moderating effect on the group if their outlook includes value for individual freedom.

In further counter-balance, openness on the part of the individual will ideally include a realization that a fresh look at established attitudes and practices does not necessarily mean that these attitudes and practices should be changed. Individuals should be open to learn the value of that against which they might otherwise rebel.

Al: Your statements are well and good, but they would draw a laugh from some people. The last thing some want is identity with groups, at least with particular groups.

That's right. In fact, some cry for freedom so intently that the freedom cry seems to aim toward a destruction of society. They fail to recognize the potential problems of anarchy. As previously stated, the horrendous probable outcomes of anarchy include wars between surviving tribes and loss of production of adequate food for the existing population. Counterbalance to that outlook is the recognition of value in group identity, which includes the realization of interdependence for economic and political needs.

Beyond these somewhat mechanical factors of political and economic need are psychologic elements, in particular the value of a focus beyond the self. As described in Chapter Seven, empathy with others is one aspect of self-fulfillment. Furthermore, when an individual has empathy concerning the needs of the group, dependability and responsibility to the group are more likely to be realized.

Some situations do indeed call for a preponderance of individual freedom over social continuity, not in the sense of total destruction of society but as a call to openness and in a promulgation of willingness for modification. There is need to balance the worth of continuity and the worth of disruption for the particular situation.

Let's draw together an overview of the relationship between freedom of the individual and the need for social continuity. Society should allow that maximum amount of individual freedom which is consistent with a social continuity that remains modifiable by minimally disruptive means appropriate for the situation. That is my summary statement of considerations that balance the needs of individuals and society. Such balance calls for an openness both on the part of the group and the individual.

9

Integrity; a Fullness of Life

In the last chapter we were concerned about the relationship of individuals to society. Now let's draw together a comprehensive view of the topics of the entire Part Two. You might want me to start this chapter with an answer to the question: what is integrity? We will get to the dictionary definition, but, before that, let's take a short look at what seems like integrity. The sense of integrity may afford some degree of a sense of fullness in life, a feeling that the "right" actions have been taken, that the "right" ideals are held, and that things in general are under control. One could feel that family life provides some degree of fulfillment, and that the acquisition of material goods has reached a certain level of satisfaction. For many who have reached this level, "rightness" is felt to be the acceptable self-image which is presented to an approving society.

However, for some, these attainments may seem unfulfilling to a degree. There may be a sense of lacking "something more," a lingering awareness that some central aspect of life is missing.

The attainments that are marks of material and social success may be seen as valuable. I do not belittle these achievements. But I do point to a priority of values.

The social stamp of approval is satisfying enough for some people. On the other hand, the attitude of social correctness has very little meaning to an individual when faced with major misfortune, serious illness or injury, or impending death. Even without major problems, some may feel an emptiness in the type of life described by Tolstoy: "... to lead a decorous life approved of by society ... above all that propriety of external forms required by public opinion" (1955).

The "proper," socially accepted life may seem hollow and empty when it is held as the primary source of life's direction. I do not disparage social cohesion, but I do question it when it assumes a primary role in a person's life. There are more fundamental and more satisfactory bases for fullness of life. Also, social cohesion has a more valid base when individuals are attuned to these fundamental qualities.

Let's get back to the word "integrity." In exploring the meaning of integrity, I will ask this: would you agree that integrity means self-righteousness?

Al: It does not.

Might you agree that integrity means knowing you are right, being certain you are making the right decisions, and believing that you have found the right way to live?

Al: It does not.

Well, what's your opinion? What is integrity?

Al: It's time to go to the dictionary. Merriam Webster's states that integrity is: 1. Firm adherence to a code of especially moral or artistic values: incorruptibility. 2. An unimpaired condition: soundness. 3. The quality or state of being complete or undivided: completeness.

All right. Follow a code. When you follow a code, you are right.

Al: This doesn't sound like you. You wrote the preceding chapters. The blind following of a code seems contradictory to what you previously said. Are you sure it all comes down to a formula, a code? Just follow a code, and then everything will be fine?

No. Don't just follow a code. You are right. I am not right.

Al: Right.

Right means left. (I don't mean to imply that this ridiculous phrase is to be taken in any political sense). Include the other side, the other side of things.

Al: Now I am confused. I don't know what you mean.

Sometimes confusion is good. Uncertainty can be a noble quality. Acceptance of doubt can mean that a person is open to a new understanding of truth. Integrity is enhanced and underpinned by a doubt that welcomes truth.

Al: Then doubt can be part of a code?

Yes, if you realize that doubt throws the code wide open. Doubt might be considered the un-code part of a code. Then you have an un-code code.

Al: It boggles the mind.

There are some self-righteousness ones for whom mind-boggling would be a healthy thing. They are the ones for whom codes of

God Unmasked; the Full Life Revealed

righteousness may lead to exclusiveness. For these individuals, a righteous feeling may delineate those who are acceptable and those who are not. Devastating comments about self-righteousness are made by theologian Karl Barth: "Vanity of mind and blindness of heart inevitably bring into being corrupt conduct. The more unbroken people march along their road secure of themselves, the more surely do they make fools of themselves, …" (122).

Furthermore, self-righteousness can lead to catastrophic consequences. The self-righteous have certainty about that which they think is right, no matter how much pain and injustice they might inflict on others. For them, rightness is a prejudice that fulfills and satisfies their sense of integrity.

The cure for prejudice is doubt and openness. We discussed doubt in Chapter Two and again in the last chapter. Doubt allows a person to be open, to be receptive to scanning those beliefs that are held, to verify or reject those beliefs. With doubt, we are open to a new comprehension of the truth.

The utilization of doubt and openness provides the climate for discernment—for clear-sighted evaluation of that which is before us. I cite a quote by Nietzsche, who describes the will to discern:

> To discern: that is delight to the lion-willed! But he who hath become weary is himself merely "willed;" with him play all the waves.
>
> And such is always the nature of weak men: they lose themselves on their way. And at last asketh their weariness: "Why did we ever go on the way? All is indifferent!" (459)

We value the ability to doubt and discern. We value openness. These qualities give us confidence. They are components of integrity, elements of a fullness of life.

Al: Then you are really referring to the second and third parts of the definition of integrity, aren't you? Integrity as completeness and soundness. These are what you are considering instead of a code. Right?

Yes. Integrity is the fullness of life. It affords a sense of completeness and soundness.

Al: Let's back up a bit. I want to question you about openness. Do you mean openness to everything? Anything goes? That sounds like relativistic ethics: nothing is wrong. "If it feels right, do it."

No. That is not what I mean. Life is more than just feelings and what "feels right." Responsibility is part of the full life. Responsibility implies an ability to act on the basis of a balanced judgment. I quote from *Hamlet* by Shakespeare:

> ... blest are those
> Whose blood and judgment are so well commingled,
> That they are not a pipe for fortune's finger
> To sound what stop she please. (*Hamlet:* III, Scene II, 690)

Al: And upon what do you base responsibility? What characteristics predispose a person toward responsibility?

Let's look back to Chapter Three in order to piece our way through this. The foundation of a positive outlook on life is an orientation of thankfulness. We have gratitude for existence—for the existence of ourselves, others, and the environment.

Al: And the basis for thankfulness is ...?

Axiomatic. It is an assumption. We assume an attitude of thankfulness. In relation to the larger sphere of existence, there is no basis for thankfulness. Rather, thankfulness is an individual, subjective attitude toward existence; there is no universal principle upon which to base thankfulness. However, we do note that, when we have an outlook of thankfulness, we tend to feel better. Thankfulness contributes to a sense of happiness. Therefore, we could consider that this contribution to a sense of happiness constitutes a utilitarian basis for an outlook of thankfulness.

The attitude of thankfulness creates a positive outlook, welcoming that which exists. The welcoming is an expression of value. There is respect and value for that which is. Furthermore, the valuing of another person tends to carry with it a sense of respect. Also, when we value someone, our actions toward that person are more likely to be responsible. We tend to fulfill responsibilities toward others when we perceive value in them.

Al: What about exceptions? What about when we don't like someone?

All right. Consider some person you may not like. Your judgment of that person may be negative in that you question or dislike his or her possible motives or actions. When interacting with that person, self-discipline will assist you in carrying out your responsibilities.

Self-discipline buys us time—time which can allow us to adjust or expand our view of the other person. Also, self-discipline allows an opportunity for the other person to change in response to our interaction with him or her.

Al: What you mean is: do what should be done, be responsible, and, if you don't particularly like the other person, you are giving that individual some "space." You remain open to the possibility for a positive view of that person. Isn't that what you mean?

That is another way of putting it. I will add that self-discipline does often call for patience. Listen to the Tao:

> Do you have the patience to wait
> till your mud settles and the water is clear?
> Can you remain unmoving
> till the right action arises by itself? (15)

I will describe a broader understanding of the value of self-discipline. In the course of fulfilling a life of integrity, self-discipline facilitates behavior that is consistent with integrity. Self-discipline—in conjunction with respect and the fulfillment of responsibility—is a bulwark of conscience. When a person has these qualities, his or her goals are not likely to be corrupted by the utilization of unsatisfactory means of attaining those goals. Conrad states: "But the fact remains that you must touch your reward with clean hands, lest it turn to dead leaves, to thorns, in your grasp" (255).

Self-discipline can strengthen the sense of integrity. To quote Dante's *Inferno*: ". . . so long, I say, as nothing in conscience troubles me, I am prepared for Fortune, come what may" (*Inferno* XV, lines 91-3).

Further along, Dante states: ". . .my own clear conscience strengthens me, that good companion that upholds a man within the armor of his purity" (*Inferno* XXVIII lines 115-7).

This last quote brings up a matter of concern. For some, a clear conscience is, indeed, the path to self-righteousness. They are clear in what they think is right, no matter how much pain and injustice they might inflict upon others. For them, prejudice fulfills a sense of integrity, but it is a warped integrity that can have negative consequences.

It is now time to talk about the antidote to the excesses of self-righteousness. A vehicle for a release from self-righteousness is empathy. The experience of empathy can lead a person to a more complete understanding of others.

The presentation in Chapter Seven about empathy included information about the impulse to avoid empathy. Also, it was recognized that clear-minded, non-reflective action may predispose a person to avoid empathy. However, when empathy has been felt, one can comprehend how that experience can be joyful and fulfilling. The ability to experience empathy is a hallmark of happiness. Furthermore, empathy and action are not mutually exclusive. The interacting flow between empathy and action was described in Chapter Seven.

Chapter Eight delineated the need for social structure—as opposed to anarchy. Furthermore, the existence of social structure is facilitated by a general inclination of individuals toward having empathy with each other. The occurrence of empathy eases the handling of the conflicting intricacies of social interaction.

Let's consider further the subject of empathy. There are three prime factors in the development of empathy. Openness allows a degree of freedom from prejudiced views; openness implies a welcoming of fresh perception of others.

The second factor predisposing toward empathy is thankfulness. Thankfulness affords that positive outlook which tends to place value on the other person and enables us to respect him or her. Openness and thankfulness then afford the capacity for seeing another person as a valued individual. These qualities also enable you to see that person with fresh perceptiveness. In this way, openness and thankfulness provide fertile ground for the growth of empathy.

Al: I understand your points, and I would expect that wonder is the third prime factor predisposing a person to empathy.

You are right. Of course, we don't mean the negative sense of the word "wonder." That would just be a questioning attitude. Wonder, in its positive sense, appeals to the imagination. In the positive mode, wonder stimulates an enlarged sense of awareness. There is a welcoming of that which is being experienced. This welcoming of experience becomes an invitation to empathy, to an enlarged understanding of people, of situations, of whatever is being perceived.

We have talked about how empathy draws a person beyond the self. The occurrence of empathy involves an opening of the self to the world beyond self. However, empathy does not preclude self-awareness. The perceptiveness of that which is around us does not require self-denial. There is reality of the self and validity in a sense of self. When an outlook of asceticism includes self-denial, such outlook is not adequate for the full life in that it avoids an aspect of reality: the existence of the self.

Regarding asceticism, James said: "If the inner dispositions are right, we ask, what need of all this torment, this violation of the outer nature? It keeps the outer nature too important. ... (When emancipated, one) can engage in actions and experience enjoyments without fear of corruption or enslavement" (280).

We are now at the end of this chapter, and it's time to take a look at the whole picture. Integrity is fullness of life, a sense of soundness and completeness. The wholeness of integrity includes the basic qualities that we talked about in Part Two: doubt, thankfulness, openness, freedom, wonder, empathy, respect, and responsibility. Wholeness—integrity—has many facets; a joy of peace and a joy of action, an acceptance of the unchangeable and a patience for that which can be changed, the changeable, an openness that frees the mind for new perceptiveness and for that access to doubt which can lead to new aspects of truth. Fullness of life includes a thankfulness for being and wonder of and joy for the gift of existence.

Al: I appreciate your drawing this together. I now have a more full understanding of the meaning of integrity. But isn't there something else? The title of this book is *God Unmasked; the Full Life Revealed*. Won't you have something to say about God and spirituality?

Right. There is a spiritual dimension to the full life. Actually, spirituality involves those qualities to which we have just referred. But the subject of spirituality gets more complex. In discussing spirituality, we will deal more extensively with the imagination and include consideration of the concept of God and religious practice. Bit by bit, we will sort this out in Part Three of the book.

There is something further I want to say about joy and happiness.

Al: I'm glad of that.

I'm glad your're glad. So now, I will finish this section with a survey: three questions. Picture these activities and ask yourself if you are happy during the activities.

1. You are walking along the Champs-Elysees in Paris on a warm spring day. Ask yourself now: "Am I happy?"

2. You are eating a gourmet dinner at a fine restaurant. Expend some thought on this question: "Am I happy?"

Integrity; a Fullness of Life

3. You are having sex. Now turn this thought in your mind: "Am I happy?"

The point of this survey is that a mindfulness of the question of happiness may cause a person to, in fact, be less happy. When there is a questioning of happiness, then the possibility of realizing happiness becomes less likely.

On the other hand, happiness is more likely when a person becomes immersed in the activity. An aliveness to the activity at hand is more wholehearted when there is an absence of mental rumination about evaluating the presence or degree of happiness. In other words, don't remain in a state of constantly evaluating everything. Question and cogitate about those things which are reasonable to question. Beyond that, live life spontaneously. Allow spontaneity in those parts of life for which trust has been developed. "How do you decide about trust?" you ask. That is coming up in Chapter Twenty-two.

I can add this: happiness and joy are not to be pursued as conscious goals in themselves. They are celebrated, but their attainment is not purposive. As previously pointed out, it is well for a person to be without some drive toward attaining happiness. Such striving is self-defeating in that the conscious effort tends to negate the possibility for attaining happiness. The feeling of happiness requires a mind that is cleared of striving for happiness as such, a mind that is free to experience the joy of the moment. Rather than striving toward happiness, it is far better to relax from striving while realizing that happiness is the natural accompaniment and consequence of living the life of integrity, the life that is full and whole. Joy is more likely to occur when there is no conscious effort directed toward it. Happiness itself is not an attainment to be gained; happiness is not to be seen as an achievement. Joy and happiness are those welcome feelings which are integral to and occur spontaneously with the peace and confidence created by the life of integrity. This is illustrated in an ancient Buddhist text quoted by Hick: "If a man speaks or acts with a pure thought, happiness follows him… " (319). And Nietzsche says: "Pure is his eye, and no loathing lurketh about his mouth. Goeth he not along like a dancer?"(431)

10

Nonsense

Al: A chapter for nonsense? That's ridiculous.

You have been thinking for nine chapters. It's time for a break.

Al: I can put the book down if I want a break.

But that's not the same thing. You officially get to continue reading the book while taking a break.

Al: I am not worried about being official.

The break comes before starting a new realm of material in Part Three.

Al: Fine. And so?

You want to be refreshed.

Al: Excuse me. I'm going for a sandwich and pop.

Which brand?

Al: I thought you would not want the brand named.

That's right, and that is a good lead-in to the use of word-symbols in Chapter Eleven.

Al: I'm taking a break.

PART III

THE UNMASKING OF GOD

11

Word Symbols and Imagination

We will now piece our way toward an understanding of spirituality. I start this chapter with a brief overview of Part III. The first three chapters provide background to Chapter Fourteen, God Unmasked. In the present chapter we consider characteristics of word-symbols and the imagination, particularly that which is termed the "cosmic imagination." Chapter Twelve takes a more objective look at the nature of the universe. In Chapter Thirteen the release from doubt and discernment is the topic, and this is one of the factors predisposing one toward experiencing a spiritual dimension. A conceptual view of God is presented in Chapter Fourteen, a view which may be acceptable to many who value the retention of an openness to doubt. Chapters Sixteen through Eighteen provide information on particular aspects of the spiritual outlook: mysticism, opposition, and individual differences. In Chapter Nineteen we will look into the nature of a religious orientation.

In the present chapter we explore the nature of words. We will find that information about language can lead to an enlarged understanding of the role of the imagination.

It is helpful to outline the chapter. We start with the subject of verbal expression and its relation to the imagination. Next is abstraction and some of the problems and satisfactions associated with the use of abstraction. Finally, we look at that degree of abstraction which is manifested as the cosmic imagination.

I begin by saying that the act of self-expression is a fundamental part of our nature. The intrinsic inclination toward self-expression is also stated by S. Suzuki: "Our inmost nature wants some medium, some way to express and realize itself" (136).

The following are some quite simple and basic statements about self-expression. A person expresses himself or herself in actions. Doing things is a form of expression. Also, expression takes the form of words, which are symbols corresponding to an entire range of facts and circumstances. We express our thoughts about things through the use of word symbols.

Furthermore, words spoken by others affect us, and our understanding of words spoken to us is modified by our individual perspectives. What we hear is molded and modified by our imaginative inclinations. Imagination plays a role in the understanding and interpretation of that which we hear and the manner in which it is spoken. The imaginative capacity which overlays our communication with others affects our understanding and responses. Imagination is, then, a subjective component in our interaction with others.

It is not uncommon for words to inspire a definite response even when there is not much objective meaning to the words. A simple "There, there" can engender a wide variety of responses, depending on the circumstances, the tone of voice, and the mind-set of the listener. A "There, there" could be calming and reassuring, or it could be taken as cynical.

In the following example of approximately 100 years ago, the psychology theorist Horace Fletcher describes the experience of a Buddhist disciple. This example shows the power of the imaginative response to two words:

> On my way back ... I could think of nothing else but the words *"get rid, get rid"*; and the idea must have continued to possess me during my sleeping hours, for the first consciousness in the morning brought back the same thought, with the revelation of a discovery, which framed itself into the reasoning, "If it is possible to get rid of anger and worry, why is it necessary to have them at all?" I felt the strength of the argument, and at once accepted the reasoning .... From the instant I realized that these cancer spots of worry and anger were removable, they left me. With the discovery of their weakness they were exorcized. From that time life has had an entirely changed aspect.... All at once the whole world has turned good to me. I am sure the change is not so much in the world as in me. I have become, as it were, sensitive only to the rays of good.... When I was a boy, I was standing under a tree which was struck by lightning, and received a shock, from the effects of which I never knew exemption until I had dissolved partnership with worry. Since then, lightning and thunder, and storm clouds, with wind-swept torrents of rain have been encountered under conditions which formerly would have caused great depression and discomfort, without (my) experiencing a trace of either. Surprise is also greatly modified, and one is less liable to become startled by unexpected sights or noises. (27-34)

I will relate a personal example of the power of a few words. These words were spoken to me by George Victor, to whom I have dedicated this book.

During most of my years in high school I worked at Hayes Restaurant, near Chicago, preparing drinks and desserts and tending the cash register. There were occasional periods of time when George Victor cooked at Hayes, alternating his time there with a restaurant up north. George Victor was an impressive person, quiet-spoken, calm, accommodating, and he had a gentle enthusiasm. I idolized George Victor and was happy when I would learn that he was returning to Hayes.

Though we were both busy and had little free time, we had occasional, short conversations. One time he surprised me when he said: "Ernie, you are a gem among stones." The comparison to those in my work environment was startling. I had considered my co-workers to be fine people, not at all like my adoptive mother, who repeatedly informed me of how despicable I was.

Even though I was suspicious of my mother's character, I tended to believe her evaluation of me. When exposure to verbal abuse starts in infancy and extends over many years, it is not surprising that any measure of self-esteem becomes incomprehensible to the victim of that abuse. That is why George Victor's words were so startling to me. This was a man of integrity, and he had expressed a very favorable view of me. Those few words he said that day were the beginning of my salvation from the depths of misery. Prior to hearing those words, I had not even realized that my life could be something other than miserable. The revelation of his words was like a religious conversion that transforms sorrow into joy.

I could talk a long time about the power of words, but I won't. However, I will quote Bachelard regarding the relationship between words and imagination:

> (Literary images) vitalize us. Through them, speech, the word, literature, are raised to the level of creative imagination. By expressing itself in a new image, thought is enriched and enriches the language. Being becomes word. The word appears at the highest psychic point of being. The word reveals itself as the immediate mode of becoming of the human psyche. (Imagination 21)

I have indicated two aspects of the verbal expression of imagination described by Bachelard. He points to a vitalizing effect and also alludes to an abstracting effect that extends beyond concrete objectivity.

Let's take a look at the nature of abstraction. The process of abstraction relies partly on objective grounds, that is, direct experience. Beyond direct experience, abstraction utilizes the faculty of the imagination to obtain an enlarged view, an understanding that transcends the immediate experience. Abstraction classifies experiences and it enlarges understanding through a correlation of discrete experiences.

The utilization of imagination can be a source of joyful experience. Bachelard talks about the delight and the power of the imagination when he describes the relationship between tranquility, words, and imagination:

> Tranquility is the bond which unites the Dreamer and his World. In such a Peace there is established a psychology of capital letters. The dreamer's words become names of the World. They have access to the capital letter. Then the World is great, and the man who dreams it is a *Grandeur*. This grandeur in the image is often an objection for the man of reason. It would be enough for him if the poet would admit to a poetic intoxication. He would perhaps understand him by making the word "intoxication" abstract. But for intoxication to be real, the poet drinks at the cup of the world. (Reverie 173-4)

Al: Big objection here. We are left with powerful words that can lead anywhere, and often do. Subjectivity and imagination have no solid base in the world of fact. I would be hesitant to dwell in a world excessively affected by imagination. Too much disaster could result from that.

You are worried about the calamitous effect that words often have. This also worried Simone Weil, who says:

> But when empty words are given capital letters, then, on the slightest pretext, men will begin shedding blood for them and piling up ruin in their name, without effectively grasping anything to which they refer, since what they refer to can never have any reality, for the simple reason that they mean nothing. In these conditions, the only definition of success is to crush a rival group of men who have a hostile word on their banners; for it is a characteristic of these empty words that each of them has its complementary antagonist. (221)

Let's enlarge the subject of the power of imagination as manifested in abstraction. Abstractions which have an emotional appeal often refer to subjects that concern identity. Some sources of identity—such as occupation, age, and marital status—do not involve a major degree of abstraction.

However, identity often centers on religious, political, or economic factors, all of which are abstractions of constellations of practices and beliefs. It is true that less abstract factors often are operative in the delineation of identity groups. Such factors may be quite extensive: life style, appearance, and so on. But concrete, objective perceptions often tend to become coalesced into summarizing abstractions of identity. And identity is often the key differentiating point through which economic and political forces operate. As a distant observer, that is the way it appears to me in some current disputes, such as in Bosnia and Northern Ireland. For instance, in Northern Ireland, I understand that the opportunity for employment is limited when the potential employee is recognized as Catholic; the Catholic identity limits the person's economic opportunity.

We have talked about both the appeal and the dangers of abstractions. I referred to abstractions concerning identity. A more broad perspective on the nature of abstraction is well described by Kenneth Burke:

> To be sure, many of the incentives towards abstraction derive from indirectnesses in a society's way of living, indirectnesses due to social and technical resources for the delegating of work to others. But the longer we have puzzled over this problem (noting for instance, how spontaneously children often take to the abstractions of card games), the more convinced we are that the impulse to abstraction is a driving force in itself. There seems to be in man an unremitting tendency to make himself over, in the image of his distinctive trait, language. It is as though one aimed to become like the pure spirit of sheer words, words so essential that they would not need to be spoken, but would be like the soundless Shelleyan music vibrating in the memory after the song is finished. (Cf.. Eliot's *Quartets*.) Thus it seems that, while the percentage of abstraction is increased by the increase of institutions and inventions that make for much indirectness in our ways of living, the very tendency of human societies again and again to develop towards abstraction (as with the Upward Way towards the "divine" in the Platonic dialectic) is due to a property ingrained in language itself. Even our terms for the closest of family relationships have an abstract ingredient that makes them readily serviceable for naming social relations not strictly familial at all (as with the adapting of such terms to the ecclesiastical order). (184-5)

At this point, let's look at the role of ambiguity in abstraction. The impulse toward abstraction may be seen as a manifestation of imaginative freedom. Attention is often drawn toward that which is not clearly seen. A desire to understand abstractions invites the imagination to freely comprehend in broad terms.

Furthermore, variety in the interpretation of abstractions implies a degree of ambiguity. It is this very ambiguity which attracts attention and stimulates the imagination because focus is drawn to the mysterious—to the incompletely delineated. William James had a word about this: "It is not only the Ideas of pure Reason, as Kant styled them, that have this power of making us vitally feel presences that we are impotent articulately to describe. All sorts of higher abstractions bring with them the same kind of impalpable appeal" (60).

Ambiguity invites attention by drawing the mind into an openness, into a freedom. This is so even though abstractions are, to a varying extent, tied to specifics. When using abstractions, specific examples are just symbolic representations of larger categories.

The tendency toward abstraction presents us with the possibility of seeing broader significance in the immediate experience. Furthermore, the inclination toward abstraction tends to have an inclusive quality. With imaginative freedom, abstraction, in its most comprehensive form, becomes universal. The ultimate abstraction, the grand scheme of the universe, can stimulate the imagination toward a free openness that provides a subjective experience of the totality of existence. It is this enlarged manifestation of the imagination that can be called "cosmic."

I do not use the term "cosmic" as some mysterious superforce. By "cosmic" I simply am referring to the entire universe. The term "cosmic" includes all existence—that tree, this table, us, all the galaxies, and so on. As defined in Webster's dictionary, cosmic means: "the universe in contrast to the earth alone."

Bachelard describes several characteristics of the cosmic imagination: beautification, personalization, grandeur, a potential for the establishment of self-importance, happiness, a welcoming quality, a sense of openness and freedom, a transcendental quality, a unifying effect, and the flowing together of the real and the imaginary. We will look into each of these. I greatly appreciate the outstanding insights which Bachelard has described, and I quote liberally from his work.

This is a passage by Bachelard that describes the aesthetic effect of poetry in stimulating the cosmic imagination:

> The lake, the pond, the still water very naturally awaken our cosmic imagination through the beauty of a reflected world. When

he is near such things, a dreamer receives a very simple lesson for imagining the world, for doubling the real world with an imagined world. The lake is a master at natural watercolors. The colors of the reflected world are tenderer, softer, more beautifully artificial than the heavily substantial colors. Already, those colors born by the reflections belong to an idealized universe. The reflections thus invite any dreamer of still water to idealization (Reverie 198).

Here is another example of Bachelard's description of the cosmic imagination: "The poet's garden is a fabulous garden. A past of legends opens a thousand paths to reverie. Avenues of the universe radiate out from the 'celebrated' object. The apple celebrated by the poet is the center of a cosmos, a cosmos where the living is good, where one is sure of living" (Reverie 156).

In *The Poetics of Space* Bachelard describes the cosmic imagination as experienced in the desert by psychologist Philippe Diole:

But then, we ask, why did Diole, who is a psychologist as well as an ontologist of under-seas human life, go into the desert? As a result of what cruel dialectics did he decide to leave limitless water for infinite sand? Diole answers these questions as a poet would. He knows that each new contact with the cosmos renews our inner being, and that every new cosmos is open to us when we have freed ourselves from the ties of a former sensitivity. At the beginning of his book (*loc. cit.*, p. 12), Diole tells us that he had wanted to "terminate in the desert the magical operation that, in deep water, allows the diver to loosen the ordinary ties of time and space and make life resemble an obscure, inner poem" (Space 206).

I will cite a general statement by Bachelard concerning the cosmic imagination: " ... the cosmic nature of images is the result of the imaginary life's tendency to magnify" (Imagination 91).

This cosmic imagination imbues the universe with the value of beauty. Bachelard states: "Along the normal axis of cosmic reverie, the perceptible universe is transformed into a universe of beauty" (Reverie 182).

There is a personal dimension within the cosmic imagination. Bachelard states: "All important words, all the words marked for grandeur by a poet, are keys to the universe, to the dual universe of the Cosmos and the depths of the human spirit" (Space 198). Bachelard further says: "It would seem, then, that it is through their "immensity" that these two kinds of space—the space of intimacy and world space—blend" (Space 203).

The cosmic view has its effect on the viewer. Per Bachelard: "A glimmer of eternity descends upon the beauty of the world. ... (Is) this intuition of the world, this *Weltanschauung*, anything other than a childhood which dares not speak its name? The roots of the grandeur of the world plunge into a childhood" (Reverie 102-3).

Bachelard does point to a particular caveat regarding the cosmic imagination, and this finds resonance as a concern in religious practice. The warning is about the occurrence of an implied self-importance during the experiencing of cosmic imagination:

> I also spoke of a spectacle complex in which pride of seeing is the core of the consciousness of a being in contemplation. But the problem under consideration in this present work is that of a more relaxed participation in images of immensity, a more intimate relationship between small and large. I should like to liquidate, as it were, the spectacle complex, which could harden certain values of poetic contemplation. (Space 190)

Returning to the positive aspects of the cosmic imagination, Bachelard speaks of happiness that is associated with the cosmic imagination:

> But the world dreamer does not regard the world as an object; the aggressiveness of the penetrating look is of no concern to him. He is the contemplating subject. It then seems that the contemplated world passes through a scale of clarity when the consciousness of seeing is the consciousness of seeing big and the consciousness of seeing beautiful. Beauty works actively on the perceptible. Beauty gives relief to the contemplated world and is an elevation in the dignity of seeing at the same time. When one agrees to follow the development of the aestheticizing psychology in the double valorization of the world and of its dreamer, it seems that one knows a communication of two principles of vision between the beautiful object and seeing it beautiful. Then in an exaltation of the happiness of seeing the beauty of the world, the dreamer believes that, between him and the world, there is an exchange of looks, as in the double look from the loved man to the loved woman. (Reverie 185)

Bachelard further states:

> ... how is it possible not to affirm that the man of reverie is cosmically happy. A type of happiness corresponds to each image. You cannot say of the man of reverie that he is 'thrown to the world.' For him the world is all welcome, and he himself is the

principle of welcome. The man of reverie bathes in the happiness of dreaming the world, bathes in the well-being of a happy world. (Reverie 157)

The cosmic imagination is also validated as valuable because of the openness and freedom it affords. It is a refreshment for the self. Bachelard describes this freedom:

> The idealizing reverie goes in just one direction, from level to ever more elevated level. A reader who does not follow the ascension closely may have the impression that the work is fleeing away from him in evanescence. But the person who dreams better teaches himself to repress nothing. The reveries of excessive idealization are liberated from all repression. (Reverie 92)

When describing the happiness which accompanies the cosmic imagination, Bachelard alludes to a transcendental quality of this imagination, transcendental in the sense of extending beyond the objective boundaries of the self:

> Through the cosmicity of an image then, we receive an experience of the world; cosmic reverie causes us to inhabit a world. It gives the dreamer the impression of a *home* in the imagined universe. The imagined world gives us an expanding *home* ... In dreaming on the universe, one is always *departing*; one lives in the elsewhere—in an *elsewhere* which is always *comfortable*. (Reverie 177)

One of the aspects of the cosmic imagination is a unifying effect, and this is elucidated by Bachelard:

> In the poet's reverie, the world is imagined, directly imagined. There, we are touching on one of the paradoxes of the imagination: while thinkers who reconstruct a world retrace a long path of reflections, the cosmic image is immediate. It gives us the whole before the parts. In its exuberance, it believes it is telling the whole of the Whole. It holds the universe with one of its signs. A single image invades the whole universe. It diffuses throughout the universe the happiness we have at inhabiting the very world of that image. In his reverie without limit or reserve, the dreamer gives himself over, body and soul, to the cosmic image which has just charmed him. The dreamer could not doubt that he is in a world. A single, cosmic image gives him a unity of reverie, a unity of world. Other images are born from the first image, come together and mutually embellish each other. Never do the images contradict

each other; the world dreamer does not know the division of his being. (Reverie 175)

This cosmic reverie does not deny the reality of the objective world. The imaginary and the real are lived simultaneously, without denial of either. Per Bachelard:

> And we live all the better in the world, living as the solitary child lives in images. In the child's reverie, the image comes first. Experiences only come afterward; they go against the current of all reveries of flight. The child's vision is grand and beautiful. Reverie oriented toward childhood takes us back to the beauty of first images. The child knows a natural reverie of solitude which we must not confuse with that of the sulky child. In his happy solitude, the dreaming child experiences cosmic reverie—that reverie which unites us with the world. In my opinion, it is in the memories of this cosmic solitude that we must find the nucleus of childhood which remains at the center of the human psyche. That is where imagination and memory are most closely interwoven. That is where the childhood being weaves together the real and the imaginary, and lives in the fullness of imagination the images of reality. (Imagination 96)

I will close this chapter with a personal experience of the cosmic imagination: It had been very foggy the prior evening. Looking back that evening, I reminisced: I had grown up in and around Chicago and at age seventeen had joined the Army. It was 1946, the year after World War II ended. After Infantry basic training at Fort McClellan, Alabama, we were processed for overseas duty at Camp Stoneman, California. On Sept. 30th we loaded our personal supplies into backpacks and duffel bags, hiked some distance, and then were trucked to the pier at Oakland. The troopship we boarded was named the *Marine Fox*, and our destination was Korea. As we left the dock and proceeded into San Francisco Bay, passing under the Bay Bridge, the fog settled in. By the time we went under the Golden Gate Bridge it was so foggy that we could barely see the lights on the bridge—our last view of our homeland. And then we could start to feel the roll of the ocean. It was night; we descended to the sleep compartments. The beds were rectangular metal tube frames with canvas stretched and tied to the tubes. These tubes were attached to posts and stacked five high with narrow spaces between.

In the morning I heard the loudspeaker: "Compartment C5: fall out for chow." We had left the dark fog of San Francisco and had slept in the troop quarters lit only by dim electric bulbs. The several flights up to the deck and to the mess hall were not crowded that first morning; many were seasick.

I ascended upward, each flight lit by electric bulbs. Then it happened: I stepped out into the daylight of October 1st, 1946. Before me was the brilliant sunshine, the white, expansive clouds, the ocean stretched out forever. The only sight from the ship was the sea, rolling and sparkling in the gentle wind. My whole being swayed in the rolling, pulsing glory of existence. The darkness of the past was gone. There was no concern about the future. All that I experienced in that moment was an indescribable joy, an all-consuming lightheartedness rolling into my being and carrying it into a universe of exuberance.

12

Universe, Hope, and Value

The Universe
Unknowns
Self and Universe
Hope
Value

THE UNIVERSE

Al: In Chapter Eleven we talked about imagination at the cosmic level, a mental view of the grand scheme of the universe. This involved an imaginative orientation, a freeing of the mind from anything solid and objective. Let's get back to objectivity and reality. What can you say about actual facts regarding the nature of the universe?

All right. Let's take a look at this now. The nature of the universe: this is the area of metaphysics. The dictionary definition of metaphysics is "a division of philosophy that is concerned with the fundamental nature of reality and being."

For many people current usage of the term "metaphysics" signifies a spirituality construed as reverence for the mystical. However, the discussion in this book does not use the word "metaphysics" in that sense. I am considering metaphysics as described in the following dictionary definition: the fundamental nature of reality.

My perspective of that fundamental nature is that it consists of a confluence of three basic properties of existence.

First, there is the mechanistic aspect of the universe. An example is the scientific description of a falling object. It falls according to the force of gravity and amount of time elapsed. The mathematical expression of this is:

$$S=½gt^2$$

A coin falling to the floor or an airliner falling to the ocean gains speed by these parameters. Regarding the mathematical formula, you don't really want mathematical symbols discussed, do you?

Al: No, thanks. I'll pass on that, and I note that your examples are not entirely arbitrary.

Examples not arbitrary; right. Good examples provide help for maintaining attention. If I think hard, I may even drum up some humor for you in the examples.

Al: You're kidding.

No; seriously. But the next sentence is a weighty one. Scientific formulae are available in a massive array for the entire realm of events that can be described by objective means. However, there also is the aspect of chance. This is the second characteristic of the nature of the universe. Predictions can be made within certain parameters, but within those parameters the outcome is random. A bolt may fall off an airplane wing now or in five years.

Al: That sounds cheerful.

Just making a point about Chaos Theory. This theory depicts the presence of chaos in order and order in chaos. Predictions—such as weather forecasting, the dripping of a faucet, the development of a heart arrhythmia—are more valid when they incorporate the element of chance, the irregularity aspect, in their projections. As I understand Chaos Theory, the shapes of all things are consequent to dynamic processes involving the interaction of order and disorder.

Chaos Theory incorporates the parameters of uncertainty in mechanisms. Outcomes are predicted as probabilities. In the journal, *The Sciences,* Amitabha Sen and Sharon Butler elaborate on this:

> Because of the Uncertainty Principle, physicists cannot predict exactly how subatomic particles will behave. "Physics," the late Richard Feynman observed, "a science of great exactitude, has been reduced to calculating only the probability of an event." However alien this idea might seem, the picture that quantum theory draws of the fundamental nature of the world has been borne out time and again .... (34)

Al: I want to say something here. When you admit that there is an element of chance or randomness in the scheme of the universe, that is tantamount to saying that things can and do happen without purpose. You say that random events happen without regard or concern for the well-being of people. How might such randomness fit with any sort of concept of meaning of existence?

Well, I understand that, for many, a sense of purpose is what gives life meaning, and this is particularly so when that purpose is seen to have originated at a grand, universal level, particularly when the purpose is viewed as originating on a supernatural level. On the other hand, look at it this way: existence itself is a consequence of events. How could there be some meaning of existence if the creation of and the course of that existence were determined partly by chance? I believe that the presence of chance and chaos in the course of events implies a lack of meaning of existence at some universal level.

It is my understanding that one of the concerns of that field which is termed "process theology" is the role of chance and randomness in a spiritual context. Those theologians who invoke some form of process theology are engaged in the reconciliation of chance and supernatural purpose. However, they start with the premise that a supernatural consciousness does exist. I have a different point of view, which you are in the process of discovering.

What happens happens. If Chaos Theory is a valid aspect of the universe, then earthquakes, floods, and all the innumerable events and circumstances that exist have no metaphysical significance beyond the fact of simply being expressions of randomness, mechanism, and the third aspect.

Al: Ah. One more aspect to go.

Yes, and this third aspect has many parts.

Al: I am fascinated. I don't know what the third aspect is, and already I know it has many parts.

Your enthusiasm is overwhelming. Well, I will announce that the third aspect is the unknown.

Al: How do you know that?

UNKNOWNS

Have patience. To begin, I have to say that the metaphysical unknown is a projection of our lack of knowledge and not a basic characteristic of the universe. If the unknown were considered a characteristic of cosmic existence, that would imply a conscious quality to the universe, albeit as a consciousness of the unknown. I do not mean to imply such a conscious quality. Furthermore, according to this point of view, since the unknowns are not a fundamental aspect of the universe, they are not to be considered as having some metaphysical reality. But these unknowns are intrinsic to our view of the universe. That being the case, the unknowns are the subjective companion to the two objective aspects of metaphysics: mechanism and chance.

Let's look at the unknowns. First, there is the unknown of mechanism. For instance, by Newton's findings, the laws of motion were revealed. These were clear-cut and without need for further clarification. There were no unknowns involved, that is, until Einstein showed the inadequacy of Newton's formulations. With hindsight there was an unknown but unrealized aspect in the formulation of the laws of motion, and this was revealed by the work of Einstein in his Theory of Relativity. Likewise, scientific formulations exist at the present time which include unknowns that are not as yet realized as incompletely known. Scientific findings discovered in the future will undoubtedly reveal some current formulations to be inadequate.

Regarding mechanism, we also have awareness of fundamental unknowns. The physicist Stephen Hawking refers to fundamental unknowns when he states: "The laws of science, as we know them at present, contain many fundamental numbers, like the size of the electric charge of the electron and ratio of the masses of the proton and the electron. We cannot, at the moment at least, predict the values of these numbers from theory ..." (125).

Al: I am not a physicist. Please do not go into detail.

I am not a physicist either. In that area, I can just tell you what physicists puzzle themselves about. We will go on. The second unknown is the one we know about. It is chance, and Chaos Theory has been cited in regard to the occurrence of chance. As another example of chance, we don't know when an earthquake will cause massive destruction and death, but within certain parameters we can predict such an occurrence.

Even the Old Testament has something to say about chance. Aside from various interpretations encompassed by process theologians, the occurrence of chance may seem opposed to that which could be interpreted as divine will. Therefore, it may surprise you to hear this quote from the Bible concerning chance: "I returned, and saw under the sun, that the race is not to the swift, nor the battle to the strong, neither yet bread to the wise, nor yet riches to men of understanding, nor yet favour to men of skill; but time and chance happeneth to them all" (Eccl. 9:11).

The third unknown is the one about which mystics, theologians, and hundreds of millions of religious followers have knowledge. In fact, for many, it is not an unknown. They often claim quite specific knowledge. It is the atheists and agnostics to whom this is an unknown.

This third unknown is the existence of the transcendent, the existence of a supreme being, force, or consciousness, that is independent of the existence of the entire universe. No matter how wondrous, grand, awe-inspiring, strange, or mysterious anything is that can be known by any objective means, the very existence of every thing which does exist means that it is a part of the universe. In contradistinction, the supernatural consciousness is seen to be separate and beyond the universe.

Al: I want to say something about that.

We both want to say more about that, and we will later in this chapter. Let's get through some of the preliminary information first. Also, I can say that later chapters will take up the delineation of that toward which there is a spiritual inclination.

We have now arrived at the fourth unknown. This is the question: did the universe have a beginning or does it exist eternally? It is not too hard to live life without having an answer to that question. However, it is of interest to many, particularly to those who want more definite answers about the nature of the universe.

In any event, both possible answers—finite duration of existence vs. existence without beginning or end—are incomprehensible except as visualized by some inadequate model. Neither finite duration nor infinite time can be comprehended except in some limited view presented by the imagination.

Al: What about the Big Bang Theory? I understand that theory is widely accepted.

According to the Big Bang Theory, the universe did have a definite beginning. However, the source for the initial impulse of this proposed event is unknown. Also, it has been postulated that the existence of things occurs as a series of expansions and contractions, with events like the Big Bang at the start of the expansions. If that were the case, then the totality of existence could be eternal and without a single point of initiation. Other scenarios of either eternal or point-originated existence may be possible.

But all the possibilities, including the source for the creation of a Big Bang, are in the realm of the unknown.

Al: You have more unknowns than I might have expected, but I can see your points.

SELF AND UNIVERSE

In fact, there are two more unknowns, and they are both personal. Even though these unknowns are personal, I bring them up at this point because they impact our view of the nature of the universe. Therefore, the personal unknowns affect the subjective part of our metaphysical orientation.

One of the personal unknowns—Number Five, for you, Al—is the occurrence of particular unknowns in a person's life. These unknowns are many and varied. For instance, one may not know that the spouse is cheating on him or her. Other examples: a person would not know that cancer will develop next year; someone does not know that there will be a heart attack tomorrow.

We tend to become more concerned with metaphysical questions, such as the meaning of life, when catastrophe has happened, instead of beforehand. However, the potential for catastrophe is always with us, and catastrophe tends to invite a questioning of reasons for these personal unknowns.

We have arrived at the sixth unknown, which is, the relation of personal life to the universe. First, let's look at the broad view. The course of the entire universe and the course of individual lives are manifestations of the same metaphysical properties. To summarize this metaphysical orientation, there are three basic aspects of existence: mechanism, chance or randomness, and the unknown. The ongoing character and interactions of all entities that exist are manifestations embodying these three qualities of existence. Furthermore, these three are characteristics of one process: the nature of the course of the universe. It is only in the abstract that the three components are considered separately.

We talked about the various unknowns, and we noted that the fifth unknown is the occurrence and timing of personal events, such as health problems and accidents. Awareness of these calamities tends to lead us to the sixth unknown: what is the nature and meaning of the self as part of the universe? Furthermore, this leads to the question: what is that course of life upon which we would ideally want to direct ourselves?

Our life is a part of the universe, a segment of the cosmic. Directions we take are personal, local expressions of the nature of the universe. If we have imaginative vision, we can realize the freedom to take different directions in life. With the release from a constricted view of choices, we may see paths that are more in tune with a sense of fulfillment. An awareness of freedom to take various directions may help us to realize that some paths may be more true to our nature than others.

Al: What do you mean by "true to our nature?" Any path which we might choose to take may be said to be an expression of our nature.

Ah. Ethical relativism. By "true to our nature," I mean: living a life that is made wholesome by taking the path of integrity. I posit that it is the life of integrity which is the most natural for us because it is the most fulfilling. Furthermore, by integrity, I mean that manner of life I described in Part Two of this book. It includes thankfulness, empathy, openness and doubt.

Al: Big disagreement here. Someone could just as well say that the life of violence, aggression, and power is the most natural for us. That sort of life seems to have been the most fulfilling for Nietzsche, at least, according to his writings.

Your point is well taken. There is no metaphysical basis with which to justify my statement about integrity. However, let us consider again the axiomatic basis for the course of life that was discussed in Chapter Three: thankfulness. Consider the outlook of thankfulness. As previously described, thankfulness is the foundation for respect and consideration. Furthermore, when a person has an outlook of thankfulness together with a free openness, these qualities tend to lead to a capacity for empathy. Respect and empathy mitigate against those courses of action which might lead to a destructiveness of self, others, the environment, and to destructiveness in general.

In confirmation of these statements regarding integrity, consider the joy and contentment that fulfills the life of someone who has integrity. I believe that you and almost everyone know such a person. Also, you are probably aware of the attraction of others to a person of integrity. Beyond these two considerations, I cannot claim integrity as a metaphysically proven, naturally ideal state for humankind.

Al: Well, then I will agree with you. The life of integrity is fulfilling. But I want to mention something. It appears that you have provided a solution of the sixth unknown. The ideal relation of life to the universe is incorporated within the process of living a life of integrity. The sixth unknown is not an unknown.

We have part of the answers. But if we become smug in the belief that we have all the answers, our solution is nullified.

Al: A Catch-22? If we think we have the answers, we don't, and if we don't, we do?

We really don't have all the answers. We only approach the discovery of that which is true for us. Openness and doubt are necessary parts of the full life. Doubt implies openness to an understanding of that which we do not yet fully comprehend; there is an openness to the unknown. The unknown is intrinsic to a full life. Our roles are not prescribed. The freedom and openness of our outlooks guide us into directions that are often unknown and uncharted.

As the sixth unknown—the unknown of our personal direction in life—we see that personal direction from a position of openness. Our course in life is not some pre-ordained, established path. We are open to explore the uncharted.

This does not mean we have to explore the uncharted. That which is expected—either by us or by others—is not necessarily wrong. There is no deterministic requirement either way. We are not obligated to follow either an expected or an unexpected course; we can be open to either, and, for assistance on our path of life, we can employ the characteristics of integrity—openness, freedom, doubt, thankfulness, empathy—to help guide us.

Al: Let me question you about something here. I wonder if you are confusing determinism in a metaphysical sense with expectation in a social sense.

In fact, in looking at the course of our paths in life, I am considering these together: the social point of view and that which can be considered metaphysical. There is not a metaphysical determinism which mandates our directions. Also, social obligation is weighed in the balance, both given full due when appropriate and held in abeyance when the characteristics of integrity guide in a different direction.

Even when we follow the constraints of fulfilling responsibilities, the mode of handling these responsibilities can include an openness to new, fresh possibilities. The unknown of newness can accompany these possibilities.

God Unmasked; the Full Life Revealed

There is an additional value to the use of a capacity for doubt that I want to emphasize at this time. In addition to doubt in regard to particular things which we do not completely understand, the utilization of doubt welcomes an unknown dimension in all that we do know. Doubt carries with it an openness to new understanding.

Al: You could just as well say that, instead of doubt, certainty should be a central theme for our lives.

I disagree. Please keep this in mind: certainty is the foundation for the pitfalls of self-righteousness. I again quote from Ecclesiastes in the Bible: "Be not righteous over much; neither make thyself over wise: why shouldest thou destroy thyself?" (Eccl. 7:16)

We know much about the dangers of an attitude of certainty. I have cited many examples in the previous chapters. I should think we all would want to avoid the pain and catastrophes created by an attitude of certainty. With that in mind, I say that doubt is a major component of integrity.

We have spoken about the nature of life. Now let's address the meaning of life.

Al: Well, that's a simple project. No sweat there. You have it figured out, do you?

I see the delineation of the meaning of life as the value we realize due to the orientation we have toward our individual existences and toward our lives in relation to the existence of all things, in relation to the universe.

Let's look at the effect presented when a person realizes that his or her personal nature is an aspect of the nature of the cosmos. Recognition of the self as an expression of the nature of the universe creates an enlargement of outlook. When we see the self as a component of the expression of the universe, there is likely to be less self-centeredness and less tendency for excess self concern. Also a view that includes a relationship with the universe may possibly expand our thoughts into the exuberance of the cosmic imagination, which I described in the preceding chapter. Bachelard has a phrase for the sense of enlarged awareness afforded by the cosmic imagination: "... the expansion of being which we receive from cosmic reveries" (Reverie 23).

This expanded awareness of the self in relation to the universe can lead to a calmness and peace that accompanies the comprehension of relationship with the larger nature of things. A relaxation can develop with the understanding of one's personal place in the universe. An acceptance of this realization of one's place in the universe—particularly an acceptance

Universe, Hope, and Value

of the limitation of duration of the self's existence—can lead to a calmness. The peace that comes with an acceptance of the fact of death—whether death is impending at the time or not—can place all the other activities and attitudes of life in perspective. A realization of what really matters can accompany the acceptance of the fact of death.

Also, the acceptance of the inevitability of death may foster an attitude of thankfulness for that length of life which we have. Thankfulness may replace anger and a sense of frustration about death.

With an understanding of existence of the self in relation to the larger nature of things, you may see with a vision that reaches into things, to feel what their essential nature might be, to know people more clearly. An enhanced capacity for empathy can become a natural way of life when the awareness of a larger perspective on life is realized.

This enlarged outlook has been recognized by others. William James said:

> ... man identifies his real being with the germinal higher part of himself and does so in the following way. He becomes conscious that this higher part is conterminous and continuous with a *more* of the same quality, which is operative in the universe outside of him, and which he can keep in working touch with, and in a fashion get on board of and save himself when all his lower being has gone to pieces in the wreck. (383-4)

From this point on, I will be speaking as if there is no supernatural power, no transcendental consciousness. I am comfortable with the concept of the natural unfolding of events. I am not comfortable with the concept of a supernatural manipulation of events. When good fortune or calamity happens, it seems to me more likely to be in the natural order and disorder of things rather than arranged by some supernatural consciousness. That is my personal orientation, not something I can prove. The supernatural cannot be proven or disproved. No one knows whether or not a transcendental consciousness exists (in spite of claims and mystical experiences to the contrary). The existence of a supernatural power is not known, but it seems to me that there is not such an existence. The randomness of events seems to point to the absence of such a power.

Physicist Stephen Hawking comments about chance and the unlikelihood of supernatural intervention:

> With the advent of quantum mechanics, we have come to recognize that events cannot be predicted with complete accuracy

but that there is always a degree of uncertainty. If one likes, one could ascribe this randomness to the intervention of God, but it would be a very strange kind of intervention: there is no evidence that it is directed toward any purpose. Indeed, if it were, it would by definition not be random (166).

In regard to the concept of a natural universe without supernatural control, William James states:

> Here we have the interesting notion fairly and squarely presented to us, of there being elements of the universe which may make no rational whole in conjunction with the other elements, and which, from the point of view of any system which those other elements make up, can only be considered so much irrelevance and accident—so much "dirt," as it were, and matter out of place. (116)

And again by James:

> It is impossible, in the present temper of the scientific imagination, to find in the driftings of the cosmic atoms, whether they work on the universal or on the particular scale, anything but a kind of aimless weather, doing and undoing, achieving no proper history, and leaving no result. Nature has no one distinguishable ultimate tendency with which it is possible to feel a sympathy. (371)

I will make another point which concerns the existence of a transcendental conscience. Even if there were no amount of chance in the workings of the universe, the presence of mechanism does not require a maker of that mechanism. It could be blind mechanism without a conscious power producing it.

Furthermore, there is no proof of a transcendental consciousness that exists beyond all that can be known to exist by objective means or by theoretical projection based on empirical information. Of course, you realize I make the statement that there is no proof of a transcendental existence without entering the field of theological argument. With a highly limited theological background, I am not qualified to provide a significant refutation of opposing positions. I speak from my experiences in ordinary life and from that background in philosophy, the sciences, and theology which I have obtained.

You might want to consider an extreme view of the non-significance of human life at a metaphysical level. This passage is not meant as a source for despair but as a realistic look at the subject of human significance. In fact, instead of despair, it could be considered a call for an increased supervision of weapons. It is possible that, within thirty or forty years, humanity will have become annihilated due to the use of weapons of mass destruction. Following such possible destruction, I consider it somewhat unlikely for some humanoid life form—with some semblance of human consciousness—to evolve again. Possible but unlikely. The universe wheels on, without any particular metaphysical significance for the existence of human life.

Let's carry this discussion forward with a consideration of the way in which a lack of transcendental meaning can affect a person's outlook. Life without transcendental meaning does not negate human values, but these values are held in a different way than those held by people who have faith in the supernatural. Although I said that there is no metaphysical basis for meaning, there is a subjective value in having a mindfulness of the universe—of the existence of the massive array of entities and the incredible expanse of time and space.

I suspect that many are afraid they will lose their sense of value if they accept the point that the universe proceeds partly by blind chance—randomness—rather than as directed by a supernatural consciousness. But then, why fear non-significance when we are, in fact, not significant in some metaphysical sense? Why fear the unavoidable? It is better to accept that which is reasonable to be accepted. Non-significance is an aspect of the nature of life. The billions of years in time and billions of light-years in distance—these which comprise the universe—do not make for a likely significance of our span of life on this earth. The mechanisms of existence, infused by chaos and chance, do not seem to point to some grand meaning of our being. As stated before, it is my inclination to believe that there is no transcendental consciousness that provides us with significance. Hick points to both the scientific and the religious outlook in characterizing this skeptical view:

> It is true that no naturalistic theory can account for the *existence* of the universe, or for its having the basic character that it has; this simply has to be accepted as the ultimate inexplicable fact. But religion also has its own ultimate inexplicable fact in the form of God or a non-personal Absolute. And the skeptical mind prefers to rest in the mystery of the visible world without going beyond it to a further invisible mystery. (111)

I feel that it is vanity to want something, some consciousness, that is transcendental, beyond all existence, and which bestows meaning as some grand metaphysical dimension. The search for meaning on a grand scale suggests self-importance at a metaphysical level. This search for meaning is mentally narrowing in that it is a way to buttress self-importance, which is restricting to the mind.

There is another possible drawback to the quest for metaphysical meaning. The search for meaning at a metaphysical level also may be seen to imply a feeling that there is a lack of meaning for individual existence at the level of daily existence.

There is no external, supernatural source for meaning. Value and meaning are arrived at subjectively. We create value; it is not established by some supernatural force. Meaning comes from that which is valued because of our sense of thankfulness and by our awareness of the self as part of the larger whole. William James has a word about this:

> Conceive yourself, if possible, suddenly stripped of all the emotion with which your world now inspires you, and try to imagine it *as it exists*, purely by itself, without your favorable or unfavorable, hopeful or apprehensive comment. It will be almost impossible for you to realize such a condition of negativity and deadness. No one portion of the universe would then have importance beyond another; and the whole collection of its things and series of its events would be without significance, character, expression, or perspective. Whatever of value, interest, or meaning our respective worlds may appear endued with are thus pure gifts of the spectator's mind (128).

It is not helpful to be too concerned with a quest for metaphysical meaning. There is more value in experiencing thankfulness for the fact of existence. Don't worry about metaphysical meaning or try to explain randomness. In relation to the dimension of chance in the course of life, it is less valuable to ponder metaphysical meaning than to just proceed with life, anticipating probable outcomes while knowing that the improbable may occur. Be thankful for that amount of gifts which we have.

What, you ask, are the effects of an acceptance of chaos and randomness as fundamental aspects of existence? How does the realization of the occurrence of chance affect us, knowing that chance is an intrinsic part of our existence and life's course?

Al: I didn't ask that.

But you wanted to.

Al: I don't worry too much about chance.

Some people do. We had better spend some time with this subject because hope is a powerful force, and the presence of hope is affected by the attitude toward chance.

HOPE

The viewpoint of William James is: "No fact in human nature is more characteristic than its willingness to live on a chance. The existence of the chance makes the difference, as Edmund Gurney says, between a life of which the keynote is resignation and a life of which the keynote is hope" (397).

But is hope always the right keynote? Without hope, life might seem to be filled with despair and resignation. However, despair is not the necessary result when there is a realization of the ubiquity of randomness. I will repeat a quote in which John Hick describes the frustration associated with a concern about randomness of events; he also indicates the thankfulness that this concern summons: "The consciousness of our chancy and insecure place in the scheme of things can nevertheless induce a swirling intellectual vertigo. It can also elicit a sense of gratitude and responsibility in the face of the extraordinary fact of our existence" (90).

Too much mindfulness of hope can blind a person to the value of that which is occurring in the present. When the present experience is extremely unpleasant, hope may be quite welcome. But, at other times, the negatives of the presenting situation might fill a person's thoughts to the point that there is limited perceptiveness of that for which there could be thankfulness and appreciation. Per S. Suzuki: "As long as we have some definite idea about or some hope in the future, we cannot really be serious with the moment that exists right now" (111).

It is also possible for hope to stifle the imagination, including that imaginative capacity which provides awareness of the larger aspects of life. T. S. Eliot gives an impressive picture of this:

> I said to my soul, be still, and wait without hope . . . .
> Wait without thought, for you are not ready for thought:
> So the darkness shall be the light, and the stillness the
>   dancing.
> Whisper of running streams, and winter lightning.
> The wild thyme unseen and the wild strawberry,
> The laughter in the garden, echoed ecstasy

Not lost, but requiring, pointing to the agony
Of death and birth. (28)

An absence of hope can allow more freedom in full expression of an activity. By full expression I mean that the realization of fulfillment by the activity is not inhibited by a mind that is preoccupied with the goal. It is fine to express hope, however, without dwelling on it excessively.

I will repeat a quote by Camus describing the freedom experienced when there is a release from hope: "... the very work, whether it be conquest, love, or creation, may well not be; consummate thus the utter futility of any individual life. Indeed, that gives them more freedom in the realization of that work ... " (Sisyphus 86-7).

Al: You mean: being more into the action than the end-product and not being blinded by the goal.

That's one way of putting it.

Al: Well, I believe in action, but the drive for a goal is important, too. I was at a high school football game yesterday evening. I shouted for our team: Go, team, go. Fight, fight, fight. Win, win, win.

Did you win?

Al: Yes, we did.

You see, that's an example of hope as fulfillment of the want for emotional expression. You wanted to enjoy the emotional high of desire for a goal. That's fine. We talked about that in Chapter Four.

Al: Right on.

I should add that, to some extent, I overstated my position on hope. However, I do maintain that, when faced with the prospect of an event over which there is no possible control, it is not helpful to dwell excessively on hope. An example would be excess concern about the possible occurrence of a rainstorm or an earthquake. Also, hope is counterproductive when it feeds a frustration that blocks acceptance of the inevitable, such as, when death is unavoidable.

On the other hand, when a possibility exists for change as a result of a person's action or attitude, then hope may lead to a widening of perceptiveness. For example, someone may feel submerged in a harsh social structure. The conditions associated with racial and religious prejudice are in this category. In such a situation, the capacity for hope may translate into an enlarged awareness of possible actions or attitude changes that could have constructive results.

Also, hope can feed valuable personal qualities, such as perseverance and patience. Hope may foster a positive outlook that can carry a person through stormy times. However, the value of maintaining hope should not negate an openness to acceptance of a realistic view of limiting factors.

Al: Let me see if I can summarize what you said about hope. You spoke about the value of having hope and the value of avoiding hope when an excess inclination toward hope would decrease a person's perceptiveness and openness. Furthermore, both of these aspects of hope refer to a personal level. In regard to the cosmic level, you say there is no metaphysical basis for hope, no supernatural consciousness that watches out for our well-being.

VALUE

We talked about the value of hope. Let's look at a more personal perspective on the subject of value. In future generations our existence will have been forgotten except possibly as notes in history books for some of us. In the distant future there may possibly be no conscious life, and all matter may eventually become transformed in the expanding or contracting universe. Our existence proceeds without value at some universal level.

Al: But we do have personal values. I value my family, my life, and many things in my life.

Yes. We value the gifts of existence: lives of selves and others, health, gifts of fortune. These values can be enhanced by a realization of our relation to all existence. We can identify with the processes of the universe and the universal within us. We are constituted by relationships between elemental entities that have evolved into our being. In the face of incredible odds against my ever having existence, I do exist. And what is my existence? It is an amazing array of chemical elements and compounds by which arrangement I have sight, hearing, movement, and consciousness. At some time in the future my life will end, the chemicals will be dispersed, and I will have no further consciousness. I am very grateful for this time in which I do have existence and the ability to be aware and to act.

Al: Just a bunch of chemicals? That sounds crude.

Why deny reality? We are an incredible arrangement of chemicals that has the capability to eat ice cream, to watch television, and much more. Of course, much more. I shouldn't make light of humankind's abilities.

If this is a new concept for some people, it may shock them. For me, it is a source of profound thankfulness that I have been given the gift of life.

Our being is one manifestation of all existence, and we can recognize ourselves each as one part of all creation. This recognition of our lives as a manifestation of the nature of all existence may elicit our thankfulness and freedom, thankfulness for existence and freedom by a release from the bindings of excess concern with the particulars of this world, the worldly values. We still have these values, but the worldly values are held with a light heart. The worldly values can be held with complete sincerity but without compulsion since they are secondary to the realization we have of the nature of the universe that is manifested in both our individual existences and the existence of all things. A degree of detachment from excess concern with worldly things is then more possible when we have this enlarged view of existence. Some degree of detachment can allow a clearer perceptiveness and nurture a freedom for openness, wonder, and empathy. We can have a detachment that remains engaged with the world but is free to have a more complete understanding of that which is.

Al: I see what you mean. Let me ask about another point. In the last chapter we talked about cosmic imagination. How does this fit into what you are saying?

Our cosmic imagination draws us to an enlarged consciousness of all existence. Awareness of a grandeur far beyond us encompasses our local world and renders the immediate world's values secondary to the value of that which glorifies our vision. Furthermore, the workings of the universe are the source of our creation and the source of our nature. We are what we are by the nature of the universe. This realization of the significance of the nature of the universe in our lives may predispose us toward having some experience of the cosmic imagination. To a mind nurtured by television, this may seem foreign. Many live in a world of reaction to the immediate. But, also, in the process of life's vagaries, many lead themselves toward a broadened and more enlightened view.

The broadened view, the enlarged sense of awareness brings to mind a poem I wrote when I was in a pine forest in eastern Washington State:

The Constant Hum

The hum
The constant hum
is not the creek
    far down the hill
not the grasses
  bending forward
      thin stalks
     wavering in
          the wind
              the wind
     the wind currents of the
           unseen
        pushing through
  all life
  all forms
currents of the unseen
while pines reach
    high up
    lift forward
      and lean back
           in the wind.
Needles glow bright green
    in the sun
      in the sunlight.
Swaying branches
    soar and
      sing into the sky

God Unmasked; the Full Life Revealed

reach into the nourishment
of light
the deep blue
the full sky
blue
that screens
the night of
black
and empty
space
empty
space
in the existence
of nothing
except
fiery bits of
matter
and burned out
existences.
Wind blows into
eternity.
I hear a raven
cry

Universe, Hope, and Value

13

Release From Doubt and Discernment

Release
External Authorization
Word-symbols
Self-righteousness
Summary

RELEASE

Al: Just a minute, here. I see the chapter title, and it alarms me. I doubt and I discern. I want to be able to figure out anything for myself. I don't want to be in some state in which I can't question what's going on. And that reminds me: your second chapter shows the value of doubt, and you have emphasized that capacity for doubt several times since.

Ah, patience. You have doubt. And when you don't doubt, you still have access to doubt— just in case it's needed. That's important. I did say that. Doubt is fundamental to well-being.

But I am not constantly in a state of doubt; I don't constantly think about things. I do not continuously maintain a process of evaluating. Instead, I use the facility of doubt when the need calls for it. Otherwise, my mind relaxes into whatever direction I'm going.

Wood chopping example again. Before I chop wood, I discern if that's the activity I want to engage in at that time. Once I start chopping wood, I don't consciously think about it unless some particular reason comes up to change my activity. When I'm doing the chopping, I'm not discerning or doubting. If the need to cogitate comes up, I do so. For instance, I stop the wood chopping if the metal axe head gets loose.

Should I mention skiing? Same thing. I just float down the hill—without consciously thinking or discerning, except in the purview of the immediate experience. By that I mean that I subconsciously continue to discern trees and rocks to avoid fracturing anything important.

Moreover, I should say that I am not recommending a total release from doubt and discernment. I am just describing the inclination toward that release. In fact, there is a human tendency toward experiencing a relaxation and peace that comes with the release from doubt. And here is an important adjunct to the statement about this tendency: the release from doubt is particularly operative in the realm of spirituality and religious practice. We will discuss this in ensuing chapters.

At times, doubt is very restrictive, tending to inhibit action and to destroy equanimity. Doubt and discernment are helpful in the process of a perceptiveness which can lead to a greater understanding of the true character of things, but excess doubt can impinge on the sense of wholeness.

EXTERNAL AUTHORIZATION

For many, a release from doubt is facilitated by the acceptance of some external authority that is trusted. This source of external authorization may have no formal status of authority in your life. It may be a friend or even some historical person. It might be an object, such as a religious icon. The source of external authorization may be imbedded in the sense of community or in the awareness of common social interests. The authority lies in the value you place in that person or on that thing. This value draws you toward the contentment or fulfillment that comes with being aware of its presence in your mental life.

It's possible for an interpersonal relationship to be an aspect of external authorization, serving to establish or to reinforce some belief or attitude. The realization of the attitudes and beliefs of others can lend an objective quality to a belief held in common, even when the belief itself is not founded on objective information. The belief of other individuals then becomes a source of external authorization. The content of information which forms the external authorization is not necessarily related to the actual belief but to the individual's perception of other human beings who manifest a commitment to the belief.

The point of external authorization is that you are drawn to something or somebody beyond yourself. This can release you from a tendency toward self-absorption.

Psychotherapist Viktor Frankl talks about directing oneself beyond the self: "(Man) finds himself only to the extent to which he loses himself in the first place, be it for the sake of something or somebody, for the sake of a cause or a fellowman, or 'for God's sake' (87).

In his book, *The Origin of Consciousness in the Breakdown of the Bicameral Mind*, psychologist Julian Jaynes refers to the direction many take toward finding an external authorization (317-38, Copyright 1976, 1990 by Julian Jaynes, Houghton Mifflin Company). The following passage is concerned with the inhibitions that may be associated with excess doubt and discernment. He points to sources of authority that can provide release from these psychological stresses:

> ...why is it that in our daily lives we cannot get up above ourselves to authorize ourselves into being what we really wish to be? If under hypnosis we can be changed in identity and action, why not in and by ourselves so that behavior flows from decision with as absolute a connection, so that whatever in us it is that we refer to as *will* stands master and captain over action with as sovereign a hand as the operator over a subject? ....
>
> We live in a buzzing cloud of whys and wherefores, the purposes and reasonings of our narratizations .... And this constant spinning out of possibilities is precisely what is necessary to save us from behavior of too impulsive a sort .... We know too much to command ourselves very far.
>
> Those who through what theologians call the "gift of faith" can center and surround their lives in religious belief do indeed have different collective cognitive imperatives. They can indeed change themselves through prayer and its expectancies much as in post-hypnotic suggestion. It is a fact that belief, political or religious, or simply belief in oneself through some earlier cognitive imperative, works in wondrous ways. Anyone who has experienced the sufferings of prisons or detention camps knows that both mental and physical survival is often held carefully in such untouchable hands.

But for the rest of us, who must scuttle along on conscious models and skeptical ethics, we have to accept our lessened control. We are learned in self-doubt, scholars of our very failures, geniuses at excuse and tomorrowing our resolves. And so we become practiced in powerless resolution until hope gets undone and dies in the unattempted. At least that happens to some of us. And then to rise above this noise of knowings and really change ourselves, we need an authorization that "we" do not have. (402-3)

The taking on of a source for external authorization frees the mind from uncertainty and inhibition of action. Careful thought, doubt, uncertainty, caution: all of these can inhibit the free flow of action and speech. Joy in the pulse of life is, to some extent, inhibited by a mind attuned to reason and propriety. The acceptance of external authorization tends to present a bypass to the strictures of the constrained mind.

Overall, there is value in both doubt and release from doubt. Early in this book, in Chapter Two, I emphasized the definite need for doubt. But there is also a need for freedom from doubt, as just discussed. In this chapter we will further explore aspects of release from doubt and discernment. Later, in Chapter Twenty-two, the conjuncture of doubt and the release from doubt will be examined.

WORD-SYMBOLS

Let's look at other sources for release from doubt and discernment. Words that express positive qualities can be used to avoid active perceptiveness or thought. Some people immerse themselves in an aura of compassion or love. When an expression of love includes the avoidance of discerning thought, it may become a sterile habit, an ideal that is separated from reality.

Many words may be used in such a way as to release a person from doubt and discernment. I have heard spiritual gatherings extol a unity of existence. Word symbols, such as "unity," may release people from patterns of thought by providing an overriding focus of attention. The use of words like "unity," employs an abstract focus. When a concept is abstract, it tends to invite increased attention because of the ambiguity often associated with abstract terms.

I do not fault the use of word symbols to obtain a release from excess concern about problems. One facet of mental health is the ability to find psychologic refreshment in what could be called "vacations of the mind." These vacations are helpful and often invigorating. The caveat to be kept in mind while on mental vacation, however, is to avoid a denial of reality and to be open to perceptiveness; a willingness to doubt should be maintained. When facts call for a fresh discernment of the situation at hand, these facts should not be denied. Even in the face of some degree of commitment to a source of external authoritization, individual responsibility should still be maintained.

We talked about some of the aspects of the use of word symbols in Chapter Eleven. Let's extend that discussion by mentioning slogans. Of course, slogans are well-known as agents that not only energize the direction of a group but also inhibit individual discernment. The consequences are, at times, catastrophic.

History is strewn with many examples of disastrous consequences toward which slogans had contributed some part. At this point, I will cite just one such result: the cry of the people of the German nation in the late 1930's for *lebensraum* (living space). This was one of the factors in the German invasion of countries to the east (*Drang nach Osten,* drive to the east).

The placing of oneself under an external authorization can take many forms. Another example of the taking up of an external authorization is the area of literal-mindedness. This literal-mindedness involves the adoption and espousal of written or spoken material while avoiding and, in fact, disputing the value of examination of that material. Words become authority. The symbol itself becomes the reality. Representations, symbols, the words, become central, and that which the words represent is secondary and more-or-less incidental to the authority of the words.

Here is an example of literal-mindedness. The word "god" is a word-symbol; that word means a variety of things to different people. To some of the literal-minded—especially if the word is capitalized—God, the word itself, becomes holy. Any meaning ascribed to the word is secondary to the holiness of the word itself. I am sure this is not entirely true for all who are literal-minded, but it is true to varying degrees for many.

The Bible is a book, a collection of word-symbols. Again, to the literal-minded the Bible as a symbol is holy. The meaning of the words in the Bible has importance to many of the literal-minded. However, for them, this meaning tends to be secondary in value to the authority of the Bible as a whole. For the literal-minded, the Bible represents God's authority, and the validity of the content exists precisely because it is part of the Bible rather than on the merits of that content.

Such literal-minded acceptance of authority can create problems. Armstrong points to problems with the acceptance of the words of the Bible as literal truth when she indicates that a deity who is totally responsible for all that happens manifests "impossible contradictions." Also, such a deity would be a "cruel and despotic tyrant" (283).

I can speculate that there are several possible mental processes which may incline a person toward literal-mindedness. Some people are more attuned to stability and control, and they tend to be uncomfortable with that which seems to invite openness and empathy. In the perception of these people, the immediate world needs to be pre-categorized and stable. They tend to opt for a stabilized content as opposed to an openness to greater understanding or empathy.

On the other hand, for some, a literal-minded understanding of Holy Scripture supports the reality of their personal spiritual transformation. This transformation may involve a movement away from obsession or despair and toward a new, enlarged sense of awareness. The world becomes wondrous and joyful. For these, literal-mindedness is a vehicle for the joyful anticipation of life.

This tendency toward literal-mindedness may be buttressed by an external authorization which feeds a sense of self-worth. Personal value can become enhanced by the external authorization. However, for many who are centered on a source of external authorization, when or if doubt arises regarding validity of claims of the authority, the sense of self-worth may also become jeopardized.

SELF-RIGHTEOUSNESS

Let's look at another aspect of self-worth. Self-righteousness, an exaggerated sense of self-worth, tends to narrow the vision. The self-righteous person has less openness and thereby less perceptiveness. Less openness implies less freedom to doubt and discern. This leaves the self-righteous person more susceptible and vulnerable to the claims and leadership of those authorities toward which they are inclined.

Also, the presence of self-righteousness and false pride may place a person under the authority of appearance, that is, how the self appears to others. Tolstoy describes the development of this vanity of social appearance in Ivan Ilyich: "All the enthusiasms of childhood and youth passed without leaving much trace on him; he succumbed to sensuality, to vanity, and latterly among the highest classes to liberalism, but always within limits which his instinct unfailingly indicated to him as correct" (1951). The path of social consciousness is also noted by Giddens: "Founded in the social bond, pride is continually vulnerable to the reactions of others ..." (66).

Finally, there is the authority of anti-authority, the authority of rebellion. For some, the authority of rebellion is the source for a release from doubt and discernment. The mood of rebellion may develop its strength, in some people, from its appeal to an emotional state that negates discernment.

This authority of rebellion stems from pride in opposing the persons and/or values held by what is seen as the external authority—another person, group, or social, political, or economic structure. The opposition extends to values ascribed to the external authority, whether true or not.

This worship of rebellion has a philosophical base in the person of Nietzsche. He praises rebellion, as if there were no need for social coherence and as if primitive power were the primary force in life:

> Its last Lord it here seeketh: hostile will it be to him, and to its last God; for victory will it struggle with the great dragon. What is the great dragon which the spirit is no longer inclined to call Lord and God? "Thou shalt," is the great dragon called. But the spirit of the lion saith, "I will." ...As its holiest, it once loved "Thou-shalt": now is it forced to find illusion and arbitrariness even in the holiest things, that it may capture freedom from its love.... (443-4)

Not only does the joy of empathy mean nothing to Nietzsche. He either does not foresee, is inured to, or would positively delight in the suffering loosened upon the world if his point of view became more generally accepted.

On the other hand, the expression of rebellion is justified at times. As a habituated state, however, the mood of rebellion is a blinder on the vision, a preconception. As such, it narrows perceptiveness and restricts the opportunity for an openness of the mind.

SUMMARY

Let's summarize. While affirming doubt as necessary in order to arrive as close to truth as possible, the value of a release from doubt and discernment is recognized. This is not to deny drawbacks in this release from doubt.

Several patterns of behavior and thought can manifest this release from doubt: non-reflective action, external authorization, word-symbols used as a non-reflective focus, self-righteousness, the authority of social appearance, and the authority of rebellion.

The next chapter will utilize the information developed in this chapter, including both a consideration of the value of doubt and the value of a release from doubt.

14

God Unmasked

Before Beginning...
The First Aspect of God
The Second Aspect of God
The Third Aspect of God
Overview of the Three Aspects of God
The Utilitarian Dilemma
Objectivity and Subjectivity
Doubt
A Note on Ending This Chapter

BEFORE BEGINNING ...

Al: Excuse me. I was looking ahead at this chapter.

There is to be no peeking ahead. If you are looking at this chapter without having read the preceding material, you will not have the background that has been developed, and the information in this chapter will then mean less to you. I can wait till you read the previous chapters.

* * * *

I have to start with a note of caution that I stated at the beginning of this book and will repeat here. This book is not expected to be of value to those who have already found God or are secure in their understanding of God. The individuals who know God may be offended by the information presented. Rather, this book is for those who have both a skeptical nature and some inclination toward realizing the validity of a spiritual direction in their lives.

I can say that a life that is lived without a spiritual base may have an empty quality. An orientation toward the larger sphere of existence can provide us with a perspective with which to measure the quality of our attitudes and goals. A confidence may accompany the ups and downs of life if you see the context of your life in relation to a more universal understanding of existence.

Without a relationship to the larger sphere of existence, the quality of life may be excessively set upon mundane goals or attitudes or it may degenerate into a hypocrisy of appearance. However, in the course of life individuals can come to realize the emptiness of superficiality.

In this chapter it is not my intention to present a broad view of various concepts of God. Rather, the chapter describes a delineation of my own view. In my view, the understanding of God involves an objective correlation, a subjective mental projection, and a salvific effect. Before you puzzle too much about what I just said, I can add that it may be more helpful to just proceed with the text and all will become more clear.

I should add this: it may appear that I am constructing a concept of God which fits specific information. The exposition of my thought may lead to such an impression. However, in the course of my life, the awareness of God is first, preceding the comprehension that I have of God. It is afterwards that I find words which allow communication of that experience.

THE FIRST ASPECT OF GOD

I will start this chapter by saying that God is …

Al: Yes?

God is …

Al: Is there more to that sentence?

God is a projection of the mind.

Al: That statement should satisfy the atheists.

Wait. There is more. As a mental projection, the word "God" is a representation of a mental reality. The word symbol "God" is a focus of attention which corresponds to an abstraction of all that exists.

Al: I see what you mean, but not clearly.

If I said: "God is all that exists," you might add that God is that stone, that tree, this jar of jam. But God is not the particulars of existence. God does not have a particular size or shape.

When I thank God for my existence, I am not thanking the particular sperm and egg from which I was created. Also, when expressing gratitude to God, I am not thanking the generations of men and women who are my ancestors. When I thank God for my life, I show gratitude for the workings of the universe by which I have been given life. Our gift of life is fantastically improbable. The events of the universe through billions of years have resulted in our presence here this very minute. To quote from Hick:

> One can be conscious of the prodigious notional improbability of one's existence, and can feel privileged to be alive, without interpreting this good fortune religiously. Nevertheless the mystery of the universe's existence and character can only evoke in any reflective mind a sense of wonder, and even awe, which if not taken up into a religious faith will most naturally find expression in mystical poetry. (90-1)

To my mind, one aspect of the word symbol "God" represents the workings of the universe. We talked about the nature of the universe in Chapter Twelve. Let's look at that again. The universe is constituted by a confluence of three characteristics: chance, mechanism, and the unknown. Mechanism and chance are concepts derived from a multitude of observations. Therefore, they are abstractions. Furthermore, the "nature of the universe" is an abstraction of the abstractions, mechanism and chance, in conjunction with the unknown. The nature of the universe is then a concept which is an abstraction of abstractions. As such, the understanding of the nature of the universe is somewhat vague.

It is my inclination to understand one aspect of the word symbol "God" as correlating with the grand view of the universe, an all-encompassing concept of existence. As an abstraction of phenomena which can be observed and confirmed, the phrase "nature of the universe" is compatible with objective reality. On the other hand, a concept as vague as the nature of the universe manifests that ambiguity which is an element of the workings of the imagination. This grand perception of all existence is a ready instrument for the music of the cosmic imagination. The enlarged awareness of objective reality is, in fact, a part of the symphony of the cosmic imagination.

The working of the imagination does not mitigate against a release back to the discerning perception of scientific investigation. In fact, the freedom of imagination can be a welcome adjunct for an elucidation of novel views of objective reality. Such novelty affords a potentiality for an advancement of scientific concepts.

The word symbol God correlates with the natural occurrence of that which exists. As such, God has no agenda; there is no purpose, no transcendental meaning. What meaning we have is that which we create. We talked about this in Chapter Twelve.

Furthermore, there is no end-stage, no heavenly utopia. We are each but one manifestation of existence, one part of the existence of all things, and each existing entity is in a state of unfolding, a state of becoming. There is not a final goal; instead, there is a present unfolding.

The naturalistic concept of God is not unique to this book. Hick refers to the naturalistic view of God as expressed by several theologians: "Although it is not completely clear whether they intend a full naturalistic reduction of the concept of God, a number of contemporary Christian thinkers write as though they do" (209). He cites particular theologians:

> The view of religion as expressing natural realities in supernatural symbols was beautifully expressed by George Santayana. It was also more cloudily and sometimes ambivalently expressed by Paul Tillich …. Religion in its many forms, then, bears witness to an aspect of our human experience that evokes this symbolism for its expression. Randall calls this "the Divine." The Divine, as he uses the term, is a dimension of the natural. Although language about it appears on the surface to be about a transcendent reality, Randall is emphatic that "the Divine" is a symbol and that religious symbols "are both nonrepresentative and noncognitive." (196)

Al: Let me take an opposite tack. To many skeptics, there is no inclination toward any mindfulness of what might be called "God."

That is true. Many see no need to invoke and overlay a mysterious word upon the processes of nature. The addition of that particular kind of ambiguity seems superfluous.

THE SECOND ASPECT OF GOD

Let's take another look at ambiguity—by way of hard facts. At the present time I exist. You exist. These statements are quite true and would not be disputed, except perhaps by some philosophical theorists.

I am thankful for my existence. In fact, I am very thankful for my existence and my ability to act, think, move, and experience. I am very thankful for my life.

A companion awareness may accompany gratitude for life. Realization of thankfulness for life can carry with it a view of the alternative: non-existence. The realization of death is fearful for many. However, the reality of personal non-existence can bring to mind the opportunity for an enlarged awareness. With the release from a centering on personal existence, I may become better able to have an openness to awareness of that which is beyond my agenda. With projection to a time when there is a loss of sense of self, I may be able to comprehend more thoroughly the on-goings of the world. An appreciation of and perceptiveness of the present may be enhanced by contemplation of those times when I have not existed or will not exist. Therefore, it is possible for awareness of personal non-existence to extend a person's view of the nature of existence. Thankfulness that is enhanced by an awareness of non-existence presents the potential for an enlarged sense of reality. By way of this enlarged awareness, thankfulness is one of the avenues to that which can be called the cosmic imagination. The cosmic imagination can be considered to be the content of the imagination when it extends to some degree of universal level. Also, the cosmic imagination is not some universal principal or essence within us; it is an extension of our imagination to the level of the universe.

This cosmic imagination does not restrict itself to a structured discernment. With the experience of the cosmic imagination, there occurs a release from doubt and discernment, a surrender to the enlarged imagination. It is within the cosmic imagination that our minds are free to experience unlimited grandeur. The vast sands of the desert, the endless, rolling billows of the ocean—with cosmic imagination our minds can wander to any part of the world and to any part of the universe. We are in awe before the vast ocean of space and massive conflagrations of matter. How limited our life is within the context of all existence!

I should state another point about the cosmic imagination: it is more a feeling than a series of visual images. In the cosmic imagination, even the smallest of things that exist are enveloped with an awareness of the larger spheres of existence. The cosmic imagination flows freely to wherever the receptive mind might be led by its undirected inclination. It can range from the feeling one might have on experiencing some concept of the vastness of space to a sense of the enormous splendor of the universe when seeing the brilliance of an insect's colors. In Hugo Rahner's book, *Ignatius the Theologian*, a description of Ignatius of Loyola illustrates this awareness of the universal in the particulars of immediate experience: "We often saw how even the smallest things could make his spirit soar upwards to God, who even in the smallest things is the Greatest. At the sight of a little plant, a leaf, a flower or a fruit, an insignificant worm or a tiny animal Ignatius could soar free above the heavens and reach through into things which lie beyond the senses" (23).

Although I referred to visual images, the primary experience of the cosmic imagination is as a sensation or feeling that is not well-delineated; it cannot easily be objectified by words. That which the mind might see is just incidental. Rather than delineated images, there is an enlarged, exuberant sense of awareness, a joy of experiencing that seeks no comprehensible form and, instead, avoids the restriction of the intellect into a narrowness of particulars. The cosmic imagination nourishes that feeling which can be characterized as enormous freedom. And a joyful peace comes with this freedom.

In addition to freedom and peace, the cosmic imagination can free a person into the world of wonder; the imagination can be freed into glorious paths. An expansiveness of imagination in poetry is described by Colette Gaudin, translator of *On Poetic Imagination and Reverie* by Gaston Bachelard. (The quote is taken from her foreward to Bachelard's book and includes a quote from another book by Bachelard):

> Images which properly fuse emotion and symbol operate neither at the surface of things nor at the surface of language. "*The poet does not describe, he exalts things*" (*The Poetics of Reverie, 163*). It is not enough to deform and transform reality. Images are the sign of an *elan*—an indication of excess. Imagination always reaches beyond what is given: it magnifies and deepens, it gathers the whole world into a simple image and the whole subject within its reverie. In this way Bachelard expresses, independently, an idea of contemporary moralists: man realizes himself only by reaching beyond himself. (Imagination, *xlix*)

Such qualities of the cosmic imagination—joy, peace, freedom, and wonder—are intrinsic to the wholeness of life. In addition, I experience these same qualities when I address God. Furthermore, in the exuberance of the cosmic imagination, I recognize the congruency of this imagination and an awareness of God; the mindfulness of God is a manifestation of the cosmic imagination. To carry this further, since I sense a similar experience by others when they are addressing God, this confirms for me that the awareness of God is a manifestation of the cosmic imagination. I expect a poet would not necessarily claim this and a literal-minded individual would disagree.

At this point I will mention lightheartedness and responsibility. The freedom of the cosmic imagination provides a source for lightheartedness. Some who are centered on God are inclined toward a spirit of wonder and joyful imagination. Those whose view of God inspires a sense of freedom and joy are likely to have an enhanced degree of spontaneity of thought and action, which are the characteristic of lightheartedness. This lightheartedness does not deny responsibility. Rather, with a centering on God, those responsibilities which are accepted may more likely become joyfully fulfilled.

A significant part of life's activity is guided by necessity. The needs of physical survival determine our actions during a major amount of our time. We have to work for food, shelter, and clothing. The needs of family and other obligations are also requirements that direct our employment.

An enlarged perspective toward obligations can provide some measure of release and relaxation concerning those obligations. This enlarged perspective may be seen to be available through some external source of authority, a separate realm from the obligations of necessities. Furthermore, it is with relief that we can have a free exercise of our will to enlist a source of authority for our direction. If we are free to choose that which we would follow, this choice is a source for the expression of our freedom. Therefore, the choice for a commitment to God can be an expression of freedom. Furthermore, the centering of our lives on God can establish a general tone of freedom in our outlook on activities and attitudes.

Of course, the freedom to choose which authority to follow can take many forms. One of the attractions of those groups which can be called "cults" is the expression of freedom in the commitment to an "alternate" source of authority. In reaction to that which is seen as "expected," some individuals find an expression of freedom in choosing to be followers of an authority which they see as alien to that against which they rebel.

Currently there is a significant segment of the population in this country who seem to be in rebellion against any source that can be construed as an authority. When individualism is manifested to an extreme degree, even interpersonal relationships may be easily broken. With such extreme individualism, one tends to rebel against such possible authority sources as God. If there is an expression of spirituality by these individuals, it may be centered on such non-authoritarian terms as "love" or "unity."

Al: Let's get back to the subject of ambiguity. As you say, the cosmic imagination is very ambiguous. There is nothing solid upon which to focus—unless we sink into the literal-mindedness of assigning facts to images of God.

I say that ambiguity is a source of the power of the cosmic imagination. By its very ambiguity do we gain freedom of the mind. In the openness of the imagination we receive a freedom to exalt and glorify. Our imagination opens us to a fullness of experience.

At this point I will cite a passage by Bachelard that presents a good description of the lightheartedness and exuberance of the cosmic imagination. This quote appears to me to be quite illustrative of the nature and the value of the cosmic imagination. Afterwards, I have several comments to make about the passage. (In using the term "material imagination," I understand Bachelard to mean objective qualities or substances that take on a more extensive significance in the realm of the imagination):

> For the *material imagination*, flight is not a mechanism to be invented, it is matter to be transmuted, it is the fundamental basis for a transmutation of all values. Our being must lose its *earthliness* and become *aerial*. Then, it will make all earth *light*. Our own earth, within us, will be *"the light one."* … But the *imaginary climate* is more important than the real one. Nietzsche's imagination is more instructive than any experience. It produces a climate of imaginary altitude and leads us into a special lyrical universe. The first transmutation of Nietzschean values is a transmutation of images. It transforms the richness of depth into a glory of the heights. Nietzsche seeks to go beyond the depths, beyond evil, and to go beyond the heights, that is to say, beyond the noble, for he is not satisfied with a tradition of prestige. He stretches *all* moral forces between these imaginary poles, rejecting any utilitarian material *progress* which would be merely horizontal, without a modification of our heavy being. Nietzsche devotes all his lyrical energy to a change from heavy to light, from the terrestrial to

the aerial. He gives to the abyss the language of the summits. The cave suddenly gives off aerial echoes: *"Hail to me ... My abyss* speaks, *I have turned my ultimate depth inside out into the light!"* Some might insist on speaking of symbol, allegory, metaphor, and ask the philosopher to designate moral lessons before images. But if images were not an integral part of moral thought, they would not have such life, such continuity. (Imagination 52-3)

This passage illustrates the experience of the cosmic imagination quite well. Also, you will note that, within the quote, there is no reference to some supernatural existence, to a god. Furthermore, I believe that neither Bachelard nor Nietzsche intended that there should be any implied reference to a supernatural existence. Therefore, it is shown that the cosmic imagination need not include any reference to a supernatural being.

However, Bachelard's following description of the cosmic imagination brings to mind a similar state of awareness when addressing God, including the times when it may be felt that this awareness is inadequate:

In the realm of imagination, every immanence takes on a transcendence. The very law of poetic expression is to go beyond thought. Undoubtedly, this transcendence often seems coarse, artificial, broken. At other times it works too quickly, it is illusory, ephemeral, dispersive; for the reflective being, it is a mirage. But this mirage is fascinating. It produces a special dynamism that is an undeniable psychological reality. We can then classify poets by asking them to answer the question: *"Tell me what your infinite is and I'll know the meaning of your universe: is it the infinite of the sea or the sky, is it the infinite of the earth's depths or of the pyre?"* The infinite is the realm in which imagination is affirmed as pure imagination, in which it is free and alone, vanquished and victorious, proud and trembling. (Imagination 23)

When I have a mindfulness of God, the experience is so similar to that of the cosmic imagination that I find no value in separating the identity of the two. Both the mindfulness of God and the experience of the cosmic imagination are expansive, ambiguous, and freeing. Furthermore, the God-symbol can be operative as a focus to draw our minds into the experience of the cosmic imagination. The word God symbolizes that which embodies the expansiveness of the cosmic imagination. I believe that many others who exult in the worship of God have the same type of experience.

In addition, the word-symbol God is readily available; it can provide an enhanced access to the wonders and joys of the cosmic imagination.

Another point about that quote by Bachelard which cites Nietzsche's experience involves a utilitarian aspect. The realization of lightheartedness can be interpreted as a positive outcome and therefore as providing utilitarian value, in spite of the comment by Bachelard. Of course, a utilitarian value could be assigned to any positive response.

Also, the buoyancy and lightheartedness expressed in the passage can find expression in any number of directions. In fact, a person could get quite an emotional high from very destructive acts. Crimes by thrill-seekers would fit this category. The dimension of doubt, as well as the other factors of integrity, must be available to modify the manifestation of lightheartedness.

Beyond these considerations, the passage by Bachelard is very valuable. It points to the exuberance of the cosmic imagination. This expansiveness is a significant part of the full life.

THE THIRD ASPECT OF GOD

This brings us to another way of comprehending God. This way is not operative if you do not have problems. Most people have some problems. Difficulties seem intrinsic to life. Even the most ideal life needs some adjustment at times.

Some people get stuck in an endless re-hashing of problems, and some are centered on finding solutions. In either event, a centering on a focus which is beyond the self can afford relief and perspective toward the problems. The focus beyond the self can provide a release from thought patterns that may be stuck in unproductive channels. Problems may seem insoluble; difficulties may seem so severe that there is not even an inclination toward a solution. A focus beyond the self can free the mind and give it a peace and relaxation that allows an openness to new, unexplored ways of looking at things. The temporary release from striving for a solution can provide the mental vacation that allows fresh perspective when attention returns to the source of stress.

There are many ways in which a person can gain a temporary relief from problems. Action is one type of release. Swimming, jogging, sky-diving, you-name-it; these all can provide a temporary release from excessive and unproductive thoughts.

In Chapter Thirteen we discussed several means of release from definitive, discerning thoughts. Although it is true that doubt and discernment are mental tools used for the solution of difficulties, it is likewise true that doubt and discernment are more effective when balanced with a degree of clearing of the mind, a free spontaneity that enhances openness and perceptiveness. A person is well-served when the definiteness of relatively objective thought is interspersed within the flow of the relaxed, cleared mind.

There are many possible sources for a focus of attention beyond the self. God is the most universal focus, the most all-encompassing, and also the most ambiguous. By dint of ambiguity, the word symbol God provides freedom of the cosmic imagination. Also, the God symbol is the most available focus beyond the self—as near at hand as the awareness of a word. For these reasons, it is valuable to rely on God both as a refuge from problems that might seem insoluble and as a source of mental release that allows fresh perspective. Consciousness of God can free us from ourselves; the destructiveness of self-centeredness can be ameliorated. Our mental outlook goes beyond the fears and desires of the self, and our minds become immersed in that which is beyond us. With a centeredness on God—or, in fact, on other modes of spiritual expression, such as liturgy or the mind-numbing that can occur when viewing the architectural elaboration of religious edifices—we can relax from self-absorption or thoughts that have become too narrowed.

At times the attainment of relief from problems includes a buttressing of the sense of integrity. The mindfulness of God can be an added source for strengthening the sense of rightness. The inclination toward an awareness of God is a positive feeling that carries with it the propensity toward personal integrity.

Again, by spiritual experience beyond self-centeredness, I do not mean to imply self-denial. Spiritual experience does not exclude access to an individual's worldly concerns, but it does put those concerns in perspective.

Let's consider why an awareness of God might incline a person to avoid recourse to reason. A mindfulness of God can be said to involve a "from" and a "to;" it is characterized by a release <u>from</u> mental effort <u>to</u> a non-reflective sense of rightness and comfort. The rest from mental effort is similar to rest from physical activity, such mental rest consisting of a release from an uncomfortable degree of reflectivity. This mental rest can be viewed in terms of freedom. Antipathy towards the employment of reason may be founded on the need for the freedom of a cleared mind. Reason implies discipline, and this might be seen as an infringement on freedom. Recourse to rational explanation might be viewed as a narrowing impingement on the open, non-reflectiveness of the cleared mind.

There is a point to be made about discernment in relation to self-concern. Discernment is not always clear-headed. Sometimes discernment is contorted into a sense of guilt. An alternate focus can provide refuge and release from guilt. This release may be counter-productive when a deserved sense of guilt could lead to action that would ameliorate the circumstance which created the guilt. However, sometimes the sense of guilt is not only not deserved but also carries with it a full realization that it is not deserved.

I do not have the inclination or the background to be able to discuss irrational feelings of guilt. But I have brought it up at this point to indicate that irrational guilt is one more opportunity for the implementation of an alternative focus to obtain refuge and release.

There is a particular term that is used to express the refuge and release provided by a focus on God. That word is "salvation." (In using the word "salvation," I do not refer to specific religious claims that may involve a commitment of faith in something which would ordinarily seem unbelievable.) Salvation is a renewal by means of relief from those stresses which diminish life. Salvation leads life from darkness to light, from distress and anguish to lightheartedness and peace.

OVERVIEW OF THE THREE ASPECTS OF GOD

At this point let's stand back and look. We have talked about three dimensions of awareness of God: God as the nature of the universe, God as manifestation of the cosmic imagination, and God as a source for refuge and release from worldly concerns.

Al: Yes. The atheist's trinity.

That almost sounds snide. Maybe you think that life should be based only on that which can be called "objective." But, life is more than objective facts. I will say this about sound facts and objectivity: life is narrowed when direction is primarily based on what could be called solid information. Known facts are, to a varying extent, tentative. An open mind can lead a person to new truth. This openness is one component of integrity. Furthermore, integrity and wholeness are dependent on the subjective outlook as well as objective facts.

Let's take a brief look at subjectivity in relation to awareness of God. Shortly, we will take up the subject of subjectivity and objectivity more extensively.

God is more than a pantheistic summation of the natural world. That is just one of the characteristics of God. With our attention directed toward God, we find the fulfillment of our subjectivity in thankfulness, wonder, openness, and freedom. We have thankfulness for the gift of existence, sustenance, and good fortune. In the reverie of the cosmic imagination, we wonder at the spectacular workings of the universe, and, in the soaring freedom of the imagination, we can receive joy and peace. With the attainment of refuge and release from worldly concerns, we find the openness and freedom of a life that is renewed and refreshed. The focus on God gives us these gifts.

The value of the subjectivity of mental life is not trivial. Subjectivity is the wellspring of our lives. As subjective beings, we experience life and direct ourselves into courses of action. Actions and reactions, emotions and commitments: these are molded by our personal outlook.

Within the subjectivity of life, we use an objective tool: doubt and discernment. With doubt and discernment we clarify as well as possible the reality of things. But objectivity is just a tool; it is not the substance of life.

Regarding subjectivity at a spiritual level, both the cosmic imagination and the nature of God are totally free and without limitation. However, in the objective realm, a vague delineation of God arises as the imaginative symbol of all existence.

The concept of God as the nature of existence could imply that there might be some essential quality of existence that transcends existence. I do not mean that God has transcendental existence; rather he is an imaginative symbol of all existence. In the objective realm we can use the term "nature of the universe" to signify God if we keep in mind that no hidden, essential quality of existence is implied. "Nature of the universe" does maintain the character of abstraction, which would possibly be lost if we just referred to the word-symbol God as meaning "all existence." This abstraction carries with it an indefiniteness that coincides well with the ambiguity of the cosmic imagination. Otherwise, someone might point to each rock, tree, and bush in sight while saying: "That's God." However, from the point of view presented in this book, a statement like that would be true if, for the individual, such sight inspired the cosmic imagination.

Al: But you said the word God referred to "all existence." Wouldn't a tree be a part of God then.

The usage of the word "god" does not lend itself to partition. Even when the presence of God is realized in the smallest leaf, a comprehensive awareness of all existence is implied.

Also, God is that aspect of the nature of the universe which finds expression in our personal creation—our existence—and in our characteristics. We pray to God in thankfulness. And we recognize that characteristic within us which reaches out in imagination to freedom, openness, and wonder. We go beyond our worldly mental pathways in surrender to God, a symbol that characterizes all existence. Also, God's processes create our minds in such a way that we have an impulse toward reverence for a vague, expansive, spiritual experience which has no objective characteristics when it is fulfilled in the exuberance of the cosmic imagination.

THE UTILITARIAN DILEMMA

We will now take up a certain dilemma of the spiritual orientation as manifested in religious practice. The positive effects pursuant to religious belief may support a claim of truth by the religious source. William James refers to this aspect of religious practice:

> ... the more complex ways of experiencing religion are new manners of producing happiness, wonderful inner paths to a supernatural kind of happiness, when the first gift of natural existence is unhappy, as it so often proves itself to be. With such relations between religion and happiness, it is perhaps not surprising that men come to regard the happiness which a religious belief affords as a proof of its truth. (76)

As indicated, the beneficial effects of religious practice may seem to certify the validity of that religious practice. However, there is an objection against the utilization of devotion to God as a means of gaining personal fulfillment. The realization of a utilitarian basis for devotion tends to nullify its effect. The protest against the worship of God for personal gain is voiced by others. An Eighth Century Islamic ascetic, Rabia, is cited in

The Mystics of Islam by R. A. Nicholson: "O God! If I worship thee in fear of Hell, burn me in Hell; and if I worship Thee in hope of Paradise, exclude me from Paradise; but if I worship Thee for Thine own sake, withhold not Thine everlasting beauty!" (115).

Despite drawbacks, the utilitarian value of religious belief is recognized by many. James states: "… so long as men can *use* their God, they care very little who he is, or even whether he is at all" (382). And: "The gods we stand by are the gods we need and can use, the gods whose demands on us are reinforcements of our demands on ourselves and on one another" (259).

Hick also indicates the utilitarian aspects of religious practice: "Religious traditions and their various components—beliefs, modes of experience, scriptures, rituals, disciplines, ethics and lifestyles, social rules and organizations—have greater or less value according as they promote or hinder the salvific transformation" (300).

Armstrong voices the same perspective: "This pragmatism would always be a factor in the history of God. People would continue to adopt a particular conception of the divine because it worked for them, not because it was scientifically or philosophically sound" (17).

I will summarize this section, taking into account opposing points of view. The utilitarian dilemma involves a realization that beneficial effects can result from a religious orientation. However, if a desire for these good effects is the source of a commitment to religious practice, the effects may become nullified.

OBJECTIVITY AND SUBJECTIVITY

Al: I want to say something here. You talk about God being a projection of the mind, a product of the imagination. How could your concept of God be effective if the concept of God is seen as having a subjective basis? Commitment to God is likely to be ineffective if God is just considered a mental projection, a product of the imagination. Do you have something to say about that?

You know I will have an answer for that. This answer does not totally refute the utilitarian question; it is impossible to do that. All human directions, action, and thoughts may be viewed as utilitarian in one way or another. The most noble endeavor can be seen as self-serving, fulfilling a person's sense of integrity, joy of service, or even of pride. This is one inescapable aspect of the utilitarian question.

To restate your question: how can there be devotion to and commitment to a god that is recognized as a product of the mind, a mental projection?

We have a partial answer to this question by noting the objective aspect of the god concept. This following information is a partial solution but not a complete answer. No complete solution is possible for the concern about the efficacy of commitment to a god that is recognized as primarily subjective.

Let's start this section by first confirming the subjective nature of belief in God. Others have voiced the view that the concept of God is created by the imagination. I quote Karen Armstrong: "Today many people in the West would be dismayed if a leading theologian suggested that God was in some profound sense a product of the imagination. Yet it should be obvious that the imagination is the chief religious faculty" (233). She also indicates that rabbis, priests, and Sufis of the three related monotheistic faiths—Judaism, Christianity, and Islam—:

> … would have taken me to task for assuming that God was—in any sense—a reality "out there"; they would have warned me not to expect to experience him as an objective fact that could be discovered by the ordinary process of rational thought. They would have told me that in an important sense God was a product of the creative imagination, like the poetry and music that I found so inspiring. A few highly respected monotheists would have told me quietly and firmly that God did not really exist—and yet that "he" was the most important reality in the world. (*xx*)

In the present discussion, the concept of God is not entirely subjective. As I elaborated earlier, God is understood as the nature of existence, which is an ambiguous abstraction referring to all that exists. There is then an objective correlation, a link to objective reality which, however, does not prove an objective existence of God. No such objective proof is possible. If it were, God would not be God; God would be just another objective phenomenon.

However, God is by nature mysterious and ambiguous. The mystery draws the attention, focuses the mind, and, by reason of its indefiniteness, feeds the beholder's capacity for freedom and spontaneity.

The objective connection of the God concept is more than a gimmick to satisfy those who would doubt. It is as real as existence itself. In fact, we have previously discussed the objective correlation of the God concept. In the objective sphere, the concept of God is conceived as a mental focus that represents the nature of the universe. As products of the natural course of events, we have thankfulness for the forces and circumstances which have resulted in the creation of our lives. We are thankful for these processes and realize that we are localized manifestations of the course of nature. Furthermore, wonder and awe of our existence and of the nature of all existence nourishes our cosmic imagination.

Taking this a step further, a limited, objective comprehension of the nature of the universe can easily enlarge into a subjective, indistinct awareness of the totality of existence. For example, the sight of the ocean waves churning up against the rocks may segue into a vague awareness of the forces of nature in general. The experience can become more general and more subjective as a vague awareness of all existence, without limit in time or space. Such experience is an aspect of the incomprehensibility and mystery to be discovered within the free, spontaneous cosmic imagination. Within this awareness we find the ambiguity of God together with an objective correlation. The comprehension of God can encompass both the objective reality of the natural universe and the grand exuberance of the cosmic imagination. The two outlooks are compatible; there is not exclusiveness of one over the other. Also, neither outlook is submerged; there is openness to experiencing either one or the other. In a state of doubt, the God symbol correlation is made with the nature of the universe, and this is not incompatible with objective fact. In thankfulness and wonder, the cosmic imagination, which is a subjective capacity, brings us into the free flow of enlarged experience.

We have looked at the compatibility of a subjective awareness of God with an objective outlook. Let's take a look in the opposite direction: the freedom of the cosmic imagination not limited by images or concepts.

I thank God for existence and good fortune. When I address God, any visual image of God that I sense is recognized as representational. Also, any image will be lightly held and easily released. Freedom of the cosmic imagination releases the mind from any definitive comprehension of God. To state this a bit differently, the freedom of cosmic imagination does not demand the restrictions of delineation; in fact, it avoids these restrictions.

Furthermore, the cosmic imagination encompasses all existence, and this imagination is free to have no focussed awareness of any particular object or character of existence. In gratitude to God, who is conceived as the nature of existence, a person recognizes this concept of God as grounded in reality. However, such understanding does not limit the comprehension of God. When thankfulness is expressed, the logic of the mind may touch the cosmic imagination to find God as representing those characteristics of the universe by which all things exist. This delineation is not channeled into a fixed mental focus; the mind's awareness enlarges beyond any limits. The essence of an awareness of God is the freedom, joy, and peace of the unrestricted cosmic imagination.

Let's look at another link that fuses these two, the objective and the subjective. We are not just bystanders, creating concepts to fit that which we want to program in our minds. We are participants in the universe. Our lives are localized manifestations of the course of all existence. We are a part of the universe, part of the reality that is known by objective means. Furthermore, it is within our nature to express an imagination that has the capacity to be expansive, to be cosmic. The inclination toward spirituality is a part of our natural existence. Subjectivity and objectivity become fused in the lives of those awakened to the joy and comfort of the free, cosmic imagination, which, as imagination, addresses the universe without trying to comprehend it.

DOUBT

In the orientation of most Western religious practice, God is usually understood as some type of supernatural consciousness. For these who so believe, God is seen as separate from all that exists, independent of the entire universe. Of course, these views usually include varying degrees of immanence of God, a presence within natural existence.

I believe it is typical for people who experience the presence of God have a feeling of certainty about that experience. A Sixteenth Century Catholic mystic, St. Teresa of Avila, said: "Then how, you may ask, can we have such a conviction, if we do not see him? This I do not know; it is his work, but I know that I am speaking truly, and I would say, that where there is not this certainty, there has not been complete union of the soul with God, ..." (45).

It is against such certainty that I place greater value in the access to doubt. My sense of integrity includes an openness to doubt, a willingness to doubt any thing which seems unreasonable to me. In this regard, the concept of a consciousness separate from all that exists seems unlikely to me. In this chapter I have expressed a different understanding of God. This understanding involves the experience of the cosmic imagination, and that includes the imaginative comprehension of the universe. This experience is the basis for a commitment to God which does not rely on a belief in the reality of a supernatural consciousness.

The correlation of God with the nature of the universe does not impinge on the availability of doubt and discernment. The existence of the natural world is indisputable, except to some students of philosophy for whom nothing may exist except perhaps some unknowable entity. For the rest of us, doubt cannot cancel the wonderful fact of existence of all things of the universe, including the self.

Also, doubt does not cancel the sense of wonder, though the utilization of doubt may question various aspects of religious dogma and practice. Doubt is a necessary part of freedom, of openness; doubt allows that detachment which frees the mind. Furthermore, in freedom, the imagination is allowed its role, and an active imagination is a precursor for the sense of wonder. Therefore, through openness, freedom, and imagination, doubt can allow an access to the joy of wonder.

A NOTE ON ENDING THIS CHAPTER

This chapter has been concerned with the conceptual aspects of God, correlating the word-symbol "god" with a vague abstraction—the nature of the universe—and seeing God as the imaginative representation of the nature of the universe. In addition, the conceptual characteristics of God have effects at a personal level. I pointed to the freedom, joy, and peace associated with the cosmic imagination. Peace is especially appreciated when attention to the problems of life has become excessive. A major degree of difficulty can be debilitating, and a source of commitment to that which is beyond our personal agendas may have a salvific effect. Spiritual expression is a means of release from the narrowness and frequent unhappiness of self-absorption.

15

Into the Air

Al: Will this be a short chapter?

Why do you ask?

Al: Every fifth chapter has been short, at least so far.

Do you want a short chapter?

Al: I wouldn't mind that.

Well, here are three short poems. We'll see if you like them. And if you don't like poetry, go directly to Chapter Sixteen.

Al: Can I buy Park Place there?

You can't afford Park Place. And this isn't a game of Monopoly.

Al: But why have poems here?

Because there is no metaphysical meaning for existence.

Al: So?

If someone says there is no rhyme or reason for existence, I can at least say there is rhyme.

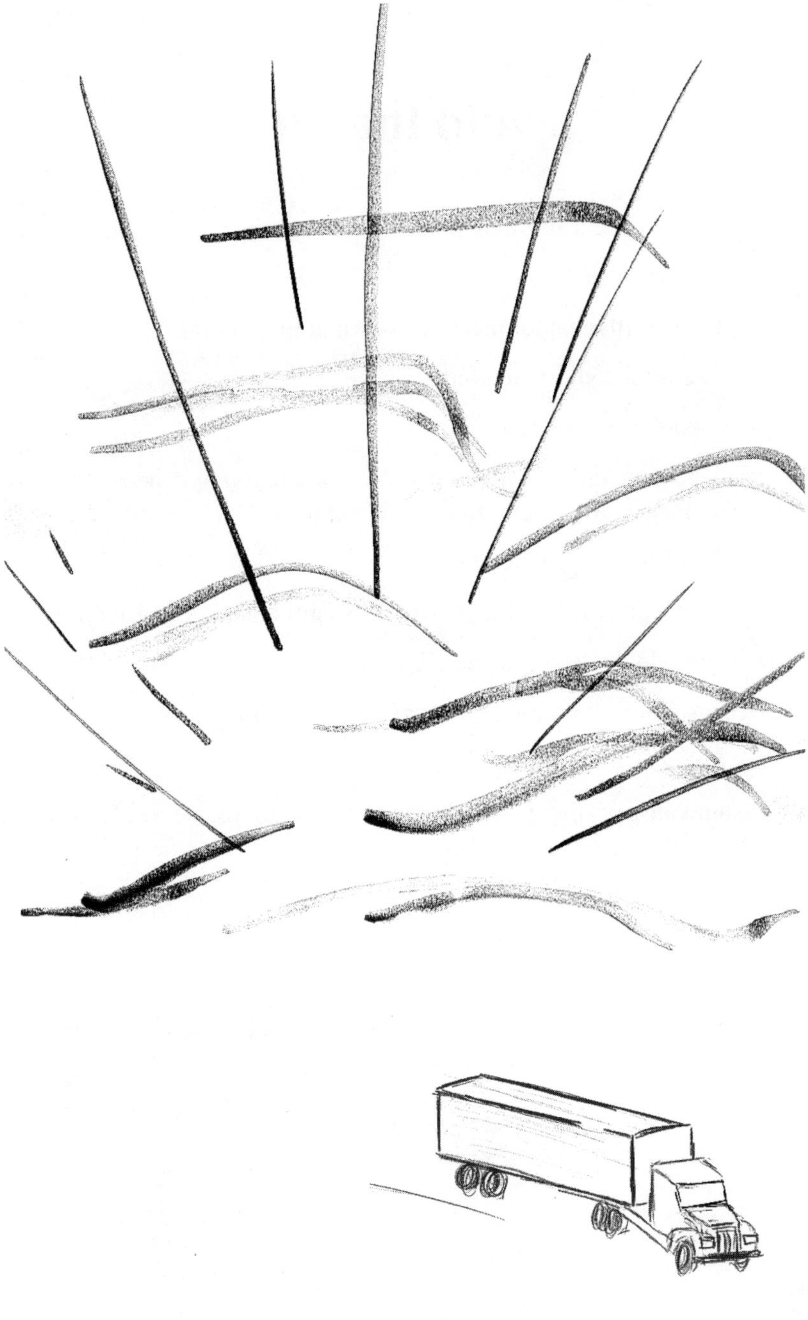

In Early Morning

(At Hoffy's Motel, Madras, Oregon, Sept. 23, 1992)

In early morning,
looking through
*   a motel window,*
past
*   the parking lot,*
past lights of a
*   slowly moving truck,*
*   beyond the truck, the restaurant,*
*   the houses,*
to the distance,
*   the horizon,*
*   the line of darkness*
*   becoming*
*   becomes*
*   light.*
*   The sky,*
*   brightening,*
*   flowing,*
*   light flows*
*   into the world,*
*   flows forward*
*   in a thousand colors.*
*   Light expands,*
*   fills into all*
*   forever.*

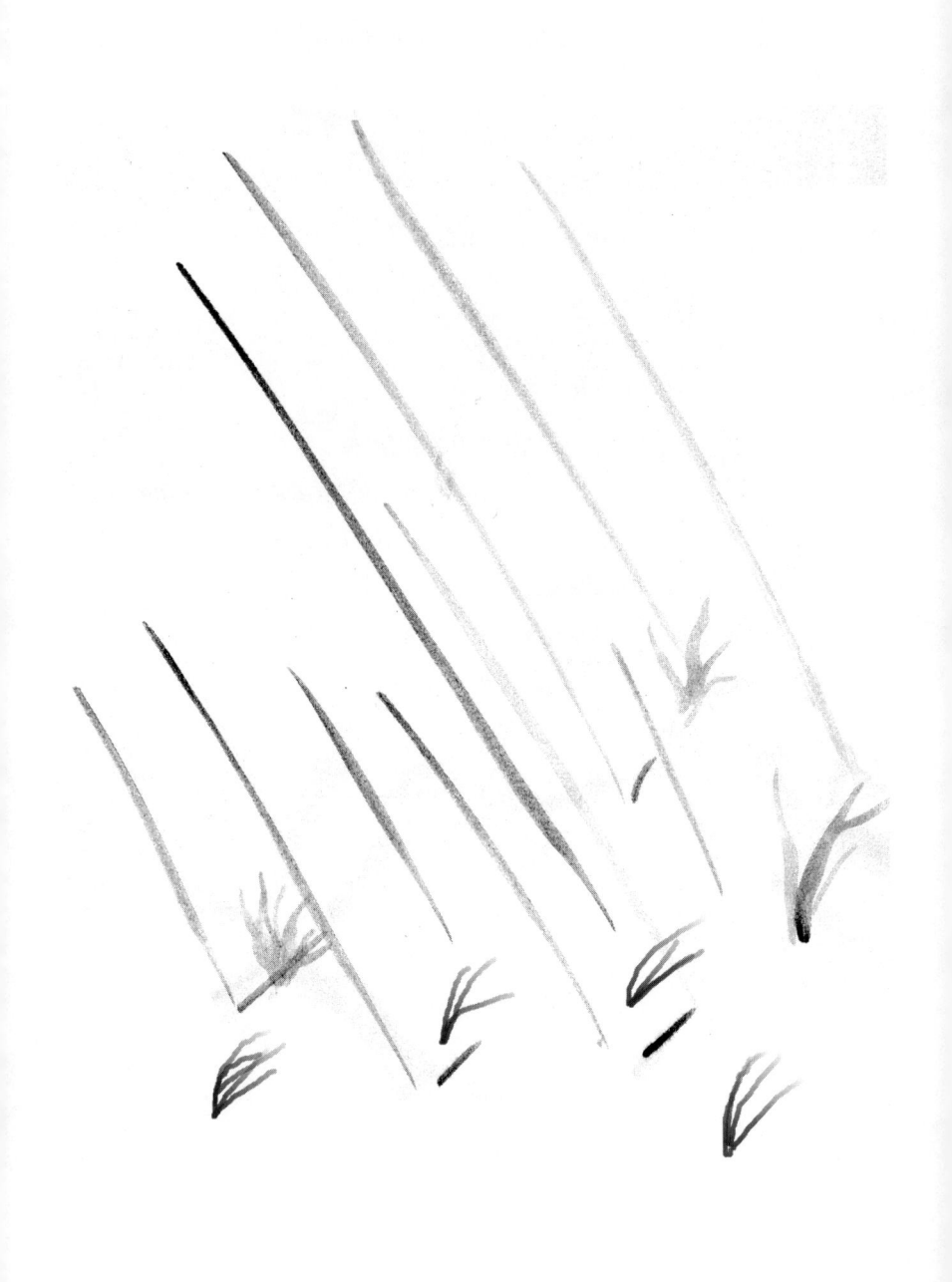

Rain

Rain
Streaks through the black
In powerful
December wind
Over the ocean
Drops push fast
Over sand
Over grass
Hard against
The motel window
Soft against
The motel window
I hear
My mind reach
For nothing
To touch
   what it hides
   from me.

The Swell of the Ocean

The swell of the ocean I am
Crashing
And rising
In joy
Pound into the water
Rise up
Heighten
In glory
Into the air
Crash down
Rise up
I live
In the kiss
Of life.

16

Mysticism: the Strength of Ambiguity

Mysticism, Ambiguity, and Freedom
The Ineffability of Mysticism
Accessing the Mystical State
The Impetus Toward Realizing a Mystical State
Individual Variation in Spiritual Receptivity
Summary

MYSTICISM, AMBIGUITY, AND FREEDOM

Al: Your poetry doesn't rhyme.

I see you are still in Chapter Fifteen. It's time to move on. We want to have a clear concept of the ambiguous.

Al: Now that makes sense: clearly know the ambiguous.

I am not trying to make sense. I am not trying to be logical. We are in that part of the book which is concerned with the concept of God, the spiritual realm, and religious practice. The essence of a religious outlook encompasses a different area than the logical.

We have talked about imagination and freedom. Let's picture how the imagination can enhance the sense of freedom. The cosmic imagination is a prime vehicle for an awareness of God. Within the imagination, the concept of God is characterized by ambiguity and wonder. Furthermore, in the realm of the ambiguous, there is no objective constraint that limits the path of awareness. And, with the absence of objective constraint, ambiguity thereby nourishes a freedom of the mind.

Also, ambiguity can be a vehicle for freedom when a person makes a choice to be aware of God. No objective constraint channels a person into that choice, unless one considers social pressure toward such a choice. Generally, the choosing to believe in God is an expression of freedom, and an awareness of God in a spirit of wonder, awe, and ambiguity is an expression of the free imagination.

How much freedom is experienced? That depends on the amount of literal-minded tendency and on the degree of tolerance for ambiguity that a person has. A strict literalist will have no doubt. He or she will have what could be called "pure faith." For that individual, freedom and ambiguity are limited by the constraints of literal understanding, which, in turn, may be related to the personal need for stability and control. We talked about this in Chapter Thirteen.

Proceeding beyond the concern about literal-mindedness, the devotion to God can find manifestation in a mystical state. This mystical state is characterized primarily by ambiguity and wonder. It is the state in which the imagination is free and open to a vague awareness of universal existence. However, I can add that, as ambiguous as the preceding statement is regarding universal existence, it is still too delineating for the cosmic imagination, which knows no bounds.

Religious significance is typically assigned to mystical states by religiously oriented individuals. However, I should note that, from what I have observed and aside from the likely assignment of factual reality to the mystical state by those who experience it, I do not believe there is a substantial difference between mystical states and the cosmic imagination. Of course, this identity of mystical states with the cosmic imagination is conjectural. Who really knows another person's state of mind? We can speculate, based on what information we have.

In seeing the mystical state as equivalent to the cosmic imagination, we find that, by looking into the nature of the mystical state, we can gain information about the cosmic imagination. In this regard, I ask you to recall that, in Chapter Fourteen, the importance of the cosmic imagination in spiritual experience was discussed at some length.

Al: Let me interrupt here. I want to say that there is no truth, no reality, to the mystical state. It's all ambiguity.

Yes; the mystical state is a subjective experience. If there were objective facts involved, it would not be mystical. As such, the mystical state is ambiguous. Inaccessibility and a realization of the inability to characterize content draws this comment by Cassirer: "The only answer that we receive from religion is that it is the will of God to conceal himself" (29).

I can say that, for some, the connotation associated with the word "ambiguity" may be so negative that this word is avoided except in a negative context. In a positive mode, they may favor the use of an alternative term, such as "enigmatic." However, consider that "enigmatic" might tend to draw people toward puzzling about an understanding of the subject at hand. Likewise, the use of the word "cryptic" might draw some toward seeking a hidden understanding.

I have placed the word "ambiguity" in a positive context in the aspiration that it can release a person from trying to understand. The word "ambiguous" may more easily predispose one toward immersion into an experience without trying to comprehend it.

Let's explore the subject of ambiguity further. As stated previously, the effects that result from the experience of ambiguity are very significant, the wonder of the ambiguous feeding a sense of freedom. Likewise, the effects of the spiritual experience, manifested as devotion to God or to some god-like representation are very real; lives may change significantly. Armstrong states: "Mystical religion is more immediate and tends to be more help in time of trouble than a predominantly cerebral faith" (212). And James says: "—that which produces effects within another reality must be termed a reality itself, so I feel as if we had no philosophic excuse for calling the unseen or mystical world unreal" (389). He also discusses mystical states as carrying a sense of truth and authority:

> Although so similar to states of feeling, mystical states seem to those who experience them to be also states of knowledge. They are states of insight into depths of truth unplumbed by the discursive intellect. They are illuminations, revelations, full of significance and importance, all inarticulate though they remain; and as a rule they carry with them a curious sense of authority for after-time. (293)

James goes on to characterize mystical states:

> In spite of their repudiation of articulate self-description, mystical states in general assert a pretty distinct theoretic drift. It is possible to give the outcome of the majority of them in terms that point in definite philosophical directions. One of these directions is optimism, and the other is monism. We pass into mystical states from out of ordinary consciousness as from a less into a more, as from a smallness into a vastness, and at the same time as from an

unrest to a rest. We feel them as reconciling, unifying states. They appeal to the yes-function more than to the no-function in us. In them the unlimited absorbs the limits and peacefully closes the account. Their very denial of every adjective you may propose as applicable to the ultimate truth,—He, the Self, the Atman, is to be described by 'No! no! Only, say the Upanishads,—though it seems on the surface to be a no-function, is a denial made on behalf of a deeper yes. Whoso calls the Absolute anything in particular, or says that it is *this*, seems implicitly to shut it off from being *that*, it is as if he lessened it. So we deny the 'this,' negating the negation which it seems to us to imply, in the interests of the higher affirmative attitude by which we are possessed. (319)

Maslow expresses a similar view, using the term "peak experience" for that which I believe is probably the same as—or equivalent to—a mystical state: "The world seen in the peak-experiences is seen only as beautiful, good, desirable, worthwhile, etc. and is never experienced as evil or undesirable. The world is accepted" (63).

Entrance into the world of ambiguity opens the potentiality for an expression of the imagination. Furthermore, such imaginative experience, while active in spiritual expression, certainly need not—and much of the time does not—imply religious significance to the experience. On the other hand, the term "mystical state" usually does connote religious significance. Let's look at a quote about the effects of the imagination when a religious significance is not implied. The positive mental effects of the imagination, discussed as experience of the "unreal," are noted by Colette Gaudin in her introduction to Bachelard's *On Poetic Imagination and Reverie*: "In all his works, but particularly in his poetic texts, values are indeed clearly polarized. The 'good' appears to depend on a healthy dialectics between the 'real' and the 'unreal.' Paraphrasing Bachelard, we could say that a true image—an image really imagined—is also an image that contains a truth about human reality. Such an image, by expanding the subject, is necessarily a source of happiness" (*Imagination*, xxviii).

Al: You have described the effects of the mystical state. I still wonder if you could give any hard, objective facts about the content of this state.

You know I won't. That is impossible by its very nature. French author Gustave Flaubert describes this lack of objective content in his short story "A Simple Heart": "She found it hard to imagine Him in person, for He was not merely a bird, but a flame as well, and a breath at other times. It may be His light, she thought, which flits at night about the edge of the marshes, His breathing which drives on the clouds, His voice which gives harmony to the bells; and she would sit rapt in adoration, enjoying the cool walls and the quiet of the church" (1828).

THE INEFFABILITY OF MYSTICISM

We have talked about characteristics and effects of mystical states. Freedom of the mind is a particularly valuable characteristic of mystical experience. The ambiguous content of the mystical state has been noted, and I will now cite several authors regarding the ambiguity and ineffability of mystical states. Following that, the discussion will center on the accessibility of a mystical state.

James discusses the ineffability of the mystical state: "This incommunicableness of the transport is the keynote of all mysticism. Mystical truth exists for the individual who has the transport, but for no one else. In this, as I have said, it resembles the knowledge given to us in sensations more than that given by conceptual thought. ... God's knowledge cannot be discursive but must be intuitive" (311). Also, James notes the awareness of inexpressible truth: " ... the sense of perceiving truths not known before. The mysteries of life become lucid, as Professor Leuba says, and often, nay usually, the solution is more or less unutterable in words" (199). Later he adds: "The subject of (the mystical) immediately says that it defies expression, that no adequate report of its contents can be given in words. It follows from this that its quality must be directly experienced; it cannot be imparted or transferred to others" (292-3).

Ambiguity is high-lighted by contradiction and paradox. James notes: "... that vertigo of self-contradiction which is so dear to mysticism" (241). Later he adds: "But these qualifications are denied by Dionysius (the Areopagite), not because the truth falls short of them, but because it so infinitely excels them ... Thus come the paradoxical expressions that so abound in mystical writings" (319-20).

A description by Kenneth Burke points to the ambiguity of the mystical state: " ... almost anarchistic indifference to traditional linguistic categories the kinds of confusion in which the mystic appears to be at home" (194).

Maslow makes a general statement regarding communication of the ineffable:

> We are taught here that the word "ineffable" means "not communicable by words that are analytic, abstract, linear, rational, exact, etc." Poetic and metaphorical language, physiognomic and

synesthetic language, primary process language of the kind found in dreams, reveries, free associations and fantasies, not to mention pre-words and non-words such as gestures, tone of voice, style of speaking, body tonus, facial expressions—all these are more efficacious in communicating certain aspects of the ineffable. (85)

On a lighter note, the English physicist Isaac Newton hardly exaggerated when he said: "Tis the temper of the hot and superstitious part of mankind in matters of religion ever to be fond of mysteries, and for that reason to like best what they understand least" (quoted by historian Richard S. Westfall, 231). This absence of understanding is also indicated by Dante: "O Light Supreme who doth Thyself withdraw so far above man's mortal understanding ..." (*Paradiso* XXXIII lines 67-8). Theologian Harvey Cox cites the anonymous Fourteenth Century author of *The Cloud of Unknowing*: "... thou findest but a darkness and as it were a kind of unknowing, thou knowest not what, saving that thou feelest in thy will a naked intent unto God ... thou mayest neither see him clearly by light of understanding in the reason, nor feel him in sweetness of love in the affection ... if ever thou shalt see him or feel him ... it must always be in this cloud and in this darkness" (92).

In a similar vein reference is made to Eastern religious sources by Hick:

> When Sunyata is understood in this sense, as referring to the ultimate reality beyond the scope of all concepts, knowable only in its manifestations, then it is indeed equivalent to what in our pluralistic hypothesis we are calling the Real. ... As Abe puts it, "Nothingness must be emphasized to indicate the necessity of going beyond any conceptualization or objectification".... "The Absolute," says Murti, expounding the Madhyamika, "is very aptly termed Sunya, as it is devoid of all predicates. Even existence, unity, selfhood and goodness cannot be affirmed of it." (291)

The ineffability of mysticism is repeated several times in the Tao:

> But words that point to the Tao
>
> seem monotonous and without flavor.
>
> When you look for it, there is nothing to see.
>
> When you listen for it, there is nothing to hear.
>
> When you use it, it is inexhaustible. (35)

Further along:

> The Tao is nowhere to be found.
> Yet it nourishes and completes all things. (41)

ACCESSING THE MYSTICAL STATE

Let's turn our attention now to the accessibility of the mystical state, particularly to the fact that it is not readily accessible. A conscious effort to reach this state is often counter-productive, resulting only in a limited aesthetic experience that could be termed " programmed joy." An effort to experience a mystical state tends to impede its realization. I believe the mystical state is more likely to be experienced when it is received without effort or compulsion. The mystical state is more accessible by means of surrender to it, by the release from effort.

The futility of conscious effort is elaborated upon by James:

> Now the history of Lutheran salvation by faith, of methodistic conversions, and of what I call the mind-cure movement seems to prove the existence of numerous persons in whom—at any rate at a certain stage in their development—a change of character for the better, so far from being facilitated by the rules laid down by official moralists, will take place all the more successfully if those rules be exactly reversed. Official moralists advise us never to relax our strenuousness. "Be vigilant, day and night," they adjure us; "hold your passive tendencies in check; shrink from no effort; keep your will like a bow always bent." But the persons I speak of find that all this conscious effort leads to nothing but failure and vexation in their hands, and only makes them two-fold more the children of hell they were before. The tense and voluntary attitude becomes in them an impossible fever and torment. Their machinery refuses to run at all when the bearings are made so hot and the belts so tight. Under these circumstances the way to success, as vouched for by innumerable authentic personal narrations, is by an anti-moralistic method, by the 'surrender' of which I spoke in my second lecture. Passivity, not activity; relaxation, not intentness, should be now the rule. Give up the feeling of responsibility, let go your hold, resign the care of your destiny to higher powers, be genuinely indifferent as to what becomes of it all, and you will find not only that you gain a perfect

Mysticism: the Strength of Ambiguity

inward relief, but often also, in addition, the particular goods you sincerely thought you were renouncing. This is the salvation through self-despair, the dying to be truly born, of Lutheran theology, the passage into *nothing* of which Jacob Behmen writes. To get to it, a critical point must usually be passed, a corner turned within one. Something must give way, a native hardness must break down and liquefy; and this event ... is frequently sudden and automatic, and leaves on the Subject an impression that he has been wrought on by an external power. (98-9)

We can see that a mystical state is experienced through an orientation of surrender of the self to the experience rather than through conscious effort. However, in the state of self-surrender the mode of response is not necessarily passive. In fact it can be quite active. It is like free-form dancing where the music is the authority and you are actively receptive to the sound and to the impulse of your body. William James describes self-surrender: "... when the characteristic sort of consciousness once has set in, the mystic feels as if his own will were in abeyance, and indeed sometimes as if he were grasped and held by a superior power" (293). The superior power, the god-symbol, focuses our attention, and we are at "active rest" in the image, actively receptive to the awareness of that which holds our attention.

Without considering the reference to the agency of a supernatural force, it is noted that the Bible does point to the negating effect of conscious effort in the spiritual realm: "... according to the power of God; Who hath saved us, and called us with an holy calling, not according to our works, but according to his own purpose and grace ..." (II Tim. 1, 8-9).

Self-surrender is to that which is "beyond," toward a "beyond all." There is a sense of "otherness," beyond all that could be definitively known, when the attention is directed toward God.

This focus on the "beyond" allows a release from worldly attachments. In a synopsis of a passage by John Caird, Scottish philosopher of religion, William James extracts the following observations:

> As a thinking being, it is possible for me to suppress and quell in my consciousness every movement of self-assertion, every notion and opinion that is merely mine, every desire that belongs to me as this particular Self, and to become the pure medium of a thought that is universal—in one word, to live no more my own life, but let my consciousness be possessed and suffused by the Infinite and Eternal life of spirit. And yet it is just in this

renunciation of self that I truly gain myself, or realize the highest possibilities of my own nature. For whilst in one sense we give up self to live the universal and absolute life of reason, yet that to which we thus surrender ourselves is in reality our truer self. (343-4)

In the same vein Dante says: "... you cannot know this state of bliss while you yet keep your eyes fixed only on those things that lie below ..." (*Paradiso* XXXI lines 112-4). This theme is also elaborated upon by Hick:

> To give up one's personal projects, desires, hopes and ambitions, as also one's fears and aversions, in absolute surrender (*Islam*) to God, or in a fading away of the ego point of view, or in acceptance of one's existence as but a fleeting moment within the interdependent flux of life, inevitably seems to most of us like plunging into darkness—even though there is the promise beyond it of peace with God "whose service is perfect freedom," or of union with Brahman as the universal Consciousness dawns within us, or of the indescribably joy of the ego-free state of Nirvana. (162)

Of course, I speak of self-surrender to the experience of a mystical state. I do not mean to infer that doubt and discernment should be disregarded. I do not recommend self-surrender to those who may be deluded or to charlatans. And, remember that wars have been fought utilizing an idealistic basis of self-surrender by large groups for suspect causes.

THE IMPETUS TOWARD REALIZING A MYSTICAL STATE

We have talked about a realization that, at times, life's goals and orientations may be found to be shallow. Sometimes we want to look beyond ourselves. The impetus toward surrender of the self into a mystical state can be fueled by a realization that exaggerated self-interest—to the point of self-absorption—can destroy a person's potential for happiness. Self-surrender allows a freedom from the narrowed perception and direction of self-interest. Self-surrender is a vehicle for freedom.

A person's outlook may also be narrowed by doubts and fears. In the course of life, situations and conditions often arise which can cast doubt on the ability to handle problems and which reveal vulnerabilities. Furthermore, the surrender of attention to an alternate focus can ease an excessive concern about problems. Relief from excess concern is addressed by Viktor Frankl in his book *Psychotherapy and Existentialism* in his discussion of the method of "de-reflection." He describes a release from the "compulsive inclination to self-observation" (156). Frankl's method includes directing a patient toward a positive focus.

A prime impetus for entering the mystical state appears to be an inclination toward a clearing of the mind. Simone Weil alludes to the blankness-of-mind aspect of spiritual experience: "Always, beyond the particular object whatever it may be, we have to fix our will on the void—to will the void. For the good which we can neither picture nor define is a void for us. But this void is fuller than all fullnesses. If we get as far as this we shall come through all right, for God fills the void" (258).

Although there is a complete focus of attention in mystical states, it is without compulsion. One senses freedom in the ambiguity and mystery of the object of focus, and this freedom likewise characterizes the mode of attention. Focus on the god-symbol is a focus on that which is without bounds, and while there is full attention, it is in a mode of freedom and therefore lighthearted and open.

INDIVIDUAL VARIATION IN SPIRITUAL RECEPTIVITY

There is individual variation in the ability to be receptive to spiritual experience. James describes the capacity for attunement to the mystical state:

> This sense of deeper significance is not confined to rational propositions. Single words, and conjunctions of words, effects of light on land and sea, odors, and musical sounds, all bring it when the mind is tuned aright. Most of us can remember the strangely moving power of passages in certain poems read when we were young, irrational doorways as they were through which the mystery of fact, the wildness and the pang of life, stole into our hearts and thrilled them. The words have now perhaps become mere polished surfaces for us; but lyric poetry and music are alive and significant only in proportion as they fetch these vague vistas of a life continuous with our own, beckoning and inviting, yet ever eluding our pursuit. We are alive or dead to the eternal inner message of the arts according as we have kept or lost this mystical susceptibility. (294-5)

Later James refers to detachment and discipline utilized for this state:

> The first thing to be aimed at in orison is the mind's detachment from outer sensations, for these interfere with its concentration upon ideal things. Such manuals as Saint Ignatius's Spiritual Exercises recommend the disciple to expel sensation by a graduated series of efforts to imagine holy scenes. The acme of this kind of discipline would be a semi-hallucinatory mono-ideism—an imaginary figure of Christ, for example, coming fully to occupy the mind. Sensorial images of this sort, whether literal or symbolic, play an enormous part in mysticism. But in certain cases imagery may fall away entirely, and in the very highest raptures it tends to do so. The state of consciousness becomes then insusceptible of any verbal description. (312)

When Armstrong repeats a point made earlier regarding the experience of God as subjective and correlates this with aesthetic expression, she also indicates the importance of discipline and warns against the degradation of the mystical state into emotionalism. Armstrong indicates that the God of the mystics:

> ... is in tune with the atheistic mood of our secular society, with its distrust of inadequate images of the Absolute. Instead of seeing God as an objective Fact, which can be demonstrated by means of scientific proof, mystics have claimed that he is a subjective experience, mysteriously experienced in the ground of being. This God is to be approached through the imagination and can be seen as a kind of art form, akin to the other great artistic symbols that have expressed the ineffable mystery, beauty and value of life. Mystics have used music, dancing, poetry, fiction, stories, painting, sculpture and architecture to express this Reality that goes beyond concepts. Like all art, however, mysticism requires intelligence, discipline and self-criticism as a safeguard against indulgent emotionalism and projection. (396)

The need for discipline is also noted by Hick when referring to the transformed consciousness of Buddha nature:

> That eternal reality cannot however be described, but only experienced, and this only at the end of a long and arduous process of de-egoisation. It is spoken of as *nirvana*, and also as *sunyata*, Emptiness—not in the sense of being nothing at all but in the sense that no human conceptuality can grasp it. (187)

I am not qualified to discuss the particulars of discipline involved in achieving a mystical state in various forms of religious practice. This discipline does seem to be centered on the focussing of attention to the exclusion of extraneous thoughts. Such focus of attention may be on a physiological function—for instance: breathing—as in the orientation of some Eastern religious practices. The focus can center on a psychological activity such as a ritualistic performance.

Regardless of the form of discipline advocated in achieving a mystical state, it can be said that the encouragement of discipline seem to be at odds with that freedom which is experienced in the cosmic imagination. There is a particular consideration that may reconcile the apparent conflict between discipline and freedom concerning the attainment of the mystical state. The mind which is cleared of extraneous thoughts through discipline is a mind that is not constricted by those thoughts and is therefore free in the service of the cosmic imagination. In this sense, discipline allows freedom.

SUMMARY

In summary, the heart of the mystical state is ambiguity and wonder. This ambiguity is manifested in the ineffability of the mystical state. Furthermore, freedom of the mind is the welcome accompaniment of ambiguity. The degree of freedom experienced varies, depending on the religious orientation, particularly regarding the extent of literal-mindedness.

The mystical state is more likely to be reached by avoiding conscious effort, that is, by surrender, a giving up of oneself to the experience, rather than by directing oneself to create it. I should add that the capacity for attunement to the mystical state tends to vary within the course of an individual's life and also varies between individuals.

Finally, there is a need for discipline in order to avoid a degradation of the mystical state into emotionalism.

17

Opposition

Al: Opposition? It seems odd to have a chapter about opposition.

You don't know the content of the chapter yet. Actually, opposition plays quite a role in the imagination and, therefore, in the spiritual life. We have talked extensively about the part that imagination plays in the spiritual life. Imagination is a vehicle for freedom and openness, and the cosmic imagination particularly nourishes these qualities.

Within the imagination, opposing images may complement each other; simultaneous reciprocal awareness enhances the appreciation of each. Also, as a complement to the primary focus of imagination, an opposing characteristic can enhance that focus. Shunryu Suzuki expresses this well:

> Before something happens in the realm of calmness, we do not feel the calmness; only when something happens within it do we find the calmness. There is a Japanese saying, "For the moon; there is the cloud. For the flower there is the wind." When we see a part of the moon covered by a cloud, or a tree, or a weed, we feel how round the moon is. But when we see the clear moon without anything covering it, we do not feel that roundness the same way we do when we see it through something else. (121)

I feel a poem coming on. The talk about opposition stimulates me to write about the sky:

A Slight Mist

A slight mist
I feel
In the sun
    light
Now becoming muted.
The golden haze
Of billowed clouds
Stretch
    pull
In the wind
    that puffs darkened blue
Into all of our
Senses.

The complementary effect of the tension of dissonance is also present in non-verbal, subjective activity, such as when listening to music. Judith Hylton, author of *Music Theory I*, describes this: "All non-harmonic tones introduce the tension of dissonance which creates the desire for release or resolution. This pattern of dissonance/resolution (tension/release) gives the music heightened expressiveness and a sense of increased forward motion" (236).

In her introduction to Bachelard's *On Poetic Imagination and Reverie*, Gaudin states:

> Moreover, every value evokes its opposite and is in constant struggle with it. Bachelard finds in poetry an application of the philosophy of values that insists on their precariousness. "Better than anyone else, a farmer knows the value of pure water because he knows that its purity is in danger" (L'Eau et les reves 188). Poetic language expresses the continuous tension within a substance. It is by virtue of the dialectic of opposite qualities that poetic matter fascinates us. (Imagination *liv*)

Bachelard elaborates on the participation of opposites in the imagination (using the term "material imagination" to indicate a dimension of the imagination that includes the heightened significance of a substance, such as water or earth):

> There are profound and durable ambivalences inherent in the fundamental matters which material imagination draws upon. This psychological property is so constant that we can formulate its converse as a basic law of imagination: a matter to which the imagination cannot give twofold life cannot play the psychological role of fundamental substance. A matter which does not elicit a psychological ambivalence cannot find its poetic double which allows endless transpositions. It is necessary then to have a double participation—participation of desire and fear, participation of good and evil, peaceful participation of black and white—for the material element to involve the entire soul. (Imagination 82-3)

The same author also indicates the enlargement of imaginative scope presented by opposition:

> Imagination that is material and dynamic enables us to experience a provoked adversity, a psychology of *opposition* that does not settle for the blow, the shock, but that seeks domination over the very heart of matter. Therefore the dreamed hardness is a hardness repeatedly attacked, which constantly repeats its stimulation. If we take hardness as the mere motive for an exclusion, in its initial *no*, we dream in its external, its intangible form. For the dreamer of inner hardness, granite is a type of provocation; its hardness offends, in a way which cannot be avenged without arms, tools, without the means of human guile. One does not treat granite with childish anger. It must be scored or polished in a new dialectic in which the dynamics of *opposition* may find the opportunity for nuances. (Imagination 68)

Bachelard further describes this energizing effect on the imagination:

> Take on in your imagination the work of the artisan. Imagine yourself putting the wood into the oven: cram the oven with shovels-full of coal, challenge the oven to a duel of energy. In short, be ardent and the ardor of the hearth will shoot its arrows in vain against your chest; you will be invigorated by the struggle. The fire can only return your blows. The psychology of *opposition* invigorates the worker. (Imagination 79)

I have described the complementary effect of opposition upon the imagination. These later quotations lead us to more awareness of another effect, the antagonistic effect of opposition. Of course, antagonism may have an impressive energizing effect. The antagonisms of social, political, economic, and religious forces can and do stimulate extensive—and at times catastrophic—actions and responses by individuals and groups. The myriad wartime events and other happenings of history certainly confirm this statement.

There is another aspect of opposition that I want to bring up, and this is more personal. This topic was covered in Chapter Thirteen: a release from painful concerns can be facilitated by having an alternate focus. Furthermore, awareness of the difficulties and pain that may be involved in these concerns can strengthen the impetus toward finding an alternate focus and may also invigorate the strength of attention to that focus.

There are several possibilities for creating such an alternate focus. It could be some activity, such as chopping wood or playing basketball. Particular attention to alternate focus was noted in Chapter Fourteen in relation to the effect of the cosmic imagination—and likewise, the effect of devotion to God—as a source for release and refuge. I will address this again in the next chapter because of its importance regarding individual differences in views of religious beliefs and practices.

In summary, there are two aspects of opposition. These two are the complementary effect and the antagonistic effect. Both effects tend to enhance the strength of attention toward the subject against which there has been opposition.

18

Individual Differences and Religious Practice

Individual Differences
The Natural World
Anthropomorphism
Self-Righteousness and Doubt
Opposition
Integrity
Silence

INDIVIDUAL DIFFERENCES

Each person brings something different to his or her spiritual quest. Particular characteristics of spiritual life vary greatly from one person to another, reflecting a variety of individual inclinations. Some find in spiritual life a fulfilling of their need to experience compassion. For some, the joy manifested in spiritual experience is the prime motivator toward spirituality. There are various sources for the spiritual inclination. William James makes a number of points about individual differences in religious practice. I find his descriptions so excellent that I will quote several of his passages, starting with: "Does it not appear as if one who lived more habitually on one side of the pain-threshold might need a different sort of religion from one who habitually lived on the other? This question, of the relativity of different types of religion to different types of need, arises naturally at this point" (118). Later he adds: "No two of us have identical difficulties, nor should we be expected to work out identical solutions" (368). James gives an interesting account of two opposite tendencies in religious practice:

Although some persons aim most at intellectual purity and simplification, for others richness is the supreme imaginative requirement .... To an imagination used to the perspectives of dignity and glory, the naked gospel scheme seems to offer an almshouse for a palace .... The intellectual difference is quite on a par in practical importance with the analogous difference in character. We say, under the head of Saintliness, how some characters resent confusion and must live in purity, consistency, simplicity .... For others, on the contrary, superabundance, overpressure, stimulation, lots of superficial relations, are indispensable. There are men who would suffer a very syncope if you should pay all their debts, bring it about that their engagements had been kept, their letters answered, their perplexities relieved, and their duties fulfilled, down to one which lay on a clean table under their eyes with nothing to interfere with its immediate performance. A day stripped so sparingly bare would be for them appalling. So with ease, elegance, tributes of affection, social recognitions—some of us require amounts of these things which to others would appear a mass of lying and sophistication. (349)

Karen Armstrong also tells of individual differences in religious experience as described by Jewish rabbis: "... God could not be described in a formula as though he were the same for everybody; he was an essentially subjective experience. Each individual would experience the reality of 'God' in a different way to answer the needs of his or her own particular temperament" (74).

Many orientations are reflected in the individual direction chosen for religious practice. Some are drawn to a particular religious practice for its calming effect, whereas others may be attracted to a different one for a vitalizing effect. Some might be inclined toward an unfamiliar form of religious practice to manifest defiance of a previously respected authority, now fallen out of favor. Others follow a particular form of religious practice to fulfill a desire to establish some external source of authority in their lives, particularly if they have become dissatisfied with self-centered directions.

Generally, an image of God is construed as an authority figure. If a mindfulness of God reinforces some degree of antagonism toward authority, a person holding such point of view would more likely be attracted to a form of spirituality which does not lend itself to focus on any sort of tangible image. Of course, such an individual may not be inclined toward any expression of spirituality.

Many are attracted to some form of religious practice to fulfill a need to both experience and express certainty. The release from doubt may assist a person in regaining a sense of control. If this orientation were taken further, a feeling of certainty may strengthen an inclination toward self-righteousness.

There are various aspects of a person's will to exert control that can find manifestation in the expression of spiritual experience. One aspect of the expression of control in spiritual experience is the desire to have a comprehensive orientation to existence, an overview of all that is. Chaos and meaninglessness are intolerable to many minds, and the idealized focus gives a sense of order and significance. Many believe in a source of conscious control that is separate from existence of all natural entities, and, for them, this belief enhances the meaning of existence. When this transcendental source is also considered to be in personal communication, then the sense of control is extended. Hopes and desires can be communicated to the transcendental source. Communication with a transcendental power then can extend the sense of personal control in conjunction with the mentally-projected, supernatural source of power.

A feeling of control can assist a person in overcoming weaknesses. The sense of control afforded by spiritual experience may provide a measure of protection against addicting tendencies or against any personal weakinee for which a person might seek help.

The act of supplication may be construed as one aspect of the need for control. I will mention a point about supplication to a higher power, and I will present an orientation that is coordinate with the outlook of this book: although supplication is in the form of a request, the intervention of some supernatural agent is not expected. There is not an expectation of an alteration in the course of that which might happen by a supplication to a supernatural power. It is true that the supplication is a statement of a result for which one hopes. However, in the context of the point of view presented in this book, instead of a request for divine intervention, the voicing of supplication indicates the result hoped for, and it also implies an easing of desire for such outcome by recognizing it to be within the agency of larger natural forces, forces which we cannot control. Supplication gives us some measure of relaxation from that over which we have either no control or limited control.

An attitude of control can be manifested in the character of spiritual expression, which, in a contrary direction, then tends to become less significant for that individual. Spiritual expression can have a programmed quality to it, seeming like a production. In fact, I suspect this is a common occurrence which can happen to anyone. When that happens, the spiritual experience becomes an endeavor rather than a surrender. The activity of the will is not relinquished; it directs the expression of the uplifted mood and finds the appropriate cosmic terms. Such spiritual expression is much more superficial than that in which the will is surrendered to the experience.

When there is disillusion with some particular form of religious practice that has been taken for granted, the activation of a desire for wonder and a desire to experience the mystery of the ambiguous may lead some into a totally different form of religious practice. The initiating factor in seeking an alternative to the previous area of religious expression may be simply a desire for an expression of freedom from that which is known, a step into the unknown with its re-establishment of wonder and mystery. Alternatively, the new religious direction may be toward the more concretely known in a literal-minded sense.

For some, the search itself, though directed toward fulfillment of spiritual expression, is not fulfilled by finding some satisfactory form of religious practice. In this instance, the search itself is a manifestation of an individual's desire to be in a state of desire. For these individuals, the need is in the looking, not in the finding.

The fulfillment of an inclination to be in a state of desire may also be the operative motivator in a continuous search for some adequate understanding of God. They don't want to find God. They want to want, and God is a ready source for which they can have an unending search.

The idealized focus, the god-symbol, is also a means of expressing the yearning-fulfillment cycle. In Chapter Four you may remember that the yearning-fulfillment cycle consists of repeated patterns of striving and fulfillment toward particular goals or experiences. In this section I will elaborate on the spiritual manifestation of the yearning-fulfillment cycle. God is always available, always there whenever the imagination calls a person in that direction. The seeking for God is a striving, and this striving is fulfilled when the mind senses that it is fulfilled. Both the desire for striving and the need for fulfillment are satisfied in the god-symbol. In this cycle of yearning and fulfillment, a person develops a sense of confidence in having a yearning that can readily be fulfilled.

Some individuals fulfill a need for intense emotional experience by their choice of a particular religious practice. James had a point of view about what he called 'coarser' religion:

Not the conception or intellectual perception of evil, but the grisly blood-freezing heart-palsying sensation of it close upon one, and no other conception or sensation able to live for a moment in its presence. How irrelevantly remote seem all our usual refined optimisms and intellectual and moral consolations in presence of a need of help like this! Here is the real core of the religious problem: Help! Help! No prophet can claim to bring a final message unless he says things that will have a sound of reality in the ears of victims such as these. But the deliverance must come in as strong a form as the complaint, if it is to take effect; and that seems a reason why the coarser religions, revivalistic, orgiastic, with blood and miracles and supernatural operations, may possibly never be displaced. Some constitutions need them too much. (136-7)

Al: Maybe you would not use the word "coarser."

I certainly don't fault William James for using that word. On the other hand, I do not want to offend any groups. In fact, I do not want to offend any individuals either. I just want to present information for self-understanding and for the understanding of others.

I believe that a more demonstrative form of religious practice can—for some—degenerate into an excessive pride in experiencing. For these, there is a sense of overt self-righteousness fulfilled in the spectacle of programmed bliss. Such programmed experience can be seen to occur often during religious services. Of course, personal inclination, in addition to social support during a religious meeting, makes this bliss very real for many.

If the need for a spiritual outlook is not dramatic, there is more likelihood that an ambiguous god symbol or its spiritual equivalent will be at the center of a person's life. But when greater emotional needs take a turn toward religious expression, the emotional investment in a religious belief may preclude an acceptance of any interpretation of Scripture which contests it as literal fact. The religious symbolism is then more likely to be regarded as literal fact.

The role of the imagination in a religious outlook has been emphasized. I particularly referred to the imagination in regard to an impression of universal existence, the cosmic imagination. Of course, this cosmic imagination can manifest great variation. It is interesting to note Bachelard's description of individual differences in the experience of the imagination: "For every appetite, there is a world. The dreamer then participates in the world by nourishing himself from one of the substances of the world, a dense or rare, warm or gentle substance clear or full of penumbra according to the temperament of the imagination. And when a poet comes to help the dreamer in renewing the beautiful images of the world, the dreamer accedes to cosmic health" (Reverie 178).

At this point let's consider the aesthetic aspect of religious practice. For many, this aesthetic character fulfills the sense of wonder and, in addition, provides a background that nurtures the freedom of spontaneity. Mental freedom is facilitated because aesthetic, emotional experience carries the mind beyond narrowed concerns and opens the imagination; it eases the flow of the mind into an open receptivity. Liturgy, repeated phrases, and similar acts draw our minds into openness and release us from the inclination toward directedness. Icons, liturgy, and church architecture are all vehicles that assist in reaching a state of mental clarity and renewal. Worship *per se* can be construed as primarily an aesthetic activity.

There is a particular point to be made about the nature of aesthetic experience and its role in religious practice. Bachelard discusses the release of anguish during the reading of a literary presentation of an anguished situation: "Reading a novel, we are placed in another life where we suffer, hope and sympathize, but just the same with the complex impression that our anguish remains under the domination of our liberty, that our anguish is not radical. Any anguishing book can, therefore, provide a technique for the reduction of anguish" (Reverie 24). Such release of anguish for the reader can be considered to be actuated by a concomitant awareness of freedom in the choice to welcome an unpleasant experience.

To carry this further, on a more profound level there may be, for some individuals who embrace Christianity, a sense of release from anguish when witnessing the image of the suffering of Christ on the cross, for them, the ultimate sacrifice. Such release may likewise be activated by an awareness of the freedom of choice evident in taking on that mentally-projected experience. If this mental process occurs, the sense of freedom would likely be supplemental to the compassion experienced.

James discusses the aesthetic dimension of religious practice and particularly notes the aesthetic character of religious doctrine. This passage describes the aesthetic value of religious dogma:

> The first point I will speak of is the part which the aesthetic life plays in determining one's choice of a religion. Men, I said awhile ago, involuntarily intellectualize their religious experience. They need formulas, just as they need fellowship in worship. I spoke, therefore, too contemptuously of the pragmatic uselessness of the

famous scholastic list of attributes of the deity, for they have one use which I neglected to consider. The eloquent passage in which Newman enumerates them puts us on the track of it. Intoning them as he would intone a cathedral service, he shows how high is their aesthetic value. It enriches our bare piety to carry these exalted and mysterious verbal additions just as it enriches a church to have an organ and old brasses, marbles and frescoes and stained windows. Epithets lend an atmosphere and overtones to our devotion. They are like a hymn of praise and service of glory, and may sound the more sublime for being incomprehensible. (348)

Al: You often quote from *The Varieties of Religious Experience* by William James. We could just read that book.

That is not a bad idea. It is true that the subject matter of some of this chapter particularly deals with the same material. But the theme of my book is different. I delineate the prime characteristics of fullness of life and then describe a spiritual orientation that is consistent with and adds to that fullness of life.

Let's talk a bit further about religious doctrine. As James indicates, a central characteristic of religious doctrine is that it can be a vehicle for wonder and imagination. For instance, no logical reasoning can adequately explain the Christian doctrine of the Trinity, three beings in one. It is a mystery. If it were straightforward and logical, it would be just another fact. For most people, the religious perspective needs some mystery, something not reasonable, in order for it to be a vehicle for wonder and imagination. To quote Paul: "Now faith is the substance of things hoped for, the evidence of things not seen" (Heb. 11:1). Armstrong also describes the need for the non-rational: "One of the reasons why the Cappadocians evolved this imaginative paradigm was to prevent God from becoming as rational as he was in Greek philosophy, as understood by such heretics as Arius. The theology of Arius was a little too clear and logical. The Trinity reminded Christians that the reality that we called 'God' could not be grasped by the human intellect" (118). And she states:"The whole point of the idea of God was to encourage a sense of the mystery and wonder of life, not to find neat solutions" (74).

There is another factor in the determination of which religious practice a person follows. This factor is the experience of a sense of transformation and can occur either when that religious practice which had been traditional for someone is seen in a new light or with a commitment to a new form of religious practice.

I am going to state something which may seem obvious but highlights the role of a sense of transformation in the commitment to a religious faith. For many who have spiritual experience, the particular conceptual content of that experience may be of lesser significance than the awareness of a sense of personal transformation. I believe it is often the case that a feeling of personal transformation is an important operative factor in religious experience. The particular beliefs of individuals can be the result of historical forces and the events that affect a person's life, rather than something that is arrived at through reasoned judgment. Instead of being based on some proven validity of the religious belief, the particular doctrine in which a person has faith may be a result of the emotional context of one's exposure to such dogma. The transmission of religious belief especially hinges on the capacity of adherents to promulgate a sense of transformation. I will put it this way: if, while promulgating a religious doctrine, someone were to convince you that your life was going to be changed in a positive direction by believing that doctrine, the anticipation of a new or renewed life may affect you more dramatically than the particular content of the doctrine.

Furthermore, I believe there is an apparent common factor among various religious practices in the sense of transformation: it is a freeing up from prior mental constrictions. With spiritual transformation there can be a liberation from thoughts and behavior that are seen to exert unwanted control over a person's life.

THE NATURAL WORLD

The natural world manifests amazing intricacies and fantastic processes. Unusual earth-shaking occurrences—volcanoes, earthquakes, and such—particularly stir the imagination. The events of the natural world have been a stimulus to the development of spiritual experience. Armstrong describes this source for spiritual manifestation: "From the very beginning, religion had helped people to relate to the world and to root themselves in it. The cult of the holy place had preceded all other reflection upon the world and helped men and women to find a focus in a terrifying universe. The deification of the natural forces had expressed the wonder and awe which had always been part of the human response to the world" (301).

Although many are attracted to a spiritual orientation in order to help them experience the mysterious and wonderful, the need for mystery and wonder need not involve inexplicable events and doctrine. The content of the everyday world is indeed amazing—if you really look at it. A piece of wood, a tree, clouds, you, me—all these are wondrous when not taken for granted. The mystery of existence of the ordinary is wondrous. James quotes from a sermon by James Martineau:

> Depend upon it, it is not the want of greater miracles, but of the soul to perceive such as are allowed us still, that makes us push all the sanctities into the far spaces we cannot reach. The devout feel that wherever God's hand is there is miracle: and it is simply an indevoutness which imagines that only where miracle is, can there be the real hand of God. The customs of Heaven ought surely to be more sacred in our eyes than its anomalies (360).

It is also true that religious practice may be such as to inhibit the sense of wonder. I quote from Armstrong: "As always, the atheists have a point. God had indeed been used in the past to stunt creativity; if he is made a blanket answer to every possible problem and contingency, he can indeed stifle our sense of wonder or achievement" (378).

Regarding seemingly inexplicable natural events, we realize that such perplexing events often occur in the workings of the natural world. We discussed the several characteristics of the unknown in Chapter Twelve. In religious practice these unknowns may be clothed in imagery, but for a skeptical mind it is well to recognize their basically unknown nature, realizing that future scientific discovery may reveal answers.

In Chapter Eleven we discussed the mental tendency toward abstraction, that is, the use of summarizing words to describe experience. Let's take another look at this tendency. It seems natural to consider all existence in some unified way. In fact, this tendency toward the correlation of diverse perceptions into unified concepts is one of the prime characteristics of scientific endeavor. We have scientific laws describing unified concepts, such as motion and energy states.

Let's consider at the tendency toward unifying concepts in the realm of metaphysical orientation. Armstrong refers to Ibn Sina, Muslim physician and philosopher, known in the West as Avicenna. In this quote she points not only to his idea of the unity of existence but also to his idea as to the derivation of existence: "Like all Platonists, Ibn Sina felt that the multiplicity we see all around us must be dependent upon a primal unity. Since our minds do regard composite things as secondary and derivative, this tendency must have been caused by something outside them that is a simple, higher reality" (182). In another passage, Armstrong points to the need for an all-encompassing view of existence: "The idea of God was essential to us: it represented the ideal limit that enabled us to achieve a comprehensive idea of the world" (315).

Although this perspective concerning existence does tend toward finding a unified concept by means of a summarizing abstraction, that does not mean that all existence is actually unified in some mystical way or that there is some sort of grand matrix. In the larger view of things, existence may be seen as consisting of diverse entities. Instead of some mysterious unification, randomness and individuality of initiative exist as characteristics of diversity.

There is a particular drawback in the tendency to see all as part of a whole. This unifying tendency may appear inadequate in the face of conflicting experience that seems to have no possible basis for inclusion in a unified view. An example would be something as horrible as the Holocaust. The massive horror of the systematic murder of millions of Jews—by a society that was considered to be advanced—appears impossible to reconcile with any sort of unified concept of existence. At least, this horrible example seems inconsistent with any unifying concept that includes a benign orientation toward human life and well-being.

Let's move on to the next topic. We have talked about the tendency toward and the drawbacks of a conceptual unification of the ongoing processes of existence. The next question is: what is the final outcome? Is there a state toward which the course of events are directed? It is my point of view that the train of events can be seen as an unfolding of tendencies rather than as having a direction toward some final state. Of course, a religious orientation might perceive any result whatsoever as a manifestation of a divine will.

Regarding the teleologic point of view, James states:

> It must not be forgotten that any form of disorder in the world might, by the design argument, suggest a God for just that kind of disorder. The truth is that any state of things whatever that can be named is logically susceptible of teleological interpretation. The ruins of the earthquake at Lisbon, for example: the whole of past history had to be planned exactly as it was to bring about in the fullness of time just that particular arrangement of debris of masonry, furniture, and once living bodies. No other train of causes would have been sufficient. And so of any other arrangement, bad or good, which might as a matter of fact be found resulting anywhere from previous conditions. (334)

A teleologic point of view is not necessary for establishment of value. Value is implicit in the attitude of thankfulness. This attitude of thankfulness fulfills the self by providing a release from self-absorption. Gratitude opens the attention; it welcomes both the self and that which is beyond the self.

ANTHROPOMORPHISM

At this time I will make a statement that is elaborated upon in the next chapter. The positive outlook afforded by thankfulness is consistent with the prime function of religious practice, which is the establishment and maintenance of values founded on attention focussed beyond the self. It is therefore not surprising that religious practice usually involves the projection of a source of value, and it is then toward this source that the self is oriented. This projection is usually manifested as an awareness of another consciousness with which we are in communication. Armstrong states:

> The anthropomorphic idea of God as Lawgiver and Ruler is not adequate to the temper of post-modernity. Yet the atheists who complained that the idea of God was unnatural were not entirely correct. We have seen the Jews, Christians, and Muslims have developed remarkably similar ideas of God, which also resemble other conceptions of the Absolute. When people try to find an ultimate meaning and value in human life, their minds seem to go in a certain direction. They have not been coerced to do this; it is something that seems natural to humanity. (394)

In the same vein, Spong says: "Human beings always form their understanding of God out of their own values, needs, and self-understanding. We do make God in our own image. We deify whatever we perceive to be the source of security and awe, and the giver of life and death" (122).

By opening the mind to a focus beyond the self, we can detach from our temporal concerns. This is not to deny problems, but we are likely to see them with clearer perspective when attention is returned to them. More valid pathways may then be seen for handling problems.

The release from the primacy of worldly concerns is addressed in the Bible: "And be not conformed to this world; but be ye transformed by the renewing of your mind, that ye may prove what is that good, and acceptable, and perfect, will of God" (Rom. 12:2), and "For what is a man advantaged, if he gain the whole world, and lose himself, or be cast away?" (Luke 9:25).

Of course, there is difficulty associated with the personification of God. This difficulty is expressed by Charles Wallraff in his book on the work of the existentialist philosopher Karl Jaspers: "Much as the modern theologian speaks of God in anthropomorphic terms even though he realizes that God is not a man, and thinks of Him as a person even though he knows that the analogy must in the end break down, the philosopher of Existenz must allude figuratively and indirectly to what his speech cannot directly and literally convey" (138).

Armstrong points to limitations of a prime focus that is not personalized: "All religion must begin with some anthropomorphism. A deity which is utterly remote from humanity, such as Aristotle's Unmoved Mover, cannot inspire a spiritual quest" (48). Proponents of some forms of Eastern religious practice may dispute that statement. Earlier in her book, *A History of God*, Armstrong did point to the well-known fact that not all religions are theistic. She does add: "In both Buddhism and Hinduism there had been a surge of devotion to exalted beings, such as the Buddha himself or Hindu gods which had appeared in human form. This kind of personal devotion, known as *bhakti*, expressed what seems to be a perennial human yearning for humanized religion .... The development of *bhakti* answered a deep-rooted popular need for some kind of personal relationship with the ultimate" (83-6).

It is interesting to note that the inclination toward anthropomorphism can extend to non-religious areas. Cassirer states: "The poet and the maker of myth seem, indeed, to live in the same world. They are endowed with the same fundamental power, the power of personification. They cannot contemplate any object without giving to it an inner life and a personal shape" (196).

Let's explore the particular qualities of personification that have an effect on those who experience God as, to some degree, anthropomorphic. There is usually at least a vague sense of anthropomorphism implied in the word-symbol "god," and, for some, it is a literal anthropomorphism. Orientation to a projected physiognomy is likely to lead to an assumed sense of reciprocal awareness by the other, not necessarily in a literal sense, but nevertheless in some inexplicable manner. Consciousness of an unseen presence—even when not experienced in a literal sense—stimulates a projected awareness of reciprocal understanding.

Also, for many, the awareness of a visage—no matter how vague an image—carries with it an anticipation of that which is unfolding in the immediate experience. Awareness of a vague impression of a visage is an effective source for focussing attention, that is, for drawing a person into a state of anticipation of the moment, becoming more fully alive to the present. Furthermore, the emotions which a person projects to the other presence are related to the perspective he or she has of that presence: critical, supportive, loving, or some other interpersonal characteristic. I believe that many people who sense an evaluation by a superior being receive a feeling of affirmation and a confirmation of integrity of the self.

If a person has an inclination to avoid being the object of attention, that person is more likely to avoid forms of religious practice that include an anthropomorphic god, a god whose presence would be felt.

Let's look further at some of the characteristics of anthropomorphism. Zen teacher D. T. Suzuki expresses the feeling of receiving peace in response to a mindfulness of Buddha: "His presence somehow had a pacifying and satisfying effect on whatever spiritual anguish they had; they felt as if they were securely embraced in the arms of a loving, consoling mother; to them the Buddha was really such" (37).

The Old Testament also refers to this pacifying effect: "The Lord lift up his countenance upon thee, and give thee peace" (Num. 6:26).

In the New Testament anthropomorphism is, of course, personified by Christ. The attributes of this personification, particularly value, love, and empathy are repeatedly expressed.

I will quote from Jesus' words as recorded by John in the New Testament to illustrate how a religious source can provide detachment from self-absorption: "Abide in me, and I in you. As the branch cannot bear fruit of itself, except it abide in the vine; no more can ye, except ye abide in me" (John 15:4). The realization of the self as mentally projected into another being can provide a sense of detachment from concerns of the self. This release from self-concern occurs because of a focus that can envelop a person in a mental state projected to be that of an ideal being.

Also, "Christ within" can provide a sense of detachment because thoughts and actions can be projected as emanating from a source within the self that is different from the self. In this way prior absorption with the self can be held in abeyance; there can be a feeling of detachment from self-concerns that may be excessive.

For Christians, the image of Christ on the cross carries with it several effects. One effect concerns the awareness of an authority figure which does not pose a threat. Let's look at this from a psychodynamic point of view. Often in the course of the dynamics of early family life, some degree of fear of or intolerance for the source of authority develops. I believe that anger at a parent has a residual effect in the lives of many adults. In adult life this anger can become transposed into discomfort with other sources of authority. To someone who is overly sensitive to the appearance of an authority figure, the image of a temporarily dead authority figure, symbolized by the Crucifix, can be less threatening and more readily accepted.

There is another significant effect of the image of Christ on the cross. The projection of an awareness of the mental state of the dead god-figure can carry a person into sensing some impression of that blankness of mind expected during death. Such cleared mind is of value in itself in that it is characteristic of the free, open outlook.

In addition, certainly wonder is created upon having an awareness of an image of death that, according to the Christian scriptures, will return to life.

Armstrong summarizes the quality of personalism in religious practice and states a *caveat*:

> Thus personalism has been an important and—for many—an indispensable stage of religious and moral development. The prophets of Israel attributed their own emotions and passions to God; Buddhists and Hindus had to include a personal devotion to avatars of the supreme reality. Christianity made a human person the center of the religious life in a way that was unique in the history of religion: it took the personalism inherent in Judaism to an extreme. It may be that without some degree of this kind of identification and empathy, religion cannot take root. Yet a personal God can become a grave liability. He can be a mere idol carved in our own image, a projection of our limited needs, fears and desires. (209)

SELF-RIGHTEOUSNESS AND DOUBT

In looking further at some of the problems of religious practice, the worship of God often becomes a base for self-justification. In this regard

Karl Barth states: "Our arrogance demands that ... some superworld should also be known and accessible to us. Our conduct calls for some deeper sanction, some approbation and remuneration from another world .... Our devotion consists in a solemn affirmation of ourselves and of the world ..." (117-8).

Armstrong notes the popular appeal of those who promote egotistic aims:

> Instead of making God a symbol to challenge our prejudice and force us to contemplate our own shortcomings, it can be used to endorse our egotistic hatred and make it absolute. It makes God behave exactly like us, as though he were simply another human being. Such a God is likely to be more attractive and popular than the God of Amos and Isaiah, who demands ruthless self-criticism. (55)

Indeed, self-criticism and doubt are necessary components of that spiritual life which is consistent with personal integrity. Self-righteousness is more appealing to the immediate emotions, but doubt and humility are necessary for a life that is not corrupted by self-serving attitudes. Look at this passage by Martin Luther (quoted by James): "For the godly trust not to their own righteousness" (113).

It is true that excess doubt and inappropriate doubt can be destructive, as previously noted. Furthermore, the centering on a spiritual theme can relieve that doubt, but doubt should not be totally excluded. The availability of doubt is necessary in order to avoid a fall into the pit of self-righteousness.

I believe there are some individuals who comprehend the essential nature of their lives as being agents of productivity. Furthermore, they tend to base their sense of personal worth on their productivity. Some of these individuals may look at the process of questioning and doubt as interfering with productivity. They may view doubt as counter-productive. Such individuals are more likely to be attracted to religious stands and beliefs which erase doubt, and they tend to be more literal-minded.

If an individual is inclined to avoid doubt, that person's outlook can become narrowed into excluding questioning thoughts. Certainty is reinforced at the price of a restricted mind. There may be a fear that a questioning of one aspect of the source of authority will put the acceptance of the entire authority at risk. This renders the commitment to authority inflexible and brittle, totally accepted without recourse to any examination.

When authority is accepted blindly and without question, it becomes a means of achieving a clearing of the mental state. The mind becomes unfettered by disturbing questions and concerns. Unquestioned endorsement of authority is a vehicle to blankness of mind which, at least for some people, gives release from sources of anguish. By means of this release, a person's mind is opened to free spontaneity, albeit in a mode consonant with the authority. However, the acceptance of authority is but one phase of a more balanced outlook. A measure of doubt will test the validity of the authority. Without the doubt phase, a blind acceptance of authority too often becomes dangerous to life, health, and morality. We have talked about this in previous chapters. There should be easy flow from a state of acceptance of authority into the doubt phase. A person should be able to question all.

OPPOSITION

In the last chapter we discussed several aspects of the nature of opposition. Let's look at some of the commendable effects of the role of opposition in religious practice. A variety of habituations and addictions can be opposed and conquered, and a realization of the ongoing need to control these vitalizes the spirit. James gives an example of an opposing constraint on an addiction provided by a religious attitude: "... 'the only radical remedy I know for dipsomania is religiomania,' is a saying I have heard quoted from some medical man" (213).

The opposing spiritual effect may be enlisted for something less dramatic than addictions. A person may look for a religious setting to relieve a vague sense of personal non-worth. James states: "The uneasiness, reduced to its simplest terms, is a sense that there is something wrong about us as we naturally stand. The solution is a sense that we are saved from the wrongness by making proper connection with the higher powers" (383).

There is another aspect of the status of opposition in spiritual life. The expression of spiritual freedom may be seen as a release from and an opposition to the worldly concerns and as a separation from habituated mental patterns. These concerns can be replaced or modified by a sense of newness, of openness, of spontaneity.

Furthermore, the view of the god-symbol as opposed to worldly endeavors is not necessarily antagonistic. This view of each in conjunction with the other may be a form of complementary opposition in which the things of the world become more appreciated by their relationship to a god who is viewed as separate from the world. This heightened experience of complementary antagonism is similar to the increased awareness of both moon and clouds when, instead of being seen separately, the sight is of the moon partly shaded by clouds.

On a more superficial level, the belief in the existence of a transcendental consciousness may be primarily an outcome of a need to experience a sense of difference from ordinary life. Of course, this need to experience a sense of difference may be manifested in a multitude of ways other than as a religious belief. Life-style examples range from the survivalist to the "flower child."

We have talked about opposition in relation to religious practice and we have pointed to various problems against which religious practice may give some degree of relief, including habituations, addictions, the sense of non-worth, and excess worldly concerns. On a different tack, some people may seek opposition in a religious setting to produce a desired emotional intensity. James describes this process, citing an inclination toward asceticism:

> Passive happiness is slack and insipid, and soon grown mawkish and intolerable. Some austerity and wintry negativity, some roughness, danger, stringency, and effort, some 'no! no!' must be mixed in, to produce the sense of an existence with character and texture and power .... Here I find the degree of equilibrium, safety, calm, and leisure which I need, or here I find the challenge, passion, fight, and hardship without which my soul's energy expires .... And it is just so with our sundry souls: some are happiest in calm weather; some need the sense of tension, of strong volition, to make them feel alive and well. For these latter souls, whatever is gained from day to day must be paid for by sacrifice and inhibition, or else it comes too cheap and has no zest. Now when characters of this latter sort become religious, they are apt to turn the edge of their need of effort and negativity against their natural self; and the ascetic life gets evolved as a consequence. (236)

For some there are more narrowed manifestations of opposition, such as the establishment of separateness from others. With such separateness there tends to be an avoidance of empathy. In fact, there may be a focus on that opposition which has the effect of greatly energizing the spiritual life. Kenneth Burke discusses the tendency to view an enemy in an absolute fashion (in this instance referring to a "secular enemy"):

The "perfection" of a secular enemy is the clearest observable instance of ways whereby the intermediate absolutizing step is involved. Given the vast complexities of the modern world, it would be hard to find a "perfect" material victim for any of our ills. But because the *principle* of a "perfect" victim is so implicit in the very concept of victimage, and because men have so "natural" or spontaneous a desire for a "perfect" view of their discomforts, they are eager to tell themselves of victims so thoroughgoing that the sacrifice of such offerings would bring about a correspondingly thoroughgoing cure. The "fragmentary" nature of the enemy thus comes to take on the attributes of an absolute. (293)

The smugness of self-righteousness, built upon the false pillar of certainty, has led to countless horrors and tragedies. I have described this in previous chapters. Simone Weil makes this statement: "The service of the false God (of the social Beast under whatever form it may be) purifies evil by eliminating its horror. Nothing seems evil to those who serve it except failure in its service" (125).

Differing religious doctrines may reinforce the energizing oppositions between religious groups. In this regard James states: "When however, a positive intellectual content is associated with a faith-state, it gets invincibly stamped in upon belief, and this explains the passionate loyalty of religious persons everywhere to the minutest details of their so widely differing creeds" (382).

A stance of opposition may be related to an attitude of receptivity. I will explain. For some, an outlook of receptivity may be narrowed to a particular content. It is possible for a person to have full receptivity toward some particular content which might be matched by an intolerance toward other contents in the same sphere of understanding. This is often the case with religious belief. If the attention is directed toward a spiritual content that is familiar, I believe the release of the self from temporal concerns and into that spiritual experience is easier than if the content is not familiar. In this instance, one may choose to avoid exposure to a source of spiritual experience that would involve a new initiative.

I will emphasize the well-known fact that a total commitment to one religious belief often is matched by an intolerance of other religious beliefs. Such intolerance is partly a function of the role of receptivity. For many, alternative beliefs seem "foreign." An understanding of other beliefs would require initiative, a "going-beyond" that which is already known. Such initiative might be seen by some as contradictory to an attitude of receptivity. For them, the active role of initiative may be seen as destructive of this orientation of receptivity, which is an essential aspect of their religious practice. If a particular religious belief is totally accepted, without the potential for recourse to doubt, examination, and alternate views, a person holding such a belief is likely to rebel against the employment of an active initiative for the understanding of alternate beliefs.

INTEGRITY

We have said enough about the various narrow paths that may be associated with a spiritual life. Let's return to a consideration of fullness of life. The need for doubt, detachment, empathy, respect—these qualities are aspects of the life of integrity and of a spirituality that is consistent with integrity. John Hick develops his thought in this direction:

> We have here, then, a philosophy of religion which respects and supports the use of traditional religious language, with all its emotional depths and reverberations, but which understands it throughout as referring, not to realities alleged to exist independently of ourselves, but to our own moral and spiritual states. Thus to say that God exists is not to affirm the reality of, in Richard Swinburne's definition, "a person without a body (i. e., a spirit) who is eternal, is perfectly free, omnipotent, omniscient, perfectly good, and the creator of all things." That "God exists" means that there are human beings who use the concept of God and for whom it is the presiding idea in their form of life. (199)

In this vein, Karen Armstrong states: "All the major religious traditions claim that the acid test of any spirituality is the degree to which it has been integrated into daily life" (279). She adds that the isolation of religious expression from moral standards "... can encourage people to think that it is not necessary to apply normal standards of decency and rationality to behavior supposedly inspired by 'God.' " (394). This, of course, raises the problem of knowing the basis for moral standards. Hopefully, by the end of this book, you will know my formulation of an answer to this concern.

Of course, it is possible for a person to experience spirituality while being free from literal-mindedness and from unacceptable religious dogma. One can be able to doubt any idea, any motivating principle. Doubt does not necessarily negate the validity of that which has been doubted.

The subject that has been examined may have been found to remain valid, in religious matters as well as secular. However, the capacity for doubt, discernment, and examination should be retained. A person should be able to hold anything up to the light of fresh perception.

If openness includes an absence of the fear to doubt, such openness can be nourished by that devotion to God which does not require a denial of a reasonable view of reality. Among those who tend to doubt and to disbelieve the existence of a supernatural reality, if an awareness of God does not imply unnatural or supernatural characteristics, the value of a prime focus on God is likely to nourish freedom from those concerns and orientations which would narrow the outlook. A prime focus on God gives release from habituated mental patterns and allows clarity of mind. Thoughts are allowed to wander into new dimensions of empathy and new patterns of discernment and doubt. Worldly things are put in abeyance; a person becomes open to freedom and newness. God is primary, and all else can be seen with new vision and perceptiveness. Surrender to God frees the mind. Other sources of direction—the worldly sources—no longer enslave the mind. The things of this world are held with a light heart. No need or desire takes ownership over you. As the First Commandment states: "Thou shalt have no other gods before me" (Exodus 20:3). In this commandment "other gods" can be interpreted as worldly needs and desires held to be important. These "other gods" are not to be placed before spiritual commitment.

As indicated in Chapter Fourteen, the concept of God presented in this book does not imply the existence of a supernatural consciousness. God is recognized as a manifestation of the cosmic imagination, a mental projection that fulfills the sense of openness, wonder, and freedom. This cosmic imagination is an expression of our nature and it correlates with awareness of the fantastic processes of nature by which existence develops and for which thankfulness is given.

SILENCE

Al: Let me interject here. We both agree that there is much variation among people in the concept of God. And belief in God leads to a variety of consequences, some of which are very destructive. It is my turn to quote someone. Martin Buber, Jewish philosopher, says: "Many men wish to reject the word God as a legitimate usage, because it is so misused. It is indeed the most heavily laden of all the words used by men" (75). He also states: "... we speak with Him only when speech dies within us" (104).

Yes. Silence is one valuable mode of spiritual life. Silence is a vehicle to the cleared mind. It affords opportunity to detach from narrowed directions and to focus on that which is beyond self-concerns. It is an avenue to awareness of God. Armstrong refers to an Eastern orthodox view that silence is "the only appropriate form of theology" (168).

A Catholic theologian, Leslie DeWart, points to the value of: "silence in discourse about God.... It may be that saying about God all we can, but being also as silent as we can regarding his name, might increase the meaningfulness of whatever religious experience we may wish to convey to others, to ourselves and to God" (214).

I quote from Psalm 46:10: "Be still and know that I am God ... ".

19

The Nature of a Religious Orientation

Until I Die
The Function of Religious Practice
Self-Righteousness and Doubt
Components of a Religious Orientation
God, Music, and Freedom
Review

We begin this chapter with a short poem which presents a particular message:

UNTIL I DIE

The little, brown frog

is not hungry. He

sits on a hill, looks

without passion or

thought at the

slender, green bug

Insect stilted

up,

still,

sways

Stops

> *Steps*
>
> *Stops*
>
> *Sways*
>
> *Not thinking about*
>
> *Death and*
>
> *Life's fortunes.*
>
> *I don't know*
>
> *the insect's consciousness,*
>
> *but that consciousness which I*
>
> *project to the insect*
>
> *tells me its lesson:*
>
> *Until I die*
>
> *I am alive.*

THE FUNCTION OF RELIGIOUS PRACTICE

Al: I get the message. Are you leading to some point?

Yes, I am, but it won't be apparent till later in the chapter. The poem sets the tone for the chapter and alludes to its primary purpose: the relationship of religion to the establishment of value.

Let's begin with some words about the nature of religion. One point of view about the function of religious practice is that it establishes, encourages, and reinforces a belief in religious doctrine. Furthermore, religious doctrine is usually founded on some basis which is ordinarily unbelievable. Ordinary facts cannot be a source for religious doctrine. The doctrinal foundation of most religious practice is some belief which defies reasonable explanation.

There is a reason for religious doctrine to be based on something which is ordinarily unbelievable. Let's take a look at the relation between emotion and the commitment to a religious practice. In order to have an emotional component of commitment, the content of religious belief must be extraordinary. Stated another way, when there is a commitment to beliefs which would ordinarily be viewed as unbelievable, there is an emotional dimension to such a commitment. Such is the case because this commitment requires the psychologic force of emotion if it is to be accepted. Acceptance of a strikingly extraordinary belief cannot be on the basis of reasonable discernment. If there is acceptance of such an extraordinary belief, an emotional component accompanies and reinforces the belief.

This brings up the subject of value. Value is defined in Webster's dictionary as "relative worth, utility, or importance." A sense of value requires a degree of emotion; value implies a feeling about something. With this in mind, it can be said that the establishment of value is a prime function of religion and that this value is usually tied to an emotion associated with a belief in the extraordinary.

There are several aspects of a religious orientation: tradition, narrative, historical context, ritual, sense of community, morality, world view, organization of one's life based on world view, and meditation or communication with the "divine." I have touched upon many of these in various sections of this book and will address them again in the remaining chapters. At this point I want to say that all of these characteristics are utilized in the establishment and maintenance of a sense of value.

Faith is an aspect of religious practice. According to one definition, faith is: "belief in the traditional doctrines of a religion." Another definition is: "firm belief in something for which there is no proof," and another is: "something that is believed especially with strong conviction."

It is typical for religious doctrine—at least in the orientation of Western religious practice—to embody a central theme that establishes a sense of awe and wonder. Such religious doctrine requires faith in order for someone to have a commitment to that which would ordinarily seem contrary to reason. Since faith involves a commitment to something which would ordinarily be unbelievable, such commitment carries with it a degree of emotional impact. A characteristic of faith is its emotional nature. In addition, emotional intensity implies worth, and when something has worth for an individual, it is of significant value for him or her. Therefore, it can be seen that, with the experience of emotion, faith in religious doctrine can establish significant value for the individual.

One point of view concerning the nature of a religious orientation is that the function of such orientation is not primarily the promulgation of doctrine as such. Rather, the primary function of a religious orientation can be understood as the establishment of a perceived, desirable, fundamental value for the individual by means of some type of religious doctrine. Even in the outlook of Eastern religious practice involving the eventual dispersion of individual identity, such process is understood to have value for the individual. The value to which I refer is fundamental for the individual, transcending values associated with temporal needs and desires.

Al: Now you've got me going. I don't believe in transcendental existence. I don't think there is a transcendental being who exists beyond all of the natural universe.

That's not what I meant. By "transcendental to temporal needs and desires" I mean a value established beyond those values toward which we are aimed in our ordinary pattern of life, such as goals and desires related to work or to other activities of the everyday world. These temporal values are not negated but become secondary.

Worldly values can be considered "false gods" when they are primary in a person's life. An example is the effort for some particular achievement or possession. Another false god—when it is a primary value—is the image of appearance to others. These values may be important, but should not be the primary value in life.

I will substantiate to some extent my statement that the primary function of religious practice may be considered to be the establishment of fundamental value for the individual, that is, value beyond personal needs and desires. In the various forms of religious practice, there are differing concepts of the nature of the universe and of that which may be considered to be beyond the universe. Regardless of the content of these concepts, the operative effect for religiously-oriented individuals includes an expansion of their outlook beyond personal needs.

At this point, it is valuable to consider some of the points made by a theologian, Paul Tillich. It is possible to disagree with the usage of the term "faith" by Tillich in his description of the nature of religious practice: "Faith is the state of being ultimately concerned. The content matters infinitely for the life of the believer, but it does not matter for the formal definition of faith (539)." Let's consider this statement in relation to some of the standard definitions of faith that can be considered to be important in the sphere of religion (as listed in Merriam Webster's Collegiate Dictionary, Tenth Edition):

    belief and trust in and loyalty to God,
    belief in the traditional doctrines of a religion,
    firm belief in something for which there is no proof,
    something that is believed especially with strong conviction,
        especially a system of religious beliefs.

All of these definitions point to the presence of belief, and more particularly to belief in that which has particular content. With these definitions in mind, the act of belief and the content of belief are the prominent aspects of the nature of faith. Therefore, I would consider that the concept of faith as presented by Tillich does not correspond to standard definitions.

On the other hand, I believe Tillich's statement to be significant. In this regard I prefer to shift to different but related terms. Rather than considering ultimate concern as the equivalent of faith, I would say that ultimate concern is the essence of a religious orientation, the essential nature of a religious outlook. I have used the term "fundamental value" instead of "ultimate concern," but the meanings are close enough to be considered conceptually the same.

How would this concept—fundamental value as the essence of a religious orientation—relate to specific religions? The monotheism of Western religious practice is centered on a commitment to God; a devotion to God is the primary aspect of religious life. For Tillich, an awareness of God represents a mindfulness of the "infinite." He states: "Man is driven toward faith by his awareness of the infinite … "(Quoted in Pojman, 541). It appears as " … restlessness of the heart … "(541). For Tillich the drive toward an awareness of the infinite begets a content which has significance for the individual who has such awareness: "God never can be object without being at the same time subject"(541). In Tillich's presentation, such content is expressed in religious symbols and myths. Furthermore, he states: "The fundamental symbol of our ultimate concern is God" (543).

To Tillich, atheism represents an absence of ultimate concern. However, Tillich's definition of God as the symbol of ultimate concern would not appear to require an existence of transcendental consciousness. God would not have to be seen as a transcendental consciousness with which a person would be in relationship. Rather, God—as ultimate concern—could be considered a subjective orientation to that which is viewed as fundamental to life. I suspect that such orientation would be considered to be atheistic for many who proclaim a commitment to God.

Regardless of whether or not there is belief in God as a transcendental consciousness, the commitment to fundamental value or ultimate concern can be operative in establishing a sense of value for those who may have a cynical or hopeless outlook on life. Also, a sense of fundamental value can give a perspective on the ordinary dealings of life. Fundamental value is apart and separate from ordinary life. As such, the sense of fundamental value can transcend the temporal values of worldly life; it can give an enlarged perspective on those mundane values that might otherwise entrap us within excessively narrowed attitudes and purposes.

I suspect that religious devotion in Eastern religious practice would have a similar effect. A mindfulness of that which is important beyond the needs and desires of the self can enlarge the perspective on those needs and desires. Such mindfulness has value, fundamental value. The primary nature of the Eastern religious outlook may be interpreted as the establishment of fundamental value for the individual, even though the doctrine involves a dispersion of self-identity. To my understanding, Eastern religious practice involves a mental purification by the process of the loss of a sense of self- identity into the totality of the cosmic reality, however that reality might be understood; the self is subsumed within the entirety of the cosmos. This implies a fundamental value for the individual in the act of mental purification; the call to release the mind into a purified state implies a value in such release.

Let's look at a more extreme understanding of the release from value. Consider the mind-set of Zen Buddhism (and Taoist thought as expressed in the Tao Te Ching) regarding not only a perspective on worldly values but a release from those values. There can be worth in releasing the mind from the narrowness of worldly values that would restrict the mind. This larger, fundamental value involves a release from lesser values. However, if taken to an extreme stage, there could be dire personal and social consequences pursuant to a total release from worldly values. I believe that a total release from values would include: not looking for food, not eating, no regard for personal hygiene. In short, a total release from all mundane values would leave a person in a state of simply vegetating.

The common theme in religions is a relegation of values which have been centered on personal needs and desires to a secondary role. In releasing our various desires to a secondary status, we are more able to release ourselves from the narrowness of self-centeredness. Regarding this release, most forms of Western religious practice include a devotion to God. The god-symbol is effective as a focus to center the mind into the cosmic imagination and away from the needs and desires of the self.

An example of the release from self-centeredness in Christian doctrine is expressed by Jesus: "He that findeth his life shall lose it: and he that loseth his life for my sake shall find it" (Matt. 10:39).

Hick makes a general statement about the release from self-centeredness, and, in doing so, the realization of human value is viewed as a salvific process:

> Experience of the transcendent is structured either by the concept of deity, which presides over the theistic traditions, or by the concept of the absolute, which presides over the non-theistic traditions. Each of these is schematized in actual human experience to produce the experienced divine personae (such as Jahweh, the heavenly Father, Allah, Vishnu, Shiva) and metaphysical impersonae (such as Brahman, the Tao, the Dharmakaya, Sunyata) to which human beings orient themselves in worship or meditation. The function of religion in each case is to provide contexts for salvation/liberation, which consists in various forms of the transformation of human existence from self- centeredness to Reality-centeredness. (14)

In a later passage Hick again refers to the Eastern and Western religious orientations when he states:

> The main motivation for seeking a comprehensive interpretation embracing both of these very different types of religious thought-and-experience comes from the perception that the personal deities and non-personal absolutes have a common effect ... in the transformation of human existence from self-centeredness to a new centeredness in the God who is worshiped or in the Absolute that is known in *samadhi* or *satori*. This transformed state is one of freedom from the anxious, sinful, self-concerned ego, a consequent realization of inner peace and joy, and an awareness in love or compassion of the oneness of humankind, or of all life. The devout Jewish or Christian or Muslim or theistic Hindu or Pure Land Buddhist worshiper, throwing him or herself in faith into the hands of the Lord, the Bhagavan, the highest Person, the all-compassionate Buddha, undergoes in varying degrees this salvific re-creation. (278)

Now we will get back to your concern about transcendental existence. As I said, the primary function of religious practice may be considered to be the establishment of fundamental value rather than the presentation of dogma. Many who hold religious beliefs and have faith in the content of religious doctrine would disagree with this statement. I can point out that it is not intended as a flat statement of fact. It is a different orientation toward the nature of religion, a different view of the fundamental role of religious practice. In this view, religious doctrine can be thought of as secondary, the primary function of religion being the establishment of value.

In Western religions a release from self-centeredness is attained by means of doctrines which include belief in a transcendental consciousness, a god. Value of the individual who follows religious practice is established by the belief in that individual's significance to God. With this outlook, a person has meaning because of that person's relationship to God. (Webster's definition of meaning: "significant quality," with "implication of a special significance.")

SELF-RIGHTEOUSNESS AND DOUBT

Furthermore, an outlook of Western religion implies that personal worth is further enhanced by following that course which is believed to be God's will. Therein lie many potential problems. The centering of life on God instead of the self gives a sense of self-assurance. When not balanced with some amount of empathy toward others and some openness to doubt, this self-assurance can inure a person to disastrous consequences caused in the name of God. The blindness of narrowed idealism can cause great pain. Throughout history group efforts to become spiritually pure have often led to great suffering.

The "original sin" described in the Bible may be understood as pointing to the lack of humility and doubt, giving an assuredness derived from narrowed—and possibly idealistic—knowledge: "And the Lord God said, Behold, the man is become as one of us, to know good and evil" (Gen. 3:22). The man described is seen to judge as if he were a god instead of being humble in the seeking of truth and in knowing that the truth he finds may not be true.

The idealism of service to others is the humanistic form of value as a primary source. Such value may have many beneficial effects. However, as a primary source of value, it is possible that—for some people—this idealism may place abstract goals above perceptiveness and responsiveness to the reality of a situation. When there is a drive toward idealistic goals, a person may lose sight of the need for openness to new information. Idealism can predispose a person to be insensitive, lacking an empathy which might reveal a more true picture of reality. It is possible for narrowed idealism to blind a person's sight to valid concerns of those who disagree.

Al: I can't disagree with that. Idealism can warp perception. Well, what are we left with for guidance? I will say this: if we knew the meaning of life, this could give us direction in learning the *summum bonum*, the primary value that may help us for guidance in our lives.

Right.

Al: But we don't know the meaning of life. Is there any meaning? Do we just exist and then die—with no significance that can be attributable to our lives? That's what you indicated in Chapter Twelve.

I believe that there is no meaning of life at some metaphysical level; our lives have significance as we create that significance. Also, I believe such creation of significance or value is most valid for our lives when it is consistent with our psychologic health, as individuals and as a society.

Al: This leads to a thought I have. I could consider that the right prescription for religion would be that which provides a basis for human value without the pitfalls of self-righteousness. The idealistic concepts which draw us to a mental state centered beyond our personal agendas must not lead us to immoral actions, actions that are destructive of human value.

Well said. In fact, I was about to say that. Human value, self-esteem, must include some access to doubt.

We have talked about the constituents of integrity in Part II. Concern about morality is included within the subject of integrity. A major component in morality is the openness to doubt. The ability to doubt beliefs and attitudes opens the possibility for new understandings and a more clear perception of the reality of things. With an openness to doubt, we may be able to get past the mental baggage of those preconceptions which are inadequate. With doubt we may be able to approach truth more closely.

Al: The outlook that you present has no place, then, for faith, does it?

Right. Commitment is not to a faith in the existence of some transcendental being. Rather, commitment is to personal integrity, including that component of integrity which maintains an access to doubt and examination. All attitudes and beliefs may be subjected to doubt and examination. Furthermore, I can say that confidence can be established in method instead of content. This confidence would be in the method of doubt and examination rather than that confidence which might be obtained by having faith in God or some other symbol of supernatural existence.

COMPONENTS OF A RELIGIOUS ORIENTATION

Doubt involves an openness to the questioning of beliefs and attitudes. Besides viewing doubt as an aspect of openness, the general nature of an outlook of openness is a welcoming of fresh experience. With openness we welcome the anticipation of the newness of experience. Openness provides us with the opportunity for enlarged awareness. Since openness can bring us to a sense of enlarged awareness, the capacity for openness is a prime source for a release from excessive self-centeredness.

By taking us beyond our personal agendas, the outlook of openness to new experience and understanding can be considered to be one of the components of a religious orientation. Openness is not a religious quality in the usual sense in which religion is understood. However, in our view of the function of religion as providing value which is beyond personal agendas, the outlook of openness is a prime component of religion. A capacity for openness is a religious quality because openness to new experience and understanding tends to move us beyond self-centeredness. Such movement beyond self-centeredness is valuable; it is a springboard to an enlarged awareness.

In this chapter I have not yet said anything about the content of the enlarged awareness of a religious orientation which might fulfill the criteria we have been discussing. These criteria of a religious orientation are:

1. Content which is beyond personal needs and desires,

2. The establishment or confirmation of that which is of fundamental value for the individual,

3. That which is not invalidated by reasonable examination and doubt.

Of course, in Chapter Fourteen we did discuss the content of a religious orientation which is consistent with and open to the value of doubt. The present chapter takes up a consideration of the religious orientation from the perspective of the establishment of human value.

A sense of enlargement encompasses an awareness of that which extends beyond personal concerns. This enlarged awareness may reach toward the universal when experiencing the world of nature as seen directly. As an example, a mountain top covered with snow and bright pink in the early morning light may stimulate an expansion of the imagination.

Also, an enlarged awareness may be created by some abstract conception of the universe. This abstract conception may be manifested by a word-symbol that an individual might comprehend to be at a level of the universe. Examples are the word "God" or "love" or "unity." In all of these, the focus beyond the self to that which is separate from self-direction can ease the detachment from the objects and patterns of self-direction. These pre-set patterns then become secondary and are therefore handled with more ease and grace because there is an enduring positive element, an enduring sense of affirmation beyond all the immediacies of life. The affirmation is created by an orientation that establishes value.

Regarding the realization of an enlarged awareness, God may also be viewed in the framework of complementary opposition. This subject was discussed in Chapter Seventeen. In this perspective, there is an imaginative fulfillment in perceiving the worldly endeavors as being in complementary opposition to God. This is similar to the sight of the clouds and the moon, complementing each other. A gentle relaxation tends to accompany worldly concerns when put alongside an imaginative presence of God.

There is a relationship between the ambiguity of the god-symbol and the sense of enlarged awareness. God, the enduring symbol, is a word that is not harnessed into objective fact, except as the vague abstraction as presented in this book: the symbolic representation of the nature of the universe. As such, the ambiguity of the god-symbol is quite congruent with the ambiguity and spontaneity which are present in the universe (re: Chaos Theory) and in the self. Furthermore, ambiguity and spontaneity are consonant with an openness that looks out to new perception and perspectives—to an enlarged awareness.

James describes the sense of enlarged awareness: "... a feeling of being in a wider life than that of this world's selfish little interests; and a conviction, not merely intellectual, but as it were sensible, of the existence of an Ideal Power" (216). This identity is focussed beyond the self, beyond the self's existence, beyond the wider social existence, beyond all existence or anything that can be conceived objectively. It is experienced with a sense of wonder and anticipation.

In conjunction with a focus on God and beyond the self, we may receive a sense of well-being and peace. In this regard James states:

> The (characteristics of the affective experience, which is the state of assurance or faith-state) is the loss of all the worry, the sense that all is ultimately well with one, the peace, the harmony, the willingness to be, even though the outer conditions should remain the same. The certainty of God's "grace," of "justification," "salvation," is an objective belief that usually accompanies the change in Christians; but this may be entirely lacking and yet the affective peace remain the same.... A passion of willingness, of acquiescence, of admiration, is the glowing center of this state of mind. (198-9)

St. Paul describes this peace: "And the peace of God, which passeth all understanding, shall keep your hearts and minds" (Phil. 4:7).

We proceed to the next step. The openness and freedom of the imagination can lead us to an enlarged awareness. Thankfulness can also lead in this direction in the following way. In expressing thankfulness, we are likely to be aware of that for which we are thankful: the gift of existence. It is fantastically remarkable that, in this universe of vast voids of space and mindless interactions of matter and energy, we have received the highly improbable gift of existence and consciousness.

Al: That's true, but it's unlikely people will have such a cosmic view of existence very often.

There is a helpful reminder. (I should note at this point that the orientation of this book does not include such concepts as "soul," "spirit," or reincarnation.) When we die, our state returns to the mindlessness of the elements. That is everyone's fate, either by cremation, by a chemical fixation of outward appearance, or by dispersion by worms and flowers. The awareness of life's termination may remind us of the uniqueness of the gift of life for each of us. A sense of wonder and an appreciation for life can be the natural consequences of the realization of life's improbability, tenuousness, and impermanence. Of course, these aspects of life might also be a source of cynicism and despair. There is no intervening force or agency that decides for us whether to be thankful for life or despairing of its brevity. Aside from differences in the quality of life flowing from the choice for an outlook of thankfulness or of despair, there is no measure that gives us direction in this choice. Therefore, I say that the choice for thankfulness is axiomatic. I have no *a priori* base from which to choose thankfulness. But I am grateful for existence, and I find the consequences of an outlook of thankfulness most satisfying. It brings me to a perspective on life that welcomes life. With thankfulness we are more likely to become open to the experiences of life. In the welcoming of the experiences of life, our outlook is likely to become enlarged, to encompass more than personal needs. With thankfulness our minds are likely to be less constricted into concerns of the self. Thankfulness takes us beyond self-centeredness. As such, thankfulness is a component of the religious outlook.

There is a reciprocal aspect to the awareness of a source of value beyond the self. The feeling of being of value to that which is beyond my self can nourish a feeling of affirmation, thereby enhancing my sense of wholeness. This is true even if the "that" referred to in the previous sentence is the gift of existence presented by the natural course of the universe. The "that" may be quite impersonal.

Al: "That" doesn't sound specific enough. I will ask again: thankfulness to whom? I don't believe there is a god; I don't have faith in a transcendental consciousness. In Chapter Twelve you even said there is no metaphysical significance of human life and no meaning of life beyond that which we create. To whom do you express thankfulness?

I'm glad you asked. The answer lies in music.

Al: I thought I was perplexed before. Now what do you mean? How does music enter the picture?

By way of words. Can you picture the music of a word?

Al: Well—the "music of a word:" I could easily think of some musical words. Anemone, for instance. Anemone sounds like a short, quick run of notes, not quite a trill. Then there's "department:" solid, deliberate notes. And a gentle flow of notes with "rhinorrhea."

Yes; the word "rhinorrhea" is much more melodic than its equivalent meaning: runny nose. Also, your musical imagination is impressive. However, let me stop you from going too far in that particular direction. The point is not about an attribution of musical sounds to words. I want to take up a different aspect of the relationship between music and a word.

Do you like to listen to symphonies?

Al: Yes; I like some symphonies.

Imagine listening to a symphony that you enjoy. The sound of the music fills your mind. The flow of the music fills your consciousness. And afterwards, when you return to the world of everyday life, the music may linger in your mind.

When we listen to music, our routine thoughts are surrendered to the flowing rhythm of sounds. We surrender ourselves to the music. The surrender to music gives us freedom because our consciousness is freed from pre-occupations and released into the flow of the immediate experience. This surrender is an open receptivity and is different from an act of the will; music is more appreciated when there is no will toward or mindfulness of the act of appreciating.

There are similar experiences in other areas of aesthetics. When we enjoy a painting or a piece of sculpture, we tend to surrender our train of thought to the flow of this enjoyment. We give up our direction, our concerns, and enter into the psychologic life of the work of art. For instance, we may feel a pulse of action when seeing the movement implied in a Rodin sculpture. We can sense the grace of a ballerina painted by Degas. Aesthetic experience draws us into a world that is beyond our usual conscious thoughts.

The Nature of a Religious Orientation

This brings us to the cosmic imagination. The imagination may be engaged in a vague sense of the universe, freely moving in an incorporeal and limitless space in unmeasured time. The imagination is not bounded by those mechanistic necessities which have been discovered by scientific method; the imagination is free from limitations.

In the cosmic imagination there may be projection of a "feel" for the totality of existence, an intuitive realization of all that exists. In freedom, the mind may encompass a vague comprehension of all existence. There is no barrier to the flow of the imagination and no restricting effect of objective discernment.

The freedom of the imagination teaches our Earth-bound selves. A surrender to the freedom of the cosmic imagination can release us from habituated thoughts. With freedom we can get beyond self-centered concerns and desires. Furthermore, when we are refreshed by the freedom of the imagination, it becomes easier to have a fresh perspective on those concerns. And our course may become enlightened by the freedom we receive from the cosmic imagination.

We now have the components for a religious outlook that is consonant with the criteria previously listed: openness, freedom, thankfulness, doubt, and imagination. These components are interrelated. Openness implies freedom, a freedom to be open. Thankfulness inclines a person toward the openness of an outlook that welcomes and appreciates life's experiences. The freedom of the cosmic imagination is likely to foster an orientation of openness. And openness includes a willingness to doubt.

The content of a religious outlook will be considered further in the next section. However, at this point, let's look again at the criteria for a religious orientation:

1. Content which is beyond personal needs and desires,

2. The establishment or confirmation of that which is of fundamental value for the individual,

3. That which is not invalidated by reasonable examination and doubt.

GOD, MUSIC, AND FREEDOM

Now we can be more definitive in the way we tie together the components of a religious outlook. This correlation will be found to fulfill the need for an emotional commitment that establishes the value which remains valid when subjected to examination and doubt. In fact, a valid religious orientation should incorporate the capacity for doubt if an openness to truth is to be maintained.

Much of our life is spent in communication with others. Almost all of us have a marked inclination to communicate. Therefore, when we express thankfulness, it seems natural that there be some recipient of this communication of thankfulness. The recipient of thankfulness may be said to be a projection of the imagination which we call "God." The awareness of God is a manifestation of the cosmic imagination. God's characteristics are not bounded by the limitations that are observed in natural phenomena. In the awareness of God, we do not delineate measurable features. In centering on God, our minds become free to experience that which we leave undefinable and inexpressible. We experience freedom in the mindfulness of God as a manifestation of the cosmic imagination. A mindfulness of God can draw us into the freedom of the cosmic imagination much like music can draw us into its rhythm and melody. This is the "music effect" of the word "God."

Also, I have found that—within myself and apparently within others—the experience of such freedom brings joy and peace. I can't explain the psychologic mechanism for the experience of joy and peace when the mind is centered on God. However, I suspect that the expansive sense of the freedom of the cosmic imagination is a major factor leading to joy and peace. The experience of an unlimited freedom of the mind is a likely valid source for positive psychologic effects.

Since the awareness of God is recognized as a subjective projection of the imagination, there is no objective claim to be defended. Doubt and examination do not invalidate the realization of God as a subjective creation. But there is an objective connection. God does not exist merely as a mental projection. That which is experienced as God in the cosmic imagination correlates with the reality of all existence. God of the cosmic imagination is pantheistic; the word-symbol "God" represents the imaginative abstraction which includes all that exists.

We do not pin down some feature of the natural universe and say that is God. We leave more definitive explanations aside when we say that all existence is God.

Also, when I say that all existence is God, I do not mean thereby to imply that all existence is unified. I do not envision any sort of grand spiritual or metaphysical scheme. Although there are interrelationships, each entity has its own existence; each life has its own initiative.

The concept of God as pantheistic is a subjective, mental projection that places the word-symbol god in a context of the natural world. This view serves the purpose of tying together the concept of God as an expression of the cosmic imagination with the view of God as representing the reality of existence. But there is another dimension to God conceived as pantheistic. There is the reality of our lives and a thankfulness for this reality of life. The forces and events of nature have combined in literally countless ways to give us life. With thankfulness we gratefully receive life. God—pantheistic God, the natural world—has given us life. For this we are thankful.

I believe many would agree that a belief in God can fulfill the realization of a source to establish value which is not consequent to a person's own initiative. In the context presented in this book, God is not a transcendental consciousness; he is a projection of the mind. It could, therefore, be considered that such a concept does not fit these criteria in that mental activity originates in the self. However, there is an external source which supports the sense of value, an external source which can be visualized as extending to the universal level. Our existence is not consequent to our own initiative; we did not create our selves. Life is a gift, a result of the fortuitous confluence of many factors in the course of the existence of the universe. If God is viewed as the imaginative representation of the course of the universe, we can realize that the centering of the mind on God so conceived does fulfill the need for commitment to a source of value which is not consequent to our own initiative.

Let's look at the second aspect of a commitment to God: the support of a source of value. This aspect is also affected by the concept of God as representing the nature of the universe. It is by the fortuitous nature of the universe that we live. We have received life; in the amazing turmoils and upheavals of the billions of years of existence of the universe, it is our good fortune to have the gift of awareness, consciousness, sight, hearing, movement, and all the capabilities which together we call life. For this life we are thankful.

The experience of thankfulness implics a feeling of emotion, and the realization of thankfulness provides an emotional content that establishes fundamental value. I express thankfulness not only for the gift of life. I show gratitude for health and good fortune. And I express gratitude for the particular nature of my existence; I am thankful for my physical and mental abilities. The capacity for openness, for freedom, for discernment: for these I am thankful. In turn, the thankfulness which I show for these gifts provides me with a welcoming outlook toward life. This thankfulness has a positive emotional content that implies value, and the value afforded by thankfulness tends to draw one into a welcoming of experience and to empathy with others.

Furthermore, fundamental value derived from a feeling of thankfulness can provide that self-esteem which is not a product of vanity or of self-enhancement above others. The self-esteem that is associated with thankfulness is the consequence of a mental orientation that encompasses the wonder of existence and gratitude for existence. The self-esteem derived from thankfulness is incidental to—and a result of—the process of showing thankfulness. Self-esteem by this route is not as likely to be manifested as self-righteousness.

God as pantheistic and God as an expression of the cosmic imagination are both mental projections. It is possible to realize the benefits of thankfulness, openness, and freedom of the cosmic imagination without recourse to the use of a word-symbol such as god. But there is value in having a readily available focus that will call forth thankfulness, openness, and freedom. The efficacy of the god-symbol as a focus will be discussed in Chapter Twenty-one.

REVIEW

We started this chapter with a poem about an insect. The poem can be interpreted as a message about the welcoming of life. This positive valuing of life is a prime aspect of religion.

The essence of religious practice is commonly considered to be centered on faith in some ordinarily unbelievable doctrine. Although the presentation of doctrine is important for religious practice, a broader view of the nature of a religious outlook has been described in this chapter. The function of religion may be understood as a commitment to fundamental value, a value that transcends temporal needs and desires. Such value is consistent with an enlarged awareness that draws a person beyond self-centeredness.

That fundamental value to which a person can be committed is integrity, and integrity includes certain qualities: openness, freedom, thankfulness, doubt, empathy, responsibility. In its multifaceted nature, integrity is the fundamental value that may be considered as the essence of religion. In addition, the access to fundamental value may be aided by the centering on a spiritual focus. Such spiritual focus can facilitate the expression of openness, freedom, empathy, and thankfulness. Furthermore, the characteristic qualities of integrity, together with an experience of the cosmic imagination (manifested as the God-symbol or other spiritual focus) can release a person from the narrowness of excessive self- absorption. Such release from self-absorption is not meant to imply a denial of responsibility.

There is a relationship between a release from excess concern about mundane problems and the imagination. The means to focus beyond the self is available in the ambiguous workings of the cosmic imagination. A person experiencing the cosmic imagination can enter into spiritual life with openness and freedom. This freedom may afford relief from constricting thoughts.

Note was made of potential pitfalls resulting from religious idealism, and it is recognized that an openness to doubt can place a religious orientation on a more firm basis. Since value implies an emotional dimension, the emotion that accompanies a religious practice should be balanced by an openness to doubt and examination. Moreover, as a vague abstraction—God as the symbolic representation of the nature of the universe—there is no claim of objective validity for this concept of God. Such understanding of God is not invalidated by doubt and examination.

With an openness to doubt, the pitfalls of self-righteousness and narrowed idealism may be avoided. A more valid foundation for self-esteem is the experience of wonder and thankfulness for the gifts of existence and fortune.

20

Soft

Al: Break time.

I know. I was looking out the window of my mind.

Al: You saw another poem?

I saw "Soft":

Soft
The rain descends
Past fir branches
Into the ground
Into small rivers—
    softly
        flows,
   uncovering
        grave sites
That flow
And fade
And disappear
Into
    the fog

PART IV

BRINGING IT ALL TOGETHER

21

The Value of Continuity

The Sense of Community
Interpersonal Relationships and Continuity
A Defective Tool of Enormous Value
Individual Continuity and Religious Practice
Continuity and Humanism
Review

THE SENSE OF COMMUNITY

In this country we place great value on freedom and individualism. With this individualism, many who are inclined toward a state of rebellion tend to look down upon and even to deride the continuity of the structures and practices of society, whether in particular instances such derision is justified or not. Autonomy is a treasured ideal, a manifestation of American individualism and freedom. Many express themselves in an orientation of freedom and each has their own individual rights. We are not "we" but a group of "I"s. And hardly a group at that; just individuals in the same location, each one alone in his and her freedom.

Consider the increased emphasis on individualism at the level of family life. Although married life is an actuality or is sought by many, for large numbers of people marriage has become a quaint memory. The concept of family size and the scope of interaction of family members are both more limited.

For many, society is something from which to be alienated. In fact, I believe the anti-government, anti-religious tone of a major segment of the population is as much a vehicle for the manifestation of a sense of rebellion as it is an expression of specific disagreement with practices and beliefs.

And how do we individuals fare? Many of us have lost a sense of community. Many have a mood of cynical doubt toward group enterprises and toward other individuals. Our traditional external sources of meaning are in retreat. In this country there has been widespread erosion of traditional respect for the authority of church and government. We have talked about some of the more obvious causes for this erosion of traditional respect. The triumphs of scientific method have unlocked a multitude of nature's secrets and predisposed the world outlook toward the direction of doubt and investigation. The mood of doubt tends to replace—or at least, to qualify—the sense of awe and wonder, which are springboards to the spiritual life. Also, the pre-eminence of doubt and discernment in the utilization of scientific method runs counter to faith, which is the usual basis for religious truth. More directly, the findings and orientation of science cast doubt on the tenets of much of religious doctrine.

The sense of community is also affected by the advances in communication. In Chapter Eight we discussed the effects of television and the increased consumerism that promote self-absorption.

Let me draw your attention to one of the more insidious forces that has had the effect of turning people away from the established authority of social and institutional arrangements of larger groups and toward an attitude of self-centeredness. This subtle effect was caused by the massive movement from an agriculture-based economy to an industrial and then to the service and communication-oriented economy we have today. The shift in the nature of the economy tended to draw people into an inward-looking orientation, a self-centeredness. I quote *The Power of Place* by journalist Winifred Gallagher:

> Around the turn of the twentieth century, the wisdom of the ages concerning the relationship between place and state was eclipsed by technological and cultural changes so rapid and vast that social scientists still debate our ability to adjust to them. In one of the least remarked of these transformations, the Industrial Revolution drew the West indoors.... Just as society began to measure time by its own doings rather than nature's, individuals increasingly looked inward rather than outward for insights into their behavior. (13-4)

The shift from an agriculture-based economy increased a corresponding shift in mental outlook away from "How are the powers of nature affecting me?" to "How do I create the conditions of my life?" Outward-looking shifted more toward inward-looking.

I have pointed to the shift of a large segment of population from farming to communication-oriented work in offices and other current occupations. In addition, other object-centered skills have been replaced by word-centered skills. Horse-shoeing, blacksmithing, carriage-making, ice-hauling—a long list—are, for the most part, things of the past. Such shift to word-centered skills has a parallel effect in diminishing that outward-looking orientation which tends to occur with awareness of concrete objects rather than word abstractions. The shift from occupations that center on concrete objects tends to lessen a general mental outlook toward the objective realities of the world. By default the mind becomes more inward-looking.

We have discussed the general mood of doubt and pointed to factors that predispose toward looking inward and self-centeredness. Self-absorption and doubt have led to a widespread distrust of interpersonal relationships. Self-centeredness is an attitude that opposes the tendency toward interaction with others.

I will present an overstatement as an extreme characterization of modern life:

Overstatement, but With Some Truth

Man and woman are fundamentally alone. They should live in a jungle, apart from each other except when together long enough to procreate, assuming that human life should be maintained and not become extinct. This aloneness is the view toward which the nation is heading: freedom of the individual, each person for himself or herself and no one else counts. Identity is directed toward individual freedom and self-absorption. Identity is directed away from involvement with other individuals and groups except in structured ways that maintain the relationships as collections of individuals who are free to disassociate whenever the urge calls.

But then, is that a fulfillment of what we are really like? Is loneliness an acceptable price for this degree of freedom? Is the threat of anarchy, the breakdown of social, political, and economic life, worth this amount of freedom? And how many people will the jungle support, each gathering an individual food supply and protecting it. Perhaps individuals would form into protective groups, and then we have tribal warfare, in which case, if there is access to modern weapons, all life would probably be quickly destroyed.

This is an extreme outlook. I'm just pointing out the general direction in which many are going. Not everyone; just a general trend which describes the emptiness and loneliness that comes with total freedom and extreme individualism. And there is the distant threat of anarchy.

The Value of Continuity

In contrast to an excess mindfulness of individualism, a sense of identity with a source outside of the self can be seen to have value. I live in Oregon. I am an Oregonian. For me this is definitely valuable. I have three great sons. My family is valuable.

In having sources of value outside of myself, I sense a value of my self. Connectedness tends to enhance a person's own sense of value.

Everyday interactions are characterized by a diversity of relationships, such as between customer and vendor, employer and employer, staff worker and manager, parent and child. That variety in the form of relationships contrasts with experiences held in a common relationship or role. However, whether experiences embody diverse roles of interpersonal relationships or experiences shared in common roles, they may provide a sense of shared identity and a sense of community.

Location is also a factor in shared identity. A neighborhood, city, region, state, nation: these may be a source of communal spirit. There are many other possible sources for shared identity, such as those involving the work group, interest group, culture, etc.

I will have to say that, for some, the feeling of estrangement from the community may fulfill a desire for emotional experience. There may be a certain emotional fulfillment in experiencing the sorrow of longing for that which is not. In *Under Milkwood* Dylan Thomas expresses the joy in experiencing life in a Welsh town. His poem may be interpreted to include a measure of sorrow in the realization of his longing to be fully a part of this life and knowing that he could not. In addition to the fulfillment of a desire for the emotion of longing, the poem by Thomas does highlight the value of a sense of community.

We have discussed some of the sources leading toward a sense of community. Another source that can strengthen the sense of community is a tenor of interpersonal civility. A general mood of mutual respect can strengthen that which can be called the interpersonal fabric of value.

Let's turn now to look at the role of religious practice as a source of the sense of community. The sharing of a particular religious practice can be a source for the establishment and maintenance of a sense of community. When the individuals of a group sense a common spiritual awareness, there is group reinforcement of that awareness. This promotes a sense of community in that each person has some degree of a sense of congruence of experience with others.

Identity through religious expression with a larger group is described by Dewart:

> Worship might be better understood as the rendering of ourselves present to the presence of God, whether in the interior prayer which sends no message to God but which receives his presence, or in the public and common ceremonies which visibly, audibly and sensibly unite us through our collective presence to each other in the presence of the present God. (206)

Group identity through religious practice is also discussed by Armstrong when she refers to Muslim practice: "As they converge on the Kabah, clad in the traditional pilgrim dress that obliterates all distinctions of race or class, they feel that they have been liberated from the egotistic preoccupations of their daily lives and been caught up into a community that has one focus and orientation" (156).

Another aspect of group identity through religious practice is the degree of integrity expected to be held by others committed to the same religious practice. When one believes in the integrity of others in the group, there can be a sense of mutual trust and mutual confidence, and this is a possible source for community spirit. In religious practice, the freedom from self-centeredness and the commitment to prime values are both features of integrity that can be sensed at a community level.

There is an additional factor of religious practice as a source of a sense of community: the history of the religious group. By providing continuity with the past, the awareness of group history tends to extend the communal spirit. For example, the knowledge of Jewish history enhances a Jewish communal spirit.

In general, religious practice takes place in a mode of continuity. An individual may pray at regular intervals. There are ongoing group arrangements for religious services. In the case of the major religions, continuity is manifested by large organizations, large buildings, and long-established beliefs and practices.

Of course, again, there are the *caveats* regarding the sense of community. The spirit of community may promote an idealism that leads to self-righteousness, exclusiveness, and intolerance of others. We have talked about this in previous chapters. Additionally, this exclusiveness can lead to psychological and even physical withdrawal of a religious group or other groups from the larger community. Referral is made to this group isolation in *Habits of the Heart*, by Robert N. Bellah et. al.: "The sectarian church sees itself as the gathered elect and focusses on the purity of those within as opposed to the sinfulness of those without .... It is tempted toward a radical withdrawal from the environing society ... " (244-5).

Another concern, not only for religious groups but for groups in general, is the balance of social and individual needs. In order for there to be a sense of community, there is a need for group identity and continuity. The workings and attitudes of the community must, however, recognize individual concerns and needs that may not be entirely congruent with those of the community. Individuals and groups must work toward a reasonable balance between opposing needs.

INTERPERSONAL RELATIONSHIPS AND CONTINUITY

We have considered the character of relationships in the larger community. Now let's look at some of the problems in personal relationships. Self-absorption and doubt can lead to a widespread distrust of interpersonal relationships. Self-centeredness is an attitude that opposes the tendency toward interaction with others. On the other hand, an active and affirming interplay of communication between individuals tends to enhance the mutual sense of value.

These interactions may be considered as expressions of a natural process. During a discussion of the subject of ethics, Hick points to the concept of personal interaction being a natural tendency. In doing so, he adds that the idea of natural interaction is valid whether there is a religious or non-religious outlook:

> Ethics, I suggest, is grounded in this *de facto* character of human nature as essentially inter-personal, in virtue of which we have a deep need for one another and feel (in many different degrees) a natural tendency to mutual sympathy. Morality is accordingly a dimension of this realm of personal interactions .... For the view of ethics as grounded in the structure of human nature is capable of being incorporated into either a religious or a naturalistic world-view.... On either view it is the aspect of our nature which generates the invisible dimension of moral value. This dimension is hospitable to a religious interpretation; but it is nevertheless not incompatible with a non-religious interpretation. (98-9)

Myers makes a point about social interaction that is noteworthy:

Observing others' faces, postures, and voices, we unconsciously mimic their moment-to-moment reactions. We synchronize our movements, postures, and tones of voice with theirs. Doing so helps us tune in to what they're feeling. It also makes for "emotional contagion," which helps explain why it usually is fun to be around happy people and depressing to be around depressed people. (126)

The converse of this observation is that the mood which we project may well be picked up by others. We are not necessarily puppets who mirror the emotions of those with whom we are in contact. In contradistinction to that, a happiness and contentment which we might express may positively affect others.

We now turn to the subject of value in close interpersonal relationships. There are a number of reasons for an attraction to a "significant other." Besides companionship, affection, and sex, there is a need to feel that one has some significance to another beyond immediate needs. This can be clearly realized if an awareness arises of the loss of being valued by another person. The realization of an absence of one's significance to another can be startling when there is a loss of that other person, particularly when the loss is sudden.

A sense of responsibility to those with whom we are in a close relationship carries that relationship through periods of ups and downs. This continuity in a relationship is likely to enhance a mutual sense of value. Loyalty to a relationship through a period of time provides a range of interaction in varying circumstances. Such a range of expression can enlarge the understanding and awareness of the character of each other's lives. It makes for a more fulfilling relationship.

At times it is right to break a relationship. Personal integrity helps to guide a person in this situation by allowing an openness to understanding the realities of the relationship and acting responsibly.

In an ideal partnership there is mutual bestowing of value. However, when there is an excess dependence on returned value, the relationship may become eroded. The person toward which excessive dependence is projected may feel stifled by being subjected to excess need.

There is another drawback to excess dependence on value by another. A person may be resentful of having a sense of worth that is excessively dependent on the approval of a spouse or "significant other." That person is more likely to ascribe anger to actions or words of the other when anger is not intended. This can be a source of interpersonal conflict.

The Value of Continuity

It is well to avoid excessive emotional dependence as this may engender resentment and strife. Excessive dependence is likely to be lessened when the need for reciprocal value is held more lightheartedly. Also, there may be a more valid perception of an interpersonal relationship when there are those types of alternative sources of value which may enhance the value of the primary interpersonal relationship. One such source is the sense of community. For example, in small towns that have a sense of community, value by others is an alternate source of worth that can release a person from excess centering on the partner.

Let's consider another alternate source of value that can ease an excessive focussing of attention on another person. In the spiritual realm, the centering of attention on God can afford a lightheartedness in interpersonal relationships. A full commitment to the relationship is more likely to be without the overbearing quality of excess need when God is first.

Not only does the primacy of attention to God tend to mitigate over-emphasized need; if there is an excess desire for freedom from responsibility and dependability, the centering on God can provide an outlook of thankfulness and empathy. The qualities of thankfulness and empathy can lead a person to a positive outlook and an openness that allows perceptiveness. With openness and perceptiveness, it becomes easier and seems more natural to have an inclination to respect the needs of the partner and to fulfill responsibilities.

There is another aspect of the effect of a spiritual outlook on interpersonal relationships: an independent sense of self-worth. When we regard the concept of God as representing the course of nature, we can say that it is by this course of nature that we exist; our lives are a gift from God. Furthermore, my sense of self-worth is confirmed by the fact that I exist. An awareness of God's gift of existence confirms my worth. This confirmation of self-worth, which is founded on the value of thankfulness for existence, can facilitate social interaction by allowing a full sense of self to interact with others. By that I mean that interaction becomes more likely to take place without the possible feeling of self-degradation that might have arisen from a mindfulness of inadequacies or from prior problems. Myers discusses this in terms of an anthropomorphic god, the Christian god:

> No longer is there any need to define our self-worth solely by our achievements, material well-being, or social approval. To find self-acceptance we needn't be or do anything. We need simply to accept that we are, ultimately and unconditionally, accepted. People who have this idea of God—as loving, accepting,

caring—tend to enjoy greater self-esteem .... There is, it seems, an interplay between our God-concept and our self-concept, our personal theology and our psychology. (192)

A DEFECTIVE TOOL OF ENORMOUS VALUE

We have talked about relationships between people at the personal and the community levels. Interpersonal relationships are facilitated by certain characteristics that involve continuity. Furthermore, continuity is one of the qualities involved in the expression of loyalty, responsibility, and of the sense of community. In these areas continuity means that there is a carryover of thought and behavior beyond the immediacy of the moment.

It is now time to take up the topic of the prime tool of continuity. Not only is it a prime tool; it is also a defective tool. We wouldn't be without it, but we fall prey to its pitfalls.

This tool that is enormously valuable is language. Language can be considered a tool, an invention that furthers our aims, created by mankind for various uses. The uses of words as tools can be advantageous or they can be destructive, just as the use of a hammer or atomic power can be helpful or destructive.

The development of language is the most significant invention of humanity, affecting the course of human events even more than the development of machines or agriculture. It is true that the character of life has changed drastically with the creation and development of machines that utilize physical and chemical properties of materials, electricity, and electronics. Such change in the way of life has accelerated dramatically since the initiation of the Industrial Revolution with the development of the steam engine by James Watt in the latter part of the Eighteenth Century.

Furthermore, if there had not been the development of agriculture—which allowed the increase of numbers of people and their concentration into population centers—it is very probable that the human population would have remained very sparse, primarily as nomadic hunters and gatherers. I can add that the emergence of agricultural practices and the development of arrangements for food storage and distribution undoubtedly contributed to a broadening of the range of language. Tallies needed to be kept and some manner of contracts recorded.

As significant as the development of agriculture and machines have been, the creation of language has been more significant in affecting the nature of man's life. Without language, agriculture and machines either would not have been developed at all or would have been developed to a very limited degree. Language is the primary means of communicating any sort of information between people: scientific, technological; any sort of concepts. In the realm of personal interaction, language gives us the means to communicate information such as impending dangers, good fortune, or whatever. I will mention as an aside that non-verbal communication is also important.

Al: Everybody knows that.

Yes. I know. I added it for completeness and to see if you would have a comment about it.

As I stated, a tool can be used constructively or destructively. A hammer can be used to smash car windows or to build a house. Likewise, as a tool—a means for communication—language also has its downside. There are problems intrinsic to the nature of language. First, word meanings and usage are easily distorted. Slogans, propaganda, and all sorts of distortions are perpetrated by the means of language.

Not only is there a downside of language as a means of communication. The use of language creates a drawback within the individual mind. It gets in the way of direct perception. Our minds are accustomed to framing as verbal expression that to which the consciousness is exposed. As we act and interact in the everyday world, a corresponding stream of words runs a course in our minds. Even when we don't openly verbalize these words, the course of words symbolizes and summarizes our perceptions and thoughts. In doing so, the condensing efficiency of our minds has the effect of allowing us to lose sight of much that might have been more clearly seen if language were not a habit of the mind. As abstract tools that abbreviate the awareness of reality, word-symbols tend to diminish the realization of that reality.

Consider an example: a person looks at the moon. The word-symbol "moon" occurs to him or her. At that point—unless the consciousness is directed to focus on the moon—the mind tends to wander into its next thought. In this process the perception of the moon usually diminishes. I believe the stream of consciousness will tend to follow the pattern of language that flows in our minds.

The condensing action of language is often valuable for productivity, but it is a disadvantage when clear perceptiveness would enlarge our

God Unmasked; the Full Life Revealed

understanding. For example, for most people, being hit on the head by a falling apple would not mean much. The event could be quickly synopsized with a few words, some of which might be unpleasant. But Isaac Newton took a fresh look at that event, and that allowed him to develop a more profound understanding of nature. Whether truth or fable regarding the development of the Theory of Gravity, this example illustrates the point that fresh perceptiveness avoids the condensing effect of language on our minds.

In the course of interpersonal relationships, direct perceptiveness is very valuable. With empathy, we become better able to comprehend the feelings and the effects of the attitudes of others. That is why, even though we use the tool of language, it can be valuable to hold language in abeyance. Although we use the symbolizing, condensing effect of language, it is well to have the ability to get beyond words in order to experience empathy and direct perception. If human interaction includes a pulse of perceptiveness, that interaction tends to be more satisfactory and satisfying. The ability to empathize greatly enlarges the breadth of interaction.

Of course, the use of language is highly valuable, in spite of drawbacks. Language is the coinage for the "economy of the mind." Communication between people bridges experiences, attitudes, and aims; language is a prime resource for social continuity.

This is a good time to mention education of the young. Individuals come into existence without the information that others have learned. Aside from cynics who may find no value in anything, most of us want to have knowledge transmitted to youngsters. The continuity facilitated by language carries the findings and value of human experience forward to future generations.

INDIVIDUAL CONTINUITY AND RELIGIOUS PRACTICE

Regarding any relationship, source of identity, belief, or need, there tends to be a natural decay of mindfulness of a subject when not periodically exposed to it. The use of words is a means of renewing awareness of those things for which we choose to maintain a consciousness. As noted above, words are the psychological coinage of our continuity; words provide an "economy of the mind" which can facilitate an access to that which we would mentally renew.

Any sort of need may be quickly brought to consciousness by a word. The words "breakfast" or "grapefruit juice" are handy symbols for creating awareness of the corresponding realities. A multitude of similar symbols facilitates our ability to manage thoughts, actions, and interactions.

Let's take a look at the need for continuity in the spiritual realm. We have talked about the value of thankfulness for the gift of existence and also about wonder for and awe of the marvelous processes of existence. In the course of life's problems, the joy of wonder and the positive fulfillment of thankfulness can be easily forgotten. Also, life and good health can quickly become taken for granted. If a sense of wonder and thankfulness is missing, a person may more likely be shadowed by a cloud of unhappiness or lack of contentment. For instance, the course of life may proceed at a subdued, mechanical pace; even bitterness and cynicism might lurk in the mental shadows if there is not some continuing, periodic spiritual endeavor. A pattern of religious practice can spark a recurring call to a spiritual outlook.

Spirituality is possible without a god-symbol. As Armstrong says: "Humanism is itself a religion without God—not all religions, of course, are theistic. Our ethical secular ideal has its own disciplines of mind and heart and gives people the means of finding faith in the ultimate meaning of human life that were once provided by the more conventional religions" (*xix*).

It is possible to speculate that Camus considered the mythologic character Sisyphus as spiritually fulfilled without the need for a god-symbol when he said:

> I leave Sisyphus at the foot of the mountain! One always finds one's burden again. But Sisyphus teaches the higher fidelity that negates the gods and raises rocks. He too concludes that all is well. This universe henceforth without a master seems to him neither sterile nor futile. Each atom of that stone, each mineral flake of that night-filled mountain, in itself forms a world. And the struggle itself toward the heights is enough to fill a man's heart. One must imagine Sisyphus happy. (*Sisyphus* 91)

Though spiritual life may be fulfilled without a conception of God, the god-symbol does present a focus for spirituality. If founded on valid grounds, reinforced instead of negated by subjection to the processes of doubt and discernment, the concept of God need not be avoided.

Furthermore, this concept, the god-concept, has value as a focus for a number of reasons. The god-symbol serves the mind as a recipient of thankfulness. God is also a source for the wonder and awe that is experienced in the cosmic imagination.

In addition, the god-symbol is easily accessible, always readily available, an inexhaustible source, without extensive need for mental preparation and discipline. With facility, an awareness of God draws the mind into a cleared openness, freeing it from worldly concerns and filling it with the expansiveness of the cosmic imagination. The availability of awareness of God facilitates the fulfillment of life's recurring need for spiritual experience. Without a ready focus that activates the cosmic imagination, spiritual life may become less accessible.

Continuity of spiritual life may be facilitated by periodic prayer. Let's look at the act of prayer more closely. Prayer is communication with God. Webster's dictionary definition of prayer is: "an address to God or a god in word or thought." And to pray is: "to address God or a god with adoration, confession, supplication, or thankfulness."

In conjunction with prayer, there is likely to be a realization of the positive aspects of life. These positive aspects include a thankfulness for life and fortune and also praise for and wonder of the fact of existence. In addition, life may more likely be viewed in a positive light when there is a focus on God because of the sense of relief afforded by a mental release from difficult problems or from a feeling of guilt, releasing to the agency of larger forces. Of course, regarding the release from guilt, we have talked about the maintenance of responsibility earlier, and I do not mean to negate the need for personal responsibility.

This positive expression occurs as a mutual welcome. I welcome life, and I project that the universe welcomes me, even at those times when there may be problems. I project this welcome to God as a vague sense of the totality of the universe. This welcome by that which is characterized by the cosmic imagination is realized to be subjective, but there is an objective aspect to it, which I have indicated in previous passages and will reiterate. Such projection of welcome is enhanced by an appreciation for the objective fact of my personal existence and by an awareness of my gifts of health and good fortune.

When I say grace at mealtime, it is an expression of thankfulness that implies a realization of the precariousness of life. Also, regular prayer is a ritual that recreates my welcoming of the experiences of life.

A reminder of thankfulness occurs in the Old Testament: "Know ye that the Lord he is God: it is he that hath made us, and not we ourselves; we are his people, and the sheep of his pasture. Enter into his gates with thanksgiving, and into his courts with praise: be thankful unto him, and bless his name" (Ps. 100:3-4).

William James discusses the welcoming sense of joyful affirmation afforded by prayer:

> At bottom the whole concern of both morality and religion is with the manner of our acceptance of the universe .... Morality pure and simple accepts the law of the whole which it finds reigning, so far as to acknowledge and obey it, but it may obey it with the heaviest and coldest heart, and never cease to feel it is a yoke. But for religion, in its strong and fully developed manifestations, the service of the highest never is felt as a yoke. Dull submission is left far behind, and a mood of welcome, which may fill any place on the scale between cheerful serenity and enthusiastic gladness, has taken its place. It makes a tremendous emotional and practical difference to one whether one accepts the universe in the drab discolored way of stoic resignation to necessity, or with the passionate happiness of Christian saints. (49)

Prayer is also a vehicle for mind-clearing and openness, and this is one of the reasons for the positive effect of prayer. In this regard, Armstrong quotes the ancient Greek theologian Evagrius Pontus: " ... prayer means the shedding of thought" (221).

James also refers to the mind-clearing openness of prayer:

> So when one's affections keep in touch with the divinity of the world's authorship, fear and egotism fall away; and in the equanimity that follows, one finds in the hours, as they succeed each other, a series of purely benignant opportunities. It is as if all doors were opened, and all paths freshly smoothed. We meet a new world when we meet the old world in the spirit which this kind of prayer infuses (359).

Regardless of the validity of the particular content of a prayer, there is commonly an effect of prayer on those who pray. Prayer has an impact on the one who does the praying. James points out that, aside from any claim for truth of the content of prayer, there is objective validity of the effect of prayer:

> It may well prove that the sphere of influence in prayer is subjective exclusively, and that what is immediately changed is only the mind of the praying person. But however our opinion of prayer's effects may come to be limited by criticism, religion, in

the vital sense in which these lectures study it, must stand or fall by the persuasion that effects of some sort genuinely do occur. Through prayer, religion insists, things which cannot be realized in any other manner come about: energy which but for prayer would be bound is by prayer set free and operates in some part, be it objective or subjective, of the world of facts. (353)

CONTINUITY AND HUMANISM

Many times I have mentioned the horrors committed in the name of God. Also, I have described qualities of God-centeredness that may be called "ennobling." These ennobling qualities are personal characteristics that enhance a sense of integrity without feeding the destructiveness of self-righteousness.

There are many who lead a life of integrity without having a reference to a spiritual orientation. However, there remains a fund of civility in society which is buttressed by a centeredness on God. In the short run, I believe that a society permeated by humanism without God would work. A residual fund of civility would linger at some level in society. However, in the broad realm of society there is a wide range of personality types and an ongoing occurrence of various sorts of interpersonal conflict. In the flux of interpersonal interactions, I believe the fund of civility would gradually become eroded if there were a total loss of God-centeredness by society.

In spite of difficulties associated with the centeredness of a major segment of society upon God, I believe these problems are outweighed by a spiritual expression that emphasizes the qualities of integrity. The positive aspects of a focus on God have been presented in this book in a context that assumes there is no transcendental existence. I believe these same positive aspects are present to varying degrees in several forms of established religious practice. Such positive characteristics include the openness and freedom of the cosmic imagination. This openness may be carried over to an openness to new perspectives, fresh perceptiveness, and empathy. Also, as previously stated, the god-symbol is the readily available source toward which is directed the welcoming and affirmation of life in thankfulness.

These attributes of the centering on God are beneficial both to individuals and to society in general. There are some who champion a humanistic orientation that would abolish any reference to God. I believe humanists assume that the general tone of civility would not be at risk in the absence of God-centeredness by at least a part of society.

Without some level of commitment to God by a major segment of society, I can visualize the erosion of the general level of integrity in time as interpersonal conflicts predispose individuals to a general tone of self-concern and self-protection. Without some general societal inclination toward a centeredness beyond individual selves, I expect that self-concern would eventually dominate thought, and, in this situation, social structure would probably become eroded and likely would disintegrate.

There is an additional consideration: in the absence of a spiritual orientation that includes some degree of focus held in common, I believe that in time the impetus toward personal integrity would also tend to become eroded. As I indicated above, without a spiritual focus external to the self, individuals would likely become more self-contained and self-centered. Without a source of fundamental value external to the self, it is possible to become excessively absorbed in the agenda of the self. The personal sense of integrity would tend to diminish in reaction to the engulfing sea of self-centeredness and self-seeking unleashed by such a communal loss of God-centeredness. This tendency might possibly eventuate in the disruption of society, ending in anarchy.

Let's compare the effects of two different types of fundamental focus: that focus which has objective content and a focus so ambiguous that any objective content which might be ascribed to it is insubstantial. Consider alternates to a focus on God—perhaps "ecology" or "compassion." Any activity, goal, or orientation that has some objective content has the potential to become too intent and exclusively focussed to the extent that perceptiveness becomes narrowed. On the other hand, such a focus upon something objective may often become taken for granted. Conversely, a focus that has no constricting effect of objective content is less likely to cause a narrowed outlook. When there are no delineating qualities that might constrict the freedom of the mind, a focus on such an ambiguous entity can allow a free-ranging outlook that is open to an enlarged perspective. Such focus may provide a balance for a more true perspective on our activities and goals. A focus that is beyond any reasoning, thinking, or observing is freeing for the mind; it may give us a better perspective on any thing toward which we direct ourselves that has objective content. I believe this freedom of the ambiguous is what gives impetus to a spiritual endeavor, to the centering of attention on God or something equivalent to a god-symbol.

Of course, non-focussed, abstract sources that have a degree of objective definiteness (as opposed to the ambiguity of the god-symbol) might be enlisted to maintain personal integrity and the social fabric.

Al: Humanists are long on integrity.

Yes. They say: be responsible, have compassion, and ... all the good stuff. I believe these would eventually have limited effect.

A particular candidate for the role of a fundamental value is "love and compassion." But any outlook or orientation can be overdone. The mind can become fixed in a monotone of pre-programmed perception and responsiveness when directed on a prescribed path. A set-pattern of interaction may be inappropriate at times. When love is grounded in the spontaneity of the open, free mind, it tends to be more valid and less stereotyped. Furthermore, there should be freedom to adjust the mode of behavior according to the situation.

Also, in the course of most individual's lives, all may be brought into question. There is a phase of rebellion that most people experience at some time in their lives, and some remain in that state of rebellion. The rebellion is an aspect of freedom, toward which we are all drawn. Freedom is a prime quality of life, more fundamental than love.

Al: Well, then, is freedom a candidate for the prime motivation in life?

No, I would say not. When the impulse toward freedom becomes an obsession, it can be narrowing, diminishing other potential modes of interaction.

Al: Well, then, surely integrity, in its meaning as a fullness of life, would be a satisfactory candidate as a fundamental quality of life.

A commitment of the self to integrity is basic, but, for a full life, there is also a need to get beyond the self, beyond those thoughts that are centered on the self. We should realize that a commitment to integrity— if such commitment remains centered in the self— could degenerate into a self-righteousness pose. It is too readily possible for a person to become sold on the rightness of the self. Such a pose may narrow a person's vision and decrease the capacity for empathy.

Even if self-righteousness is not involved in a person's trust in their own integrity, an enlargement of outlook to include an awareness of a projected "other"—such as someone recently departed or an image of God—can be valuable. Of course, a *caveat* is that, if the "other" is God, the calling forth of a mindfulness of the projected "other" should be done without invoking a feeling of self-righteousness that might be established because of a commitment to that "other."

One of the values of an awareness of a projected "other" is that it can facilitate some degree of detachment from the concerns, needs, and desires of the self. This detachment may allow a more comprehensive view of the self and of the situation at hand. In addition, such detachment may possibly be facilitated and the perceptiveness of the self enhanced by a projection of how the "other" views the self.

Such mental projection of another also is an avenue to a sense of enlarged awareness. This enlarged awareness may nourish the freedom of the imagination, including the cosmic imagination. The enlarged world of the imagination becomes readily available when the word-symbol "God" is used by someone who is amenable to the use of that word. This can lead to experiencing those valuable characteristics of the imagination that we discussed in Chapters Four and Eleven, including a positive outlook on life, a sense of openness and freedom, and the joy in experiencing grandeur.

There are three particular types of individuals who, I expect, would not look to a spiritual focus as an aid for detachment. First are those for whom the inclination for detachment is a customary stance and for whom everything is tentative, doubted, and examined while trust and relaxation are held to a minimum. I will discuss a balance of doubt/examination and trust/relaxation in Chapter Twenty-two.

Another group who would not look to the spiritual as a source of help in detaching from an excessive centering on concerns are, of course, those who rebel against the expression of anything spiritual. Third are those who are in rebellion against anything that can be construed as a source of authority.

I will state a particular view of a life centered on God: a major aspect of the full life is the ability to project some type of ambiguous, freely imagined, idealized consciousness. Such a consciousness is recognized as a mental projection. Furthermore, such mental projection—typically understood as God—is seen to view us according to the responsibilities and joys of integrity.

There are many who don't care either way. They do not wave the idealistic banner of either the God-centered or humanist movements; many don't bother with a declared stance. However, I believe some of these have an understanding that a significant segment of society is God-centered. They rely on this understanding, realizing perhaps that it underpins social structure. Furthermore, of those without a declared stance, many incline themselves toward a level of personal integrity that might be viewed as consonant with a God-centered society. If there were not some level of general understanding that a significant part of society was God-centered, then, in the course of generations, I feel that the level of integrity would tend to become eroded as individuals became more individual-centered. And, at its extreme, the individual-centered society ends in anarchy.

Al: What we really need to do is test what you say: have two civilizations, one of which has a significant element of God-centeredness and the other having no awareness of God. Then we could see the ultimate consequences in a number of generations.

Yes. Of course, for your test, there could be no communication between the two civilizations. They would have to be on separate planets. I can just visualize the civilization without God twenty generations down the line: a few individuals viewing the perplexing, intriguing ruins of our current civilization—a lost Atlantis—incomprehensible to wandering, warring, stone-age tribes.

Al: Someone could say that both points of view—God-centeredness and an absense of an awareness of God—tend to evolve toward the same end, regardless of the initial orientation of a society.

That may be true. But for the purpose of some degree of comparison, we can at least conjecture what the outcomes might be.

REVIEW

There are several important aspects of the subject of continuity. Continuity may be manifested at the individual level, in interpersonal relationships, and at the level of society. At the social level, we have witnessed an erosion of the sense of community and social continuity. Such decrease of the sense of community correlates with a shift toward increased individual freedom and narrowed self-absorption.

At all levels—the larger community, interpersonal, and individual—there can be both value and drawbacks in the various expressions of religious practice. Group identity may be enhanced by religious practice, but exclusivism and narrowed idealism may result in destructive consequences.

At the interpersonal level, excessive self-absorption may be relieved or diminished by the religious focus that can put mundane concerns in perspective. Such release may allow a fuller mutual enjoyment and possibly facilitate the fulfillment of responsibilities.

The broad view of language confirms its enormous value and its potential for causing problems. At an individual level, the use of word-symbols in the spiritual realm can activate the freedom and openness of the cosmic imagination. Also, the use of the word-symbol God may recall or reinforce an outlook of thankfulness with its attendant sense of affirmation.

All three levels—community, interpersonal, and individual—may manifest an increased sense of continuity through the expression of spirituality. On the other hand, it is a concern that, in time and under the pressure of varying amounts of disagreement and conflict between varying types of individuals, a society which would be devoid of religious experience may possibly disintegrate. Such is the potential threat if humanism were to become a general outlook of humanity, universalized beyond the province of those humanists attuned to the value of integrity.

22

Minimizing the Maximum

The Cleared Mind
Doubt
The Focus on God
A Balance, Phases, and Trust

THE CLEARED MIND

Al: I am curious about the title of this chapter.

That's not surprising. I will start with a clear statement. I enjoy action. It's fun to run. Within limits, I enjoy pulling weeds.

Al: You won't catch me doing yard work.

Everyone has their own enjoyments. Different actions please different people. For some it may be the handling of playing cards. For others it may be skiing or sky-diving. Enjoyment fills the mind with the experience of that moment. There is joy in the experience of the immediate moment, without sidetracking into analysis, examination, or doubt. The mind is momentarily cleared of other thoughts, that is, until needs and responsibilities nag into view.

In fact, if and when responsibilities are accepted, we do well if we fulfill these responsibilities with clear-minded action. Once responsibility is accepted, mulling over that acceptance is counter-productive. When you accept a responsibility, just center your mind on it; don't question the responsibility without a significant reason. A clear-minded action, in completing the responsibility, is more fulfilling than regrets that cannot be satisfied.

Most of us enjoy experiences that clear the mind of momentary, extraneous thoughts. For instance, music has great power to envelop us and release us from thoughts that are unrelated to the mood of the music. Many activities that concentrate our focus also clear out other activities from our minds. For examples, games such as chess or basketball do a good job of clearing other thoughts from the mind.

Some activities tend to be addicting, partly because their concentrated mental focus clears the mind of other thoughts. For example: television-watching or playing slot machines.

On an opposite tack, for many of us, doubt—when in association with cogitation and analysis—is often a fulfillment, either in work or as avocation. In this setting, doubt is a welcome asset rather than a detriment. I would not try to detract from the employment of doubt when it is used as a source of fulfillment. A mind cleared of cogitation, in association with doubt and examination, certainly is not and need not be sought by all or at all times. There are pleasures of cogitation, realizing correlations such as those involved in scientific investigation, reading or viewing mystery stories, games, and the like. In addition, the utilization of doubt is valuable for problem-solving when doubt is employed in a constructive mode.

However, the experience of doubt and uncertainty often is accompanied by some measure of distress. Doubt can be disruptive of that calm which occurs with a cleared mind. Often there is concern about unsettled questions, and the possible solutions may raise more doubts than answers. Particularly, in the face of serious illness or catastrophe, fundamental values and meaning may be questioned. With concern about fundamental values, an ongoing state of doubt can make the cleared mind unattainable.

The impetus toward having a cleared mind is a theme that runs through the work of Nietzsche. I believe that Nietzsche considered empathy as a constraint on a free, clear mind. He rebelled against a feeling of compassion. We talked about this in Chapter Seven.

There is a different way to view the relationship between a cleared mind and empathy. A cleared mind can be considered as a substrate for an openness to fresh perception and empathy. The cleared mind can allow receptivity to fresh perceptiveness.

Now we can consider word-symbols in relation to the cleared-mind state. Word-symbols can be a source for either mind-clearing or mind-obfuscation, depending on how they are used. Words as such can cloud the mind in confusion and anguish. For instance, a fear of spiders may be increased by an overactive response to a recall of the word "spider."

On the other hand, focussing on word-symbols as slogans can lead to a mind-clearing state—a psychological state which is the opposite of mental obfuscation. I make this statement regarding mental activity alone, aside from the objective accuracy of slogans. Slogans often employ words that characterize a condensed view of something. As slogans, they tend to by-pass objective fact in favor of an emotionally committed attitude. When the mind moves in the direction of a clarity of abbreviated thoughts, word-symbols as slogans reinforce the tendency for mind-clearing.

Let's talk about identity in relation to the cleared mind. One of the facets of a sense of identity is in the employment of words that provide a feeling of personal affirmation by making a declaration of either the location, vocation, attitudes, or activities for which a person stands. Certain sources of identity which are valued have the effect of conferring value back upon the one who expresses the value.

For example, I am an Oregonian, a Northwesterner, an American, and I value my identity as such.

Some people sneer at that. Proud to be an American? That's a "No" for some. They may be in rebellion against anything that implies pride. They are proud of their anti-pride identity.

Self-identity is one benefit of a cleared mind. The word-symbols of self-identity may have been examined at some point in time and then accepted without a resort to continuous questioning. However, it is characteristic for self-identity symbols to trigger unexamined stances, short-cuts to the joy of an uncluttered mind. The word-symbols of self-identity seem to have a life of their own, apart from the circumstances in which they are expressed. For example, I know someone who took great pride in informing others that she was a sixth generation Oregonian. Second thoughts about that statement of identity occurred after she had declared it to someone with a much longer duration of identity in the region, a Native American.

Al: Someone probably laughed at that. But, are you implying that we should not use words for things which give us a pride of self-identity? Are you saying that we should remain in a state of constant examination of everything?

No. Examination and discernment as constant, unending processes would be burdensome. Instead, I am all for maximizing the cleared mind, but not at the price of a loss of openness to insight, understanding, and truth. It is well to point out that the cleared mind is more valuable when combined with an access to doubt and discernment.

Minimizing the Maximum

A narrowed mental outlook occurs if an openness to new perception and understanding is avoided. One could say that freedom from new thoughts and new understanding may seem to be a way to maintain the cleared mind, but this concept of freedom is constricting. It crowds the cleared mind and makes it less clear than it would be with an openness to new information, no matter how unsettling that might be. Openness to new information may trigger questioning and doubt, but these are indispensable for obtaining an approximation of truth. The willingness to consider new thought and understanding is essential for maintaining an outlook that does not avoid truth.

Al: How many times have you made that sort of statement?

I don't know. I repeat it in different contexts. Let's get back to the subject of identity. The openness to new understanding can be operative in the area of self-identity. The continuing openness to truth does not mean that there should be no settled sources of identity. These sources of self-identity may provide a sense of personal affirmation and orientation to people and circumstances. However, to avoid a constricted outlook, the sense of self-identity should be secondary and subordinate. Self-identity should be secondary to openness. The free, spontaneous, cleared mind that is open to truth: this is primary. Openness of the mind should generally take precedence over the affirmation of a sense of self-identity.

There are several sources for mind-clearing. Aside from particulars of the situations, a prime impetus for taking up and involving the self in these sources is, in fact, the mind-clearing effect they produce. I mean by the term "mind-clearing" the state of filling it with non-critical experience, free from agitation and doubt. Several sources have a mind-clearing effect: action, music, games, addictions, and word-symbols as slogans and sources of identity (such as location, vocation, and avocation). Also, as indicated, the tendency to avoid empathy can be viewed by some as an effort to keep the mind cleared.

Certainly, the inclination to avoid doubt and uncertainty is enhanced by a desire for a blankness of mind, a cleared mental state that doesn't require mulling over and endless examination. The uncritical acceptance of authority is another example of the manifestation of a non-discerning mental state. An example would be the mentally-blinded followers in a religious cult.

Joseph Conrad comments on the uncritical acceptance of authority in describing the central figure in his book, *Lord Jim*:

He stood there for all the parentage of his kind, for men and women by no means clever or amusing, but whose very existence is based upon honest faith, and upon the instinct of courage. I don't mean military courage, or civil courage, or any special kind of courage. I mean just that inborn ability to look temptations straight in the face—a readiness unintellectual enough, goodness knows, but without pose—a power of resistance, don't you see, ungracious if you like, but priceless—an unthinking and blessed stiffness before the outward and inward terrors, before the might of nature, and the seductive corruption of men—backed by a faith invulnerable to the strength of facts, to the contagion of example, to the solicitation of ideas. Hang ideas! They are tramps, vagabonds, knocking at the backdoor of your mind, each taking a little of your substance, each carrying away some crumb of that belief in a few simple notions you must cling to if you want to live decently and would like to die easy! (50-1)

In the opposite direction, there may be a rebellion against authority. This rebellion may occur as unreasoned behavior in an antagonistic mode. Such rebellion would then be founded on a preprogrammed mind-set embodying the avoidance of discernment.

Apathy and superficiality may both be seen as characteristics of a mind attuned to the minimizing of cogitation. As such, these mental qualities are examples of the avoidance of discernment. For instance, in the place of cogitation which (though indicated for the situation at hand) could be stressful for a person, an outlook of a cleared mind may be maintained. In consequence, that person remains apathetic. In this instance I suspect that, paradoxically, it might take some mental effort to suppress thoughts about that subject toward which someone is apathetic.

At the level of social organization, slogans and other symbols commonly represent authority in the workings of these societies. Authority symbols can be a source for clearing the mind of extraneous thoughts. The symbols may be employed as motivators of commitment that derive their strength partly because they are accepted blindly and not examined. To state this another way, blind acceptance may be a desirable goal for someone who is seeking a clearing of the mind. There are a variety of sources of authority that might fulfill that person's desire to be in a state of blind acceptance. Such sources are often symbols of political or religious authority.

In this regard, I will repeat part of a quote of Hoffer's work that I cited in Chapter Two: "The effectiveness of a doctrine does not come from its meaning but from its certitude .... It is obvious, therefore, that in order to be effective a doctrine must not be understood but has to be believed in" (76).

DOUBT

Although the inclination toward having a cleared mind is valuable, the propensity toward mind-clearing can also lead to problematic consequences. We have talked about problems that can develop due to an absence of doubt and critical thought. At the interpersonal level, unreasonable attitudes are damaging to relationships. At the level of larger groups, slogans and symbols are often fuel for hatred and war. The capacity for and employment of doubt and examination are necessary in order to avoid the destructiveness of the cleared mind. Slogans, actions, attitudes, beliefs—these all must be open to doubt.

That is not to say that a person should live in a continuing state of doubt. Unceasing examination is an uncomfortable state in which to be. Too much doubt can foster cynicism, suspicion, distrust, and insecurity. It puts a negative tone on life.

However, the repression of doubt is not a valuable option. Doubt repression requires an active will that blanks out the possible realization of new aspects of truth and of previously unseen realities. In addition, as stated above, the avoidance of doubt and discernment can have disastrous interpersonal and social effects.

Also, it should be realized that there are no available answers for some concerns. The fortunes of life can take surprising turns. Examples: A work position may suddenly be terminated. A spouse may be found to be cheating. Will my spouse love me in ten years? We can question what the future will bring, but we don't have answers. Such unanswerable questions point to the value of an openness to doubt and, definitely, a tolerance for uncertainty. Doubt about the future can certainly be unsettling. But, by the acceptance of the uncertain nature of some concerns, we can move on, without dwelling on that which we cannot know.

There is also a broader aspect of doubt and uncertainty. Some ultimate questions don't have answers. Where does blame fall when an infant dies in a no-fault accident? Why should I get this serious illness? What's the meaning of all this human endeavor? Why is there life?

There are some things we don't know and can never know. There just are no answers to some questions. We can doubt any possible answers, but also we can live in a state of doubt and uncertainty, not expecting some questions to be answered. In fact, we can accept doubt as a necessary component of our lives of integrity and wholeness. Instead of remaining in a state of uncertain anguish, we can accept doubt and uncertainty as a natural part of our full life.

Furthermore, in the welcoming of doubt and uncertainty as an expected part of our lives, we no longer need to fuss and anguish over that which we cannot know. By a complete and maximum openness to doubt, we can minimize the anguishing attention that doubt might command. We can minimize the maximum.

The best way to reach the comfort of a cleared mind, the best way to relieve doubt and uncertainty, is to give doubt a full play. Repression of doubt is counter-productive; be open to doubt. Examine the subject at hand, then reach conclusions, even when these conclusions are accepted as tentative. Allow that openness to doubt which bolsters reassurance for the path taken because of confidence in an openness to truth. An attitude of willingness to realize new approximations of truth enhances confidence.

THE FOCUS ON GOD

Openness to truth requires both the ability to detach from one's own agenda and a positive attitude toward looking beyond oneself. Here we get back to basics, to the qualities of life described in previous chapters. Let's take another look at those qualities of outlook which facilitate detachment. Thankfulness is a mental attitude which creates a positive tone on life.Thankfulness provides a welcoming outlook toward the self and toward surroundings. Also, the freedom of the imagination can nourish a positive outlook. Both thankfulness and imagination can be nurtured by a type of focus that is beyond all possible known objective reality, beyond anything which might crowd the imagination. Thoughts tethered to objective experience are likely to be less free-ranging than the flow of consciousness which has no restricting objective representation.

If I were asked about the nature of the focus that is beyond all objective reality, such a question would lead back to the realm of spirituality. A metaphysical concept so abstract that it defies objectification is one such possible focus, and this sort of ambiguous abstraction is typical for a spiritual orientation. Of course, the focus that this conversation is leading to is God, that word-symbol which is beyond all meaningful delineation. The god-symbol can activate the cosmic imagination. Furthermore, a devotion to God frees a person from excess concentration on the self; it allows a detachment from the self's agenda. When the attention is centered on God, a person may be able to see himself or herself and those nearby from a position of detachment. Such detachment can allow an openness to a fuller understanding by allowing some degree of release from intenseness that may be associated with a focus on personal goals. A focus on God provides an alternative to worldly concerns. The concept of God—as a characteristic of the cosmic imagination—is of value to us because it is an expression of both freedom from excess absorption into worldliness and freedom from domination by temporal needs and wants. Previous statements have described how this concept of God, ambiguous by necessity, is correlated with a vague-but-objective abstraction, the nature of the universe. This correlation of God with the totality of existence may be satisfying to those minds which would have some correspondence of objective reality for the use of the word symbol "God."

There is another reason to correlate the word "God" with the nature of the universe. It is by the confluence of many events through billions of years that we now exist. Thankfulness for life is a part of the full life. This thankfulness may be expressed toward God, which is that word representing the nature of the life-giving universe. Also, the abstraction implied by the word "God," as correlating with the nature of the universe, is vague enough so that the cosmic imagination is not crowded or hindered. In fact, this vague abstraction is a ready complement for the cosmic imagination. A person's mind may easily flow from the total ambiguity of the cosmic imagination to that indistinct abstraction in which the god symbol represents the nature of the universe.

Most religious practice involves a more substantive symbol than the vague abstraction and ambiguity which we have discussed. Most religious practice centers on something specific, something which more definitively satisfies the need for content. For many, a presence of objective content in the god-concept may provide emotional satisfaction. Many can find a release from cares and worries by means of a blind acceptance of God as a figure of authority. A commitment to that which is beyond ordinary reason becomes empowered with the strength of blind emotion. I can surmise that it is this degree of unquestioning emotion which seems necessary for those caught in more frustrating problems. Such strong commitment aids in releasing the mind from more severe difficulties.

Furthermore, a more substantive focus is necessary for the young in order to attune them to values beyond their own self-interest. They need an authoritative preparation for the time when they will mature into individuals able to have a healthy expression of doubt and freedom. It should be hoped that the specifics of the authoritative focus presented to children will be constructive and not harmful.

The many potential problems of structured religious practice have been discussed. Belief can often lead to self-righteousness, intolerance, exclusiveness, and worse. Such destructive directions may be affirmed and enhanced by a fabric of support by others. Justification of destructive acts is not uncommon. I will cite one example that I consider destructive and immoral but which I am sure many would consider just the opposite. A defining moment in the Old Testament was the stay of murder of a son as a sacrifice to God (Gen. 22). The substitution of a ram at the last moment stopped Abraham's sacrifice of his son. Theological analysis has shown this event to be justified as evidence of God's redeeming quality, and the depth of emotion at the scene exemplifies a very impressive degree of religious experience. But theological gymnastics do not justify a call to murder. Obedience to God is not a justification for the threat of or the production of misery and death.

After I have disparaged theologic gymnastics, I must confess that I am tempted to try such gymnastics myself with one particular interpretation of the thwarted human sacrifice. In God's call for the sacrifice of human life, it could be understood that Abraham suddenly realized the impending murder was not God's instruction but instead was his warped comprehension of the guidance of God. Possibly, Abraham developed an enlarged understanding of God as a source for an awareness of empathy and for human value in an altered way, realizing that a ritualized sacrifice of life was not expected. Then, with that enlarged awareness, Abraham changed his course and stopped the impending execution of his son Isaac.

A BALANCE, PHASES, AND TRUST

The example of Abraham's experience again shows the need for doubt and examination. We need openness to become mindful of effects on ourselves and others. Destructive attitudes and acts should not be maintained or initiated. However, the propensity toward doubt and the inclination to avoid doubt should be balanced according to the realities of the situation at hand. We do not want to remain in a state of constant, all-consuming doubt. We do commit to that which is found by examination to be valid; we act upon that which we learn. With an openness to doubt and discernment, we move forward. Our action remains open to modification by the new understanding of truth, knowing that there is no absolute truth. There is always the accessibility of doubt and openness to examination.

Therefore we have phases.

Al: Phases? That sounds like moon-talk.

What I mean is, there is a dimension of time in our expression of the full life. We are not in a state of doubt and a state of cleared mind at the same time. At times we are in the process of experiencing something without any mindfulness of doubt, examination, or attempts to comprehend. And, with an openness to perception and understanding, we can easily shift our minds towards doubt and delineation. Also, we can easily shift back to the cleared mind state when the needs discovered by discernment are handled.

I will give you an example. When I chop wood, I first examine the situation. I allow a full expression of doubt. Is there an overhanging wire that could catch the upswing of the axe? Is the chopping block on level ground? Is the chopping block high enough?

Al: And now you are ready?

Yes. The needs are met. I go ahead and chop wood. If I were to put a blank space on this page, it would represent the cleared portion of my conscious mind while chopping wood. But now there is an asterisk*.

*This fir pad is too large. I need a wedge and sledge.

Though I was chopping wood with a cleared mind, I was open to examination and doubt, and that aspect of my consciousness takes over. After that, the mind blanks into the full experience of wood chopping again. Just like life. I am not in a continuous fuss with doubt, but doubt serves me well when activated.

This is a path to the minimization of doubt. Give doubt full rein and tolerate doubt and uncertainty for the unanswerable questions. Examine what needs to be examined. Arrive at some conclusion, however tentative it might be. Then go with it. Release yourself into the flow of activity, always keeping the capacity for doubt available. This is the way for maximizing the cleared mind and a flow of spontaneity. Maximum availability of the capacity for doubt allows a settled confidence in the path for tentative truth. There is no repression of any thought which could create doubt. With a full openness for doubt, tentative solutions might be found and proceeded upon. A maximum capacity for doubt can minimize doubt when combined with decisiveness. With an openness to doubt in coordination with decisiveness, we can accept tentative solutions and act on them in full measure. Such action entails an openness to the further revelation of truthful understanding of the situation at hand. This is the pathway of phases of doubt and cleared mind. It is the doubt/cleared-mind cycle.

This doubt/cleared mind cycle is valuable in interpersonal relationships. Doubt opens the door to truth, and the cleared mind state is established as a sense of trust when the reality of the relationship warrants it. Although openness to doubt remains, we are not in a perpetual state of examination and uncertainty. Following the resolution of difficulties to whatever extent is possible, life can proceed with a cleared mind; life can become spontaneous, with an uncluttered mind. A person can become open to the joy of life.

In interpersonal relationships, an openness to doubt about possible preconceptions can lead to a firmer base for the relationship. Rather than proceeding in the relationship with possibly unrealistic views of the self and the other, the employment of doubt and discernment may afford more accurate information for the relationship. Interactions and communication which include room for doubt and discernment can eventually lead to a replacement of doubt by trust. When there are satisfactory grounds for trust, the doubt can stop, yet always remain available.

The same is true in considering larger groups. Individuals in social settings who remain in a state of constant doubt are prone to moods of suspicion and cynicism. For example, many of us know rebellious young adults who manifest such cynicism.

It may be possible for observers of the cynics to dispel or diminish the suspicion which cynics may have. With good will, the content of problems may be delineated more fully by the utilization of doubt and discernment on the part of all contending parties. Hopefully, an improved mutual understanding of the difficulties might then allow the problems to be processed in some satisfactory manner. Such processing of disagreement can lead to trust between individuals and toward the group as a whole. This is a basis for the expression of a sense of community.

There is one more sphere to consider regarding the doubt/cleared-mind cycles. That realm is the spiritual life. Traditional views of God serve the function of clearing the mind quite well, focussing the mind on a quite specific source of authority. However, the usual views of God may be undermined by a doubt of the reality of the transcendental, the supernatural. In this book, the concept of God is not transcendental. As correlated with the nature of the universe and as our expression of the cosmic imagination in freedom and thankfulness, the conception of God remains valid in the face of doubt and examination. Also, God remains a source for a clearing of the mind. Excess involvement with the concerns of life is alleviated and seen with more balance and detachment when there is devotion to God.

In all of these dimensions—personal, spiritual, interpersonal, and community relationships—we would do well to maximize the availability of doubt and discernment. The ready availability of these two mental resources allows us to approach truth more closely, giving us confidence in our approach to life. Such confidence is an aspect of our wholeness, our integrity. It allows a fullness of experience and expression, unhindered by nagging doubts about that which may have been repressed. We allow doubts to be processed. Discipline, responsibility, whatever it takes—these can be employed to handle information brought forth by doubt and discernment.

Of course, the resolution of concerns that have been brought forth by an openness to doubt and discernment frees the mind from dwelling on those concerns. A maximum openness to doubt allows the development of a cleared mind. Such cleared mind is characterized by a minimized need to continue doubting because there is a confidence that doubts can be handled as well as possible when they arise. With a ready availability of doubt and an openness to change when needed, beliefs and responsibilities may be lightly held—without compulsion—while being thoroughly followed. Full rein for doubt lets us process the doubts and then to put doubt to rest, snoozing but not sleeping. By being open to doubt and handling the information revealed by doubt, we are able to "minimize the maximum." Openness to doubt is maximized, leading to a minimization of the need to actively doubt.

Al: Your point about openness to doubt seems like a statement of Christ in the Sermon on the Mount: "Blessed are the meek ..." (Matt. 5:5).

Yes. There is a similarity. A release from self-righteousness and an openness to doubt can be labelled as humility, which would be characteristic of the meek.

To continue, in interpersonal relationships and at the community level we can direct ourselves toward "minimizing the maximum." We can aim toward recognizing and handling our doubts and the doubts of others. Such personal actions and attitudes feed a sense of trust among us by creating a climate of openness to the understanding of problems and to their solutions. The maximization of an openness to doubt may lead to a minimization of the need to doubt, and therefore, lead to a sense of trust.

Also, trust between individuals can enhance the possibility of enjoying shared experiences because, when there is trust, interactions are not hindered by concerns about the relationship.

An atmosphere of trust, buttressed by the availability of doubt when it is needed, can extend the feeling of good will between people. The more we feed this trust, the more that we can contribute toward an environment that mirrors our inclination toward the spontaneity, joy, and peace of a cleared mind.

23

Review

Al: I see we're getting to the end of the book.

Yes; it's time for a comprehensive view.

Al: You will pull everything together now?

In fact, no. First, in this chapter let's look at a brief overview. We'll touch on the subjects in the order in which they were presented.

In the initial remarks section I indicated that this book may be of value to those who have some inclination toward the experience of and the expression of spirituality but who doubt the content of that experience. They are likely to be unaware of ways to express their spiritual inclination that do not sacrifice their willingness to doubt; the content of many forms of spirituality may seem meaningless to some. This book can be of benefit to these people.

Also, the initial section included some of the reasons why people seek spirituality. In addition, I gave some personal background.

In Part II, I presented information about the several components of integrity. In using the term "integrity," I mean more than moral integrity. "Integrity" includes morality, but the word "integrity" as used in this book is meant as a more general term, referring to a wholeness of life.

There are many components of integrity. The availability of doubt is a prime characteristic of integrity. It is valuable to be able to question and to doubt any information. Doubt allows an openness for examination and discernment; doubt is the path to a closer approximation of truth.

A cautionary note was made against being stuck in some morass of excess doubt. Instead of a continuous orientation of doubt, we would do well to accept and to act upon tentative truths, always remaining open to doubt and to a new discernment of truth.

Let's move from truth to space.

Al: Can I make the sound effects?

Don't help me that much. To resume, the space of the universe is an unbelievably enormous expanse, speckled with huge, fiery masses that we call stars. Within this array, on a rock we call Earth, we exist. Against fantastic odds in the interplay of the forces of nature and history, we exist. For this remarkable fact of our existence, we are very thankful, or, at least, I encourage that we should be very thankful. For life, health, and that amount of good fortune which we have, we can be very willing to express thankfulness and gratitude.

Chapter Four takes up another dimension of the full life. At times, mental life may be narrowed by an excess need for control or self-justification. On the other hand, some detachment from excess needs tends to allow a relaxation, a releasing of drives, directions, and attitudes. This relief from an intense, narrowed direction may allow for a fuller perceptiveness. With greater clarity and perception, a person might modify an orientation or a goal toward a more productive direction.

I have used a term "engaged detachment," and by that term I mean a detachment that remains engaged in the situation at hand but to some degree holds the mental outlook apart from the situation. This may afford a degree of clarity of perception. The utilization of detachment tends to release a mind that is too narrowly focussed. With detachment there is an opportunity for a widened perspective, for openness, for freedom of the mind. With openness and mental freedom, greater understanding of the present experience may become possible as well as greater intuition about future potentialities.

Imagination plays a role in the orientation of openness and freedom of the mind. When the mind is released into the flow of imagination, then freedom, spontaneity, and perceptiveness are likely to be enhanced.

In Chapter Six I pointed to the problems of self-absorption and indicated certain factors that tend to feed self-absorption: perfectionism, excess indulgence, excess desires. There is much value in being able to look beyond the desires and needs of the self. An ability to look beyond these needs can allow greater openness to a perceptiveness of reality. Also, the capacity to see beyond a self-centered orientation may ease the access to more fundamental values.

In the next chapter emphasis was made on the value of an ability to look beyond the agenda of the self, to be able to see people and situations with some degree of empathy. In that chapter we also talked about the flow of physical action. Action that is carried forward in a wholehearted way is more satisfying than action which is hesitant and stutters along in uncertain fashion. However, there may at times be problems with wholehearted action. During action it is helpful to maintain some awareness of the surroundings, an awareness that can include empathy. It is well to have an easy shifting of mental awareness between the outgoing orientation of empathy and the physical flow of action.

The following chapter took up the consideration of a balance in the needs of individuals and society.

In the last chapter of Part II we centered on the nature of integrity, the unifying concept of Part II. Again, by integrity I mean more than moral integrity, although moral integrity is included. The broader definition of integrity is a wholeness, a sense of completeness.

The subject matter of Part III is the spiritual life. The content of spirituality is recognized as being within the subjective realm, that is, in the inclinations of the mind. Either the objective verification of the content of spirituality is not possible or spirituality is founded on abstractions so vague as to defy objective evaluation. Ambiguity is, in fact, a requirement for spirituality. It is within ambiguity that the imagination gains its freedom, and mental freedom is a valuable outcome of spiritual expression. The initial chapter of Part III discusses this, particularly at the level of the cosmic imagination. The word "cosmic" refers to the universe, all of existence. Nothing spooky is meant by the term "cosmic."

In Chapter Twelve we take the opposite tack, discussing what can be objectively known about existence and how this relates to the establishment, or rather, to the non-establishment of human value on some metaphysical basis.

Chapter Thirteen discusses a release from doubt and discernment and leads into the following chapter, which is a presentation of the concept of God as comprehended in this book. This concept of God manifests the value of the cosmic imagination but also remains valid when subjected to doubt and examination.

Ensuing chapters characterize particulars of spiritual life: mysticism, opposition, individual differences in religious practice, and the nature of a religious orientation, particularly the function and components of a religious outlook.

Part IV brings together information previously developed. The first chapter of Part IV points to the value of continuity in personal life and in interpersonal and community relationships. Of particular note is the

Review

recognition of the inherent problems in the utilization of language for maintaining continuity.

The following chapter again takes up the subject of doubt. It is pointed out that the mind may be most easily released from anxiety about doubt when there is complete openness to doubt, allowing a consideration of questioning thought. A healthy tolerance for doubt can lessen the insecurity which may be associated with the possible effort of avoiding doubt.

There is a social aspect regarding the prevalence of a mood of doubt. When there is trust between people, there is usually less need for doubt. Therefore, actions and behavior that enhance trust are helpful in minimizing the inclination to doubt.

That brings us to the present chapter, the summary. And here we are at the end of it. What more can I say in the next chapter? We'll see.

24

The Psychologic Body

Overview

A Metaphor

Openness

Freedom; the Cosmic Imagination; God

Values

Final Considerations

Last, Short Verse

OVERVIEW

I have said everything I want to say in this book.

Al: I don't believe that. I know there is this last chapter. What are you covering in the final chapter?

You are right; there is more. This is a summarizing chapter, and it will integrate the information more thoroughly than the last chapter.

First, an overview. The beginning of the chapter presents a metaphor that will facilitate an understanding of the full life by integrating its various components. Then we look at the psychologic quality of openness in relation to spontaneity, discipline, doubt, decisiveness, and perceptiveness. This leads to the subject of freedom and the value of the imagination, particularly the cosmic imagination. We will take another look at the nature of God as presented in this book, particularly in relation to the role of doubt and self-centeredness. We then turn to the subject of values and end the chapter and the book with some final statements.

A METAPHOR

A metaphor will be helpful in bringing disparate concepts together into a meaningful whole. Picture the mind as a physical human body. This will help in seeing some of the interrelationships between the psychologic factors that we have been discussing. Also, the metaphor of mental activity viewed as a physical body draws together the understanding of mental life as an integrated whole. The psychologic components of our lives are then more easily seen in their totality.

I should point out that the metaphor is just meant to indicate relationships between components; nothing literal is implied.

This discussion is not meant to be a general characterization of human psychology. It is a depiction of those characteristics which have been presented in this book and which are seen as fundamentally significant for the full life.

Let's start with the heart, that organ which is our vital center. The psychologic counterpart of the heart is openness. In this representation, the heart is the openness of a receptive outlook, ready to be in touch with an awareness of ongoing events, attitudes and emotions. A largehearted person has a generous disposition, open to becoming aware of that which is.

The heart of the psychologic body, which is openness, pumps the blood that is freedom, the blood of freedom which nourishes the entire body.

The continuing stability of the body is the spine, which, speaking in terms of the metaphor, is thankfulness, providing us with a sense of value and affirmation. The spine is that stable foundation upon which the other components act and interact. Likewise, thankfulness provides the stable foundation of a positive attitude—and thereby provides affirmation—for the psychologic body. This positive attitude creates a tone of welcome to life.

As a manifestation of openness, the receptive attitude toward doubt is a part of the function of the heart. However, the process of doubt and examination is performed by the head (or should I say, brain).

Al: Empathy would be the eyes and ears. Right?

Yes. And, since imagination is wide-ranging in openness and freedom, the bodily metaphor for the imagination is that organ which is permeated by the wide-ranging air that we breathe: the lungs.

God Unmasked; the Full Life Revealed

Here's another part of the metaphor. The skin represents the continuing appearance we present to others and to ourselves. When interaction between individuals occurs in a mode of integrity, the appearance of behavior and attitudes over a period of time presents the possibility for creating a sense of trust. There is continuity of interaction involved in the creation of trust. As an aspect of appearance, we can consider the skin as that part of the body which represents continuity of behavior.

OPENNESS

We talked about openness in Chapter Four and related it to freedom and spontaneity. Let's further integrate these characteristics of the full life with other aspects of life. First we'll review Webster's dictionary definitions. To be open is to be "willing to hear and consider or to accept and deal with;" an open orientation is "responsive."

Behavior that is spontaneous tends to be more possible when there is an open outlook. Spontaneity implies that a person is open to the experience of the present moment. Spontaneous means "proceeding from natural feeling or native tendency without external constraint."

Al: Well, you have worked yourself into a corner. You say that openness is responsiveness and that spontaneity proceeds without external constraint. Openness and spontaneity seem like opposites, on one hand: being responsive, and on the other: acting without constraint. How can you relate such opposites?

Openness and spontaneity both involve an outlook in which preconceptions and beliefs do not blind a person to comprehending the reality of the present. Both involve an attunement to the immediate experience. I think that will answer your concern.

Now let's look at the differences between openness and spontaneity. This requires an understanding of the workings of the actual nervous system. In this instance I am not referring to the metaphor but to actual nervous system physiology. The activity of the nervous system includes sensory and motor segments. The sensory part involves input from the various sense modalities, and, of course, the motor part is active in guiding bodily movement. And now returning to the metaphor, one difference between openness and spontaneity is that openness is on the sensory side of nervous system activity and spontaneity is on the motor side. Openness involves an orientation toward sensory input, and spontaneity is a characteristic type of motor activity.

There is another difference: certain mediative qualities are operative in counterbalancing the expression of spontaneity, and these do not apply to the experience of openness. A total commitment to spontaneity would be destructive of society and destructive of self. A completely spontaneous life would have no restraints and, therefore, no consideration for the ongoing needs of the self or of the group. Just to maintain life by arranging to obtain food requires a certain amount of narrowing away from a spontaneous orientation. The needs of life require some degree of pre-programming.

In Chapter Eight we discussed the choice for an acceptance of social structure rather than anarchy. With this acceptance comes the need for discipline and responsibility. Both self and society are served by such pre-programmed constraints as discipline and responsibility. It is valuable to have an agenda, a predisposition toward anticipated consequences. The maintenance of self and society are served by such attitudes and preconceptions as those which involve discipline and responsibility. In such instance a preconception might be viewed more favorably, without its pejorative connotation, if it is called a "belief." We discussed this in Chapter Two.

It is valuable to have both spontaneity on one hand and pre-programming on the other. The freedom of spontaneity can be balanced by the practical needs of self and society.

These practical needs of self and society are not necessarily expressed in a reasonable manner. Beliefs and loyalties can be maintained with minimal recourse to reason and may be expressed with non-reflective spontaneity. There may be minimal restraint manifested along with a suspension of reason. However, such beliefs and loyalties may have either reasonable or deleterious consequences. Such spontaneous expression brings up a consideration of what is reasonable and how a person should integrate reasonableness with spontaneity.

During spontaneous interaction the recourse to doubt and examination becomes limited; reason may be held in abeyance during spontaneous acts. However, a balance may be developed between the roles of spontaneity and reason. We pointed to the nature of spontaneity at an individual level. There is also a manifestation of spontaneity intrinsic to the workings of society. In individual and social life, the fabric of consistency in the life of an individual and of society is woven with beliefs and loyalties. Once established, the network of beliefs and loyalties may be expressed spontaneously, without forethought.

A major factor in the development of loyalty is the establishment of trust. We discussed this in Chapter Twenty-two. Trust between people can be a source of comfort and happiness. One reason for this happiness is a release from the need for doubt and discernment. Such release allows a measure of spontaneous interaction. It is, therefore, valuable to be able to have a set of beliefs and loyalties as the basis for spontaneous actions. However, an openness to doubt and examination can allow either reinforcement of existing beliefs and loyalties or the establishment of more valid ones. The maintenance of an openness to doubt and reason can provide the safeguard for an establishment of beliefs which are less likely to be destructive.

Furthermore, a maximum openness to tolerance for doubt is likely to eventuate into a minimized concern about doubt because any lingering doubt about a belief is not suppressed. All that we hold as important or valuable may be doubted. No thought need remain unexamined. Any belief may be overthrown or established more securely in the course of examination. And we accept doubt and uncertainty about unanswerable questions as an integral part of our lives. As a consequence, the maximization of tolerance for doubt may lead to a decreased need to anguish about doubt and therefore afford greater spontaneity.

This brings us back to the metaphor, the psychologic body. The muscles are the symbolic representation for action.

Al: That's hardly a symbol. The movement of muscles is, in fact, the way we express action.

Right. But the metaphor gets a little more complex. The actions of some muscles complement each other, and there are opposing movements of many muscles. If I throw a baseball, several muscles in my right shoulder combine their actions to create a smooth flow of action. It is not only the complementary muscle groups that smooth the flow of action: opposing muscle groups do likewise. For example, in lifting a sack of flour, the biceps and triceps, which have opposing muscle action, are both activated to a degree that fulfills the action without a jerkiness that might occur with totally unopposed action.

In relation to the metaphor, we can now think of one group of actions—those that involve pre-programming, such as beliefs, discipline, and the actions which fulfill responsibility—as one set of opposing muscles. The muscles in opposition to that set represent spontaneity. The

The Psychologic Body

pumping action of the heart provides openness that feeds both groups of muscles. All act in concert. Openness nourishes the capacity for a variety of types of action. At times the muscle groups act out the needs that are pre-programmed. At other times the action is more spontaneous. And sometimes the action is a mix of the two, programmed and spontaneous. Both spontaneity and programming can be available simultaneously in the manifestation of action. The expression of one need not inhibit a shift to the opposite mode.

There is a note of caution about the possibility of an outlook of openness that, in its extreme, might inhibit action when action would be timely. It's all well and good to be open, to stay in tune with what's going on. But if I just sit there or stand there, being in tune with everything, I never do anything. I could just stay in a state of being in touch with things, open to what is and to what could be.

However, openness need not imply being stuck in a state of observing the situation while weighing the various options of direction. When the situation calls for action, the initiation of action need not be resisted by endless hesitancy.

In *Julius Caesar* Shakespeare characterizes decisiveness:

> There is a tide in the affairs of men,
> Which, taken at the flood, leads on to fortune;
> Omitted, all the voyage of their life
> Is bound in shallows and in miseries (4.3.217-20).

Openness and action can be more than interspersed; it is often valuable for them to be present simultaneously. I can liken this to musical counterpoint, a melody accompanying an existing melody. In our metaphor, muscle action proceeds simultaneously with the action of the heart, that organ which is our bodily symbol for openness. The muscles and the heart work in counterpoint, each providing its characteristic output. Likewise, action and openness can occur simultaneously, in counterpoint, in concert as the music of the psychologic body.

This information may seem trivial, something to be taken for granted. However, the implications are important and far-ranging.

An outlook of openness feeds the sense of spontaneity. With openness we are more alive to the ongoing changes in ourselves, in others, and in situations. We become attuned to the reality of things. Openness releases us from the narrowness which our direction might assume. Excess concentration on the end result would destroy this spontaneity and might warp our awareness of reality. If there is excess concentration on action and its end result, it is possible that a person could lose sight of that which might be of greater value. Therefore, an outlook of openness may enhance productivity.

I will give some examples. Consider the re-setting of time on a stopped clock for which time-setting is mechanically difficult. I may proceed in a usual course of action by setting the correct time, albeit with difficulty. However, with openness, I may realize that I can ease the task by just leaving the clock as is till it shows the later correct time—or close to it, with minor adjustments.

Another example: this was when I was practicing medicine, before I retired. Evaluation of the symptoms and examination of a patient would point me in a certain direction for the diagnosis and treatment of that patient's illness. However, new information might develop, such as significant laboratory findings or a different emphasis in the symptoms. For the sake of a patient's health, I found it useful to remain continually open to new understanding and to be able to change the course of action in treatment of the patient.

As could be shown in many examples, increased efficiency is the likely result when an outlook of openness accompanies the will towards some particular direction. With openness, the perception of reality tends to become broader and more inclusive. The enhanced perceptiveness may modulate a person's direction toward a more favorable course of action.

FREEDOM; THE COSMIC IMAGINATION; GOD

Let's leave the discussion of productivity and move from the subject of openness to a closely related topic, freedom. Openness enlarges the awareness of paths among which there is a freedom to choose. With freedom, a person can choose to delay the initiation of a course of action. In fact, with freedom, a person can also choose decisiveness, responsibility, spontaneity, whatever. Freedom is the blood of the psychologic body that feeds all of the capabilities which someone can choose.

Freedom for these several capacities can be combined with a reasoned judgment that is afforded by doubt and examination. Freedom is not a chaotic expression of random impulses. Nor does freedom mean a rebellion against reason and examination. Freedom means having choice. This choice can even include the utilization of discipline and responsibility, although these might seem to be opposites of freedom. The outward appearance of disciplined conformity to some sort of appearance or toward some end result need not negate the basic freedom of choice for that direction.

Al: Discipline and responsibility. I believe that you are back to the subject of productivity.

I was talking about freedom just now, and that subject led back to productivity. In fact, there is something else I want to say about productivity. I can add parenthetically that one of the great challenges of the capitalist economic system is the maintenance of a human dimension in the face of the dehumanizing effect of a narrowed concentration on productivity. Competition can increase productivity and be stimulating. However, under the stress of competition, a concentration on productivity may cause people to lose sight of themselves and others as human beings. The availability of the fundamental human quality of openness is at risk in the grinding path of total concentration on productivity. The loss of the human dimension is unsettling. Some might conform to that loss and become machine-like, productive but with a decreased or absent sense of fulfillment. Others might rebel or withdraw.

I won't stretch my opinions about economic matters any further.

Al: Even aside from the broad economic picture, it is possible for the fulfillment of duties to become a treadmill that narrows the vision. I frequently tend to become pre-occupied with goals, losing sight of the value of openness and freedom. It's not all that easy to maintain an openness, a freedom and spontaneity.

It is too easy to become narrowly focussed on the concerns of everyday life. The press of work will often channel a person's outlook into a disciplined single-mindedness that can be carried beyond that reasonable degree which is needed for the work. In addition, worries can become repetitious; a person can get stuck in various stages of partial understanding or partial resolution of problems.

A regular recall to a state of mental freedom is helpful in releasing the mind from thoughts that may have become too narrowly focussed. As previously stated, one such resource for rest and release from worldly concerns is the imagination, and particularly, the cosmic imagination as commonly experienced in an awareness of the god-symbol. A mindfulness of God may give us rest from cares and also help us to see our cares with a refreshed understanding. Regular prayer to God gives us a recurrent opportunity to renew ourselves. Prayer is a valid part of the full life if it is done in a mode of integrity rather than self-righteousness.

Experience of the cosmic imagination can lead us to a free and open state of mind. Without regular recourse to prayer, the mindfulness of God is more likely to become a forgotten resource for the access to openness and freedom. On the other hand, with prayer to God, the wonder and joy of the cosmic imagination can fill the lungs, the imagination, like a breath of fresh air, nourishing the blood of freedom. This freedom is manifested in the awareness of the vaguely perceived and totally undelineated experience of that which is found to be profound in the cosmic imagination.

I can point to other values that come with regular prayer. Thankfulness implies a sense of value; thankfulness provides an affirmation for life. Regular prayer to God is a recurring source for this expression of thankfulness. Also, a wonder of and thankfulness to God can enlarge the feeling of awareness and refresh the mind with freedom and openness.

Furthermore, in looking with an objective viewpoint, the understanding of God as a representation of the natural universe need not undermine the value of the cosmic imagination. Thankfulness for existence ties the objectivity of the reality of existence to the subjective value of the imagination. In both, the objective realm of existence and the subjective realm of the imagination, God is a valid source for wonder and thankfulness.

Periodic prayer may also activate a person's conscience toward the path of moral integrity. I quote from the New Testament: "But in a great house there are not only vessels of gold and of silver, but also of wood and of earth; and some to honour, and some to dishonour. If a man therefore purge himself from these, he shall be a vessel unto honour, sanctified, and meet for the master's use, and prepared unto every good work. Flee also youthful lusts: but follow righteousness, faith, charity, peace, with them that call on the Lord out of a pure heart "(II Tim. 2:20-2).

Hick addresses the subject of a religious call to moral integrity:

> Nor of course is it the case that religion always offers consolation. It also offers challenge. God is not only our "strength in time of trouble" (Psalm 37:39) but is also "like a refiner's fire" (Malachi 3:2), and "the word of God is quick, and powerful, and sharper than any two-edged sword, piercing even to the dividing asunder of soul and spirit, and of the joints and marrow, and is a discerner of the thoughts and intents of the heart". (Heb. 4:12) (113)

The use of words can provide continuity. The recall of a word can call forth longstanding meaning in individual lives and for groups. As an enduring symbol, the word-symbol "god" can provide a sense of continuity, even when the word "god" is understood as an imaginative abstraction of the nature of existence. In the interest of continuity, the availability of a focus, the god-symbol, is valuable for both individuals and groups. This focus can facilitate the recall of fundamentals, the fundamental value of the life of integrity, with all that it connotes.

In considering continuity for individuals as well as for the group, let's look at the value of prayer as expressed in a group setting, that is, in religious services. The traditional-minded would favor services that are centered on the worship of God and in which God is understood as some type of transcendental reality. Consider the value of prayer for those who do not believe in such transcendental reality. The centering on God can also be valuable for many who do not believe in the existence of a transcendental consciousness. There can be value in a mindfulness of God for those who recognize God as a projection of the mind. I will reiterate certain points. Some non-believers may value a mindfulness of God because of the mental freedom which the cosmic imagination provides. Other non-believers may be inclined to center on the god-symbol as the source toward which they would wish to express thankfulness. In addition, the search for a moral pathway would incline some toward an awareness of God, even while harboring doubt about the existence of God. They would value God because the mindfulness of God carries with it an inclination to follow a path of integrity and wholeness. This inclination toward a life that is whole and full may be recalled and refreshed by regular prayer to God. For this, the word "God" is a focus, and this focus is not necessarily to be seen as Transcendental Existence. The god-symbol can be seen as the imaginative representation of the nature of the universe.

In the economy of the mind, the cosmic imagination is not always activated when addressing God. At times, prayer to God may provide the realization of a more limited degree of an enlarged awareness, without immersion into the total freedom of an expanded imagination. This lesser degree of enlarged awareness has some effect in getting us beyond the concerns of the day.

Since I describe a regular recall to the mindfulness of God, it is obvious that I do not have—nor would I expect to have—a continuous awareness of God. Most of the time I have no consciousness of God at all. We can conjecture that some religious individuals maintain a relatively continuous awareness of God. However, for most of us who are mindful of God, this awareness is intermittent.

A continuing awareness brings up the subject of compulsion. If I were to impose an imaginative symbol continuously on my mind, I might be creating a mental narrowness. If there is any compulsion toward mindfulness of God, my outlook might tend to become constricted. It is possible for a mental awareness of something highly valued to become too programmed and exclusive. Any excess programming of the mind might diminish the range of human possibility. Openness and freedom can be maintained by the easy flowing of mental currents between the cosmic imagination and the needs and pleasures of the everyday world.

Let's look at another aspect of a mindfulness of God: he does not exist as some supernatural being. God is a mental projection, something we create in our minds, a product of the imagination that relates to the entirety of existence. As a mental creation, the awareness of God is a manifestation of our nature, a characteristic of our being.

Furthermore, we realize that, for each of us, personal existence is a localized manifestation of existence in general. Every individual is constituted as a particular, local expression of the ongoing processes of all that exists. Therefore, keeping in mind the pantheistic nature of the god-symbol, our lives are components of the manifestation of God.

Al: I got lost. Could you elaborate?

Certainly. We described God as a product of the imagination. Also, looking back to Chapter Fourteen, we discussed the concept of God as corresponding to all that exists. God of the cosmic imagination correlates with an abstraction of objective reality. As a manifestation of the cosmic imagination, God is an imaginative symbol of all existence. Since each of us is a part of the existence of all things, we are each a part of the expression of God.

As a product of the imagination, God does not have objective existence. The concept of God is subjective. The lack of objective reality does not detract from the efficacy of the god concept. In fact, the concept of God is empowered by its very lack of objectivity. With an absence of the constricting discipline of hard reality, the mind is liberated to engage the imagination in openness, allowing a person to surrender their thoughts to the freedom of the cosmic imagination. Therefore, God—as non-existent in an objective sense (except as the imaginative representation of all existence)—is effective for our lives precisely because of being non-existent. As a manifestation of the cosmic imagination, the mindfulness of God can bring joy by providing the experience of freedom.

Of course, many would strongly disagree that God is non-existent. At this point let's look at one of the possible reasons for a view that God exists as more than a projection of the imagination. The expression of faith in God may fulfill the want for a value that is indestructible. All else has some finite existence. Values held during life tend to change. Self-esteem is a manifestation of value, but the value of self may be suspect at times. Most of us have felt guilt or despair at some point in life.

There is the value of existence itself. In looking for an unchanging source of value, an individual will likely discount his or her own existence, knowing that life will end. In fact, all life forms will die. Even the mountains and seas will disappear. The universe itself is expected to self-destruct in billions of years, at least, according to current scientific theory.

But, for many who have faith in God, he is all-knowing and all-powerful, beyond any limits that could be known. For many believers, God is the indestructible source of value.

Some people are more predisposed than others toward having an indestructible source of value, particularly one that is all-powerful. Individuals may associate themselves with the power of God for a variety of reasons. These reasons frequently involve an element of opposition. A person may want to realize the potency of God's will in fighting an addiction. Anxiety about many sorts of mental and physical stresses may precipitate the supplication to a higher power.

The call for God's power may be invoked not only because of the stresses which someone experiences. There are some who aggressively seek out some form of opposition. They may, in fact, create an opposition that would form in reaction to their aggressiveness. Some of these individuals may invoke the name of God as a power on their side. Indeed, who would be better to have on their side than he who is all-powerful?

We have talked about some of the dangers and potential for destructiveness that may be associated with the concept of God. More beneficially, the awareness of God is of value in the renewal of thankfulness, openness, and freedom. In instances where a mindfulness of God has the opposite effect, it is well for the mind to become relieved from such constricting orientations.

For each individual, the efficacy of the awareness of God may be regarded by the degree to which that awareness is consistent with and fulfills that person's sense of wholeness and integrity. This integrity includes the characteristics we have been considering: openness, freedom, spontaneity, empathy, responsibility, thankfulness, discipline, openness to doubt.

Al: You say that the god presented by religious practice provides a source of value that is indestructible. Another way of saying it could be that religion sells certainty; it markets the obliteration of doubt. With that point of view, the details of religious dogma might be considered incidental.

If that description has some validity for you, then you may be open to a religious outlook that includes the capacity for doubt. In fact, as previously stated, doubt can be an intrinsic part of such a religious orientation, and that has been amply described in this book. I know that it is comfortable to live without doubt. It is relaxing to proceed without the hesitancy associated with questioning and examination. However, in Chapter Twenty-two, I described the minimization of doubt through a maximum openness to doubt. Through accepting doubt and being open to new dimensions of truth, a confidence develops in the ability to perceive reality as clearly as may be possible. A person does not then feel hindered by declarations of certainty that may suppress an understanding of reality. A full openness to doubt and a processing of the substance of this doubt by examination and discernment can lead to a settled mind, confident and at peace. With the absence of suppression of doubt, with full openness to doubt, the need for concern about doubt becomes minimized.

Also, it is well to accept doubt as a component of healthy mental life. There are uncertainties inherent in the nature of life. It is helpful to relax about the uncertainties of life and to accept them as uncertainties. I don't know if I will have a good day. I don't know how my health will be this year, or how long I will live.

There are uncertainties about the future and often doubts about the validity of present understanding. What does someone think of me? How will they respond to my actions? I don't know, though I do have some suppositions in answer to such questions.

As long as I follow the path of integrity and accept doubt and uncertainty as components of my integrity, I can have confidence that my inclinations are valid and right for me.

Al: I want to say something here. It is true that doubt and uncertainty are important parts of a life of integrity. But they could not be called components of a religious outlook.

The Psychologic Body

Again, looking at Webster's dictionary definitions, religious is "relating to or manifesting faithful devotion to an acknowledged ultimate reality or deity." One definition of acknowledge is "to express gratitude for or obligation for;" another definition is: "to recognize as genuine or valid." "Ultimate" may refer to fundamental reality instead of implying commitment toward some supernatural being.

We now have a definition for religion that is applicable for a life of integrity when integrity is understood to include a dimension of doubt. This definition of religion is: devotion to the fundamental validity of a life of integrity.

Al: But integrity is a quality of personal character. This definition could be seen as self-centered.

Your point is well-taken. However, the major components of integrity, as described in this book, are openness and thankfulness. Other characteristics of the life of integrity—including empathy, respect, responsibility, discipline, and spontaneity—are either modulated by or derived from the qualities of openness and thankfulness.

Regarding self-centeredness, it is true that openness includes a receptivity not only to the understanding of others but receptivity also to the understanding of self. In addition, thankfulness is directed toward the forces that have been instrumental in the creation of ourselves and of other beings and entities. Though we are thankful for lives and health, the tone of thankfulness is directed beyond our selves. Though there is a personal aspect in the manifestation of both openness and thankfulness, these qualities are not self-centered. They are both significantly inclusive of that which is beyond our personal existence.

Al: I will say this. It is a stretch to call your presentation a religion. Most people would disagree with that. But what you have presented could be called a religion in that it is a fundamental commitment. Why would you want this even to be considered a religion?

The word "religion" points to a fundamental commitment. Many have a need for a fundamental commitment. The drift toward materialism and overindulged individualism is unsatisfying to many. There is a need for a type of commitment that is consistent with personal integrity. Doubt of known religious dogmas turns many off toward religion. Furthermore, doubt is a necessary part of integrity. In the presentation of this book, doubt is a component of the life of integrity, and the wholeness of integrity is the source of fundamental commitment which may be called "religious."

There is another aspect to this. The mindfulness of God is a manifestation of the cosmic imagination, and the cosmic imagination is the imaginative representation of the nature of the universe. There is wonder and joy in the freedom of the cosmic experience. Also, the mindfulness of God gives us a focus of fundamental importance beyond the self and, therefore, releases a person from self-centeredness. This release from self-centeredness gives us freedom. In turn, the experience of wonder, joy, and freedom confirms the value of the cosmic imagination and of the awareness of God.

In the presentation of this book, the cosmic imagination does not necessitate a belief in the actuality of a supernatural being. The cosmic imagination is recognized as a projection of the mind. The recognition of the cosmic imagination as mental projection does not negate the value of the freedom which accompanies the experience of the cosmic imagination.

Furthermore, the freedom of the cosmic imagination is a valuable part of the full life. This cosmic imagination is an aspect of spirituality, a manifestation of religion. Therefore, the joy of freedom of the cosmic imagination is a part of religious expression.

It is well at times to direct oneself toward release from any preconceptions and word-symbols, including the god-symbol. To the extent that total openness is possible, a mind is released from all that might constrict it. The more that an open, cleared mind is experienced, the more likely that a return to usual thought patterns will reveal new, fresh perspectives, including the perception of God.

VALUES

At this point, let's have a look at the subject of value. To bring this subject more into focus, I will point to a personal example. When I was a youngster, I wanted to be a doctor. That was my direction. I valued that direction. And there were other things that I valued along the way, both related to and unrelated to the training for the medical profession. Different sorts of work experiences provided income in order to continue my course toward earning an M. D. degree. In addition, I also enjoyed experiencing various work settings.

Other people pick other directions. Some want to be engineers; some want to be architects, and so on. Also, we choose more immediate goals, such as wanting to see a certain movie. The point is that we decide what to value. These choices are not imposed on us by some higher scheme of things, some metaphysical Grand Direction. We each have our own initiative.

When I say that value is self-created, I do not mean to deny the enormous effect on our choices by the influences around us. We have been particularly influenced by those who nourished us and those to whom we were subjected while growing up. In various degrees, these influences become parts of our mental constitution.

As I previously stated, I do not have value in some metaphysical sense. There is no grand scheme in the universe by which my existence derives meaning. The universe consists of the various forms of existence—galaxies, centipedes, volcanoes, us—that evolve and express changes according to the characteristics by which each is constituted. We experience and express the unfolding of our nature, and that is what all things do. The unfolding is not directed by some universal consciousness or inclination.

We talked about the absence of value at a metaphysical level. Also, at a certain personal level I do not have value. I believe that when life ends, we are gone. We may be remembered for awhile, but it will not be many generations before we become just ancestral curiosities to those living in a future time.

In a more particular way, there is worth in the ability to release from sources of value, such as the values of self-image and the particulars of interpersonal life and material life. If I become too engrossed in the values which I have created, my perspective and my judgment may become warped. It is necessary to occasionally be able to release the self from temporal values in order to maintain perspective.

That does not mean that a person should not have values. Values are a part of life. Consider this example of value: if you love or have loved someone, you know that the love is directed toward that person whom you value very highly.

On the other hand, if problems arise in interpersonal relationships, it is not well to live in a state of denial of the reality of those problems. The realization of value is not a blank check that guarantees eternal value. A person needs to maintain the ability to detach from that which is valued when necessary in order to see with a more clear vision. With some relief from narrowed perceptions, a fresh look at things may reveal previously hidden aspects.

Of course, we recognize the needs of self and society; we have values regarding self and society. However, these values, while very important in the fabric of life, are not exempt from being examined with an open mind. A person manifests the freedom of a cleared mind when there is an orientation that includes the possibility of an absence of valuation. Valuation involves preconceptions and beliefs. A capacity to release oneself from preconceptions may allow a freedom from narrowness and a fresh look.

Values may become established or renewed in the course of an open outlook. Freedom of the mind may often enhance values; they tend to become enriched by having been subjected to the openness and freedom of examination. Such values are enhanced by freedom rather than constricted by preconceptions. In other words, with openness to new perspectives, the outcome of an examination of values may be either the maintenance or modification of the same desires and values or a turn toward something different. By allowing fresh perception, the ability to detach from values provides an opportunity to realize a firmer base for these values.

I have talked about having values and having the capability to release from values that are held. Life is best served by a confluence of both orientations. Both are experienced when there is an easy flow between a mindfulness of that which is valued and the openness, freedom, and spontaneity of the absence of value awareness. With a realization of the availability of freedom and openness, it is possible to be more fully committed to that in which you are engaged, though open to change when appropriate and necessary. Openness and freedom are characteristics of lightheartedness. With freedom and openness a person can be fully committed to that which is valued and at the same enjoy a lightheartedness.

Al: Do you have a place for this in your metaphor, the psychologic body?

Yes. Again, the heart represents openness, and freedom is the blood. Values and hope are muscle groups. Heart, blood, and muscles all work together in the harmonious flow of life. The heart is always pumping: openness is always available, as is the nourishing blood of freedom. Action is engendered by values, and this action may be held in abeyance pending examination and discernment by the mind, the brain.

Al: I see what you mean, but you slipped the word "hope" in there.

Hope is not a different subject, apart from value; people place value on hope. If you hope for something, that hope is for something of value.

Furthermore, hope is a desire for that which may come to be. With hope, we aspire to some outcome. However, at times such aspiration may restrict our outlook to the point that our actions or attitudes become unrewarding or destructive. It is well to be able to detach from hope when it is excessive to the point of harmfully restricting the outlook. At times a detachment from hope can give us a freedom of mind that allows openness to new understanding.

Identity also involves value. An awareness of identity can feed our sense of affirmation, a feeling that our lives are validated by that which establishes our identity. However, an excess pride of identity can also lead to the destructive effects of self-righteousness. Examples are in the occurrence of feelings of racial or religious superiority. We have discussed this several times. It is well to be able to release oneself from the sense of identity at times in order to have a fresh perception of that identity and to become renewed in fresh understanding.

I will again mention one way to facilitate the release from an exaggerated sense of self-value. When there is a mindfulness of the ultimate vulnerability—the ultimate return of the self in death to the mindless elements of the universe—then the sense of self-worth may be held more lightly. An awareness of the nothingness of self in the ultimate context may temper the sense of self-value.

In releasing from an exaggerated sense of self-worth, I do not mean to negate self-value. Furthermore, in respect to the ultimate context, a realization of the temporary nature of life might intensify a sense of self-worth. Since the "self" is a one-time "deal," we may be led to make the most of it.

FINAL CONSIDERATIONS

I want to say a few words about responsibility and then tie in several of the points just mentioned with the subject of continuity and the relation of continuity to openness. Discipline and responsibility usually involve self-monitored actions through some period of time. Also, by providing a sense of trust, discipline and responsibility afford a base for continuity in interpersonal relationships. On the other hand, the freedom of an open mind tends to allow new perceptiveness. This open perceptiveness may be of value in reinforcing that course of action for which discipline and responsibility are expressed. Also, new insight could lead to a different direction.

Several qualities—value, hope, identity, discipline and responsibility—all involve continuity with respect to time and interpersonal relationships. I have pointed out the value of balancing these expressions that imply continuity with the freedom of an open mind. In fact, there is value in a course of mental flow that conjoins these opposing tendencies, making the opposites always available. A fullness in the range of mental life becomes available when there is an access to each of the opposites in the pair characterized by openness and the various manifestations of continuity.

It may be helpful to review the metaphor of the whole psychologic body. The heart, the physical metaphor for openness, is a central source for the full life, pumping the nourishing blood of freedom. At the center of stability for the body is the spine, the physical counterpart for thankfulness, which is a prime orientation for all of the activities of the psyche. Doubt and discernment are represented by the brain, and empathy is the eyes and ears. The imagination is the lungs, those organs which are at the interface of the body with the wide-ranging, unseen air. Continuity of behavior is how we present ourselves, and, in the metaphor, continuity is represented by the skin.

A large part of the body are the groups of muscle masses. Many of the muscles provide opposing actions, working in coordinated harmony. These opposing muscle groups are the metaphor for many aspects of the psyche. Consider some muscles as spontaneity in counterbalance with discipline and responsibility. A person is well served to be able to exercise discipline and to fulfill responsibility as well as having a capacity to enjoy the freedom of spontaneity. Spontaneity counterbalances the direction of discipline and responsibility: each side of the balance is valuable. The availability of one side should not exclude the opposing tendency.

The heart muscle action maintains an openness to fresh understanding. Some of the limb muscles can be considered to represent values. If values excessively restrict the inclination toward openness, it is time to re-examine the values. For instance, the values of a workaholic might be modified if that person's outlook becomes opened to a broader understanding of life's values.

(In looking at the interaction between openness and the functions represented by the muscles, a literal interpretation of the metaphor is not possible. For example, the heart, as openness, would not have an opposing effect to the muscles.)

In addition, consider the interplay of openness and decisiveness. Openness need not inhibit action if the situation calls for it. Action, represented by muscles, need not be inhibited by openness if that openness would delay action that should be timely. And, furthermore, such timely action can carry with it an openness that makes allowance for a possible change in direction when called for.

There are various opposites that may be operative in coordination for the expression of a full life. The opposites include spontaneity vs. discipline and responsibility, decisiveness vs. doubt and examination, values vs. a release from values in the experience of open receptivity. An openness to the availability of each of the opposites presents a person with a full range of psychologic orientations by which to experience and express life. These are the components of a life of integrity and wholeness. Commitment to a life of integrity is a source for self-confidence. But caution should be maintained so that self-confidence does not degenerate into self-righteousness.

In the course of life, particular sources of value will usually become modified. The sense of identity usually includes reference to location and work activity, and these may change. Hopes can change. Discipline and responsibility may become directed along different channels. The content of life is likely to change, but the basic characteristics of the full life remain. The capacity for empathy and for discipline and responsibility remains available to the full life. In particular, openness and freedom are always there, along with the capacity for doubt. These are permanent qualities. There is always the freshness of moment in which they operate. With openness, mental life can freely explore the experiences of the present time. Mental content is ever-changing, but, to the receptive mind, the availability of doubt, freedom, and openness is ever present.

One more thing. The value of thankfulness does not change; gratefulness for existence is always of prime importance. In the metaphor of the psychologic body, thankfulness is represented by the back. The back is the center of support and stability. Likewise, thankfulness supports psychologic life and provides life with a sense of affirmation. Gratefulness carries with it an affirmation of life, an affirmative reception of the gift of life. Furthermore, this affirmation of life is not established by a reliance on some basis arrived at either by the use of reason or by some transcendental principle; it is axiomatic. The choices to express thankfulness for life and the welcoming of life do not have a rational basis. Such choices are axiomatic for the life that would be full; there is no reasoned basis for an outlook of thankfulness other than the positive outcome which it provides.

We are grateful for life and for that good fortune which we have. In the fullness of life, we are thankful.

The *a priori* nature of the affirmation of life is one possible interpretation of this Old Testament quote: "... I have set before you life and death, blessing and cursing: therefore choose life ... " (Deut. 30:19).

Al: We're at the end of the book. The title of this book is *God Unmasked; the Full Life Revealed*. How come you're not ending with more about God?

I'm glad you asked that. God is unmasked. He is a projection of the mind, an imaginative representation of all existence. God is not at the psychological center of a person's life, but also he is. The fundamental commitment is to integrity. And integrity includes more than that about which we can feel right. In fact, with integrity, self-righteousness is to be avoided. Integrity includes an openness to doubt, an openness to freedom, a release from self-absorption, an openness to empathy. The word-symbol God can help to release us from self-absorption and open us to the joy of freedom and to the wondrous and thankful welcoming of life and fortune.

The book is complete. Let's take a break. We have been talking all day. It's time for a rest. Get a good sleep.

Al: Great. I need a rest.

LAST, SHORT VERSE

And now it's morning—in springtime:

The cool, spring morning air

Freshens the green stems,

filling them with

New light

and new

Life.

Works Cited

Alighieri, Dante. The Divine Comedy. Trans. John Ciardi. NAL: New York, 1970.

Armstrong, Karen. A History of God. New York: Knopf, 1993.

Bachelard, Gaston. On Poetic Imagination and Reverie. Dallas: Spring, 1987.

———. The Poetics of Reverie. Boston: Beacon, 1960.

———. The Poetics of Space. Boston: Beacon, 1969.

Barbour, Ian. Religion in an Age of Science. San Francisco: Harper, 1990.

Barth, Karl. Karl Barth: Theologian of Freedom. Ed. Clifford Green. London: Collins, 1989.

Bates, Tom. "When Good Turns Bad." Oregonian 4 Dec. 1994: E1, E5.

Bauman, Zygmunt. Legislators and Interpreters. Ithaca: Cornell UP, 1987.

Bellah, Robert N. et al. Habits of the Heart. New York: Harper, 1985.

Berdyaev, Nicholas. The Meaning of History. Cleveland: World, 1962.

Buber, Martin. I and Thou. New York: Scribner, 1958.

Burke, Kenneth. Permanence and Change. Indianapolis: Bobbs, 1965.

Burns, Robert. The Complete Poetical Works of Robert Burns. London: Nelson.

Campbell, Bob. "'Quiz Show' Sounds Buzzer on Public Trust." Oregonian 16 Sept. 1994.

Camus, Albert. The Fall. New York: Vintage, 1956.

———. The Myth of Sisyphus. New York: Vintage, 1955.

Carroll, Lewis. "Jabberwocky." The Pocket Book of Verse. Ed. M. E. Speare. New York: Pocket Books, 1940.

Cassirer, Ernst. An Essay on Man. Garden City: Doubleday, 1954.

Cervantes, Miguel de. Don Quixote, Part I. Mack.

Conrad, Joseph. Lord Jim. New York: Lancer, 1968.

Cox, Harvey. The Seduction of the Spirit. New York: Simon, 1973.

Dewart, Leslie. The Future of Belief. New York: Herder, 1966.

Dostoevsky, Fyodor. Introduction to Notes from Underground. Editorial note. Mack 1850-1.

Eliot, T. S. Four Quartets. San Diego: Harcourt, 1943.

Flaubert, Gustave. A Simple Heart. Mack 1828.

Fletcher, Horace. Menticulture; or, the A-B-C of True Living. Chicago: Stone, 1899.

Frankl, Viktor. Psychotherapy and Existentialism. New York: Pocket, 1985.

Gallagher, Winifred. The Power of Place. New York: Poseidon, 1993.

Gardner, Marilyn. "Soccer Unable to Slake U. S. Craving for Action." Oregonian 28 June 1994: A10.

Gaudin, Colette. Preface and Introduction. On Poetic Imagination and Reverie. By Gaston Bachelard. Dallas: Spring, 1987

Giddens, Anthony. Modernity and Self-Identity. Stanford: Stanford UP, 1991.

Goethe, Johann Wolfgang von. Faust. Mack 1644.

Hamilton, Geoffrey. An Ultimate Truth. Beaverton, Oregon: High Ground, 1997.

Hampshire, Stuart. The Study of Human Nature. Ed. Leslie Stevenson. New York: Oxford UP, 1981.

Haught, James A. "Charting Terror in the Name of the Lord." Oregonian 22 April 1993: E7.

Hawking, Stephen. A Brief History of Time. Toronto: Bantam, 1988.

Hick, John. An Interpretation of Religion. New Haven: Yale UP, 1989.

Hoffer, Eric. The True Believer. New York: Harper, 1951.

Homer. The Iliad. Trans. Richmond Lattimore. Chicago: U of Chicago, 1951.

Hylton, Judith. Music Theory I. Portland, Oregon: Noteworthy, 1994.

James, William. The Varieties of Religious Experience. New York: Triumph, 1991.

Jaynes, Julian. The Origin of Consciousness in the Breakdown of the Bicameral Mind. Boston: Houghton, 1976.

Leopardi, Giacomo. The Broom. Mack 1771-2.

Machiavelli, Niccolo. The Prince. Mack 1067-8.

Mack, Maynard et al, ed. The Norton Anthology of World Masterpieces, Fifth Continental Ed. New York: Norton, 1987.

Maslow, Abraham H. Religions, Values, and Peak-experiences. New York: Penguin, 1964.

Merriam Webster's Collegiate Dictionary, Tenth Ed. Springfield: 1993.

Myers, David G. The Pursuit of Happiness. New York: Morrow, 1992.

Nicholson, Reynold A. The Mystics of Islam. London: G. Bell and Sons, Ltd., 1914.American, 1965.

Ortega y Gasset, Jose. The Modern Theme. New York: Harper, 1961.

Pascal, Blaise. Pensees. Trans. A. J. Krailsheimer. New York: Penguin, 1966.

Perls, Frederick S. In and Out of the Garbage Pail. Toronto, Bantam, 1972.

Pfaff, William. "A Critical New View of the United States is Turning Allies Off." International Herald Tribune 24-25 June 1995: 8.

Plato. "The Apology of Socrates." Mack 436.

Pojman, Louis P. Philosophy of Religion: An Anthology. Belmont, Calif.: Wadsworth, 1998.

Putnam, Robert D. "It Isn't the Old Men who are Grumpy in America." Oregonian 31 Dec. 1995: E5.

Reynolds, David K. Playing Ball on Running Water. New York: Quill, 1984.

Rahner, Hugo. Ignatius the Theologian. Trans. Michael Barry. New York: Herder, 1968.

Rainwater, Janette. You're in Charge. Marina del Rey: Devorss, 1979.

Rousseau, Jean-Jacques. Confessions. Mack 1634.

St. Teresa of Jesus. The Interior Castle or the Mansions. London, Sands, 1945.

Sen, Amitabha and Butler, Sharon. "The Quantum Loop." Sciences Nov./Dec. 1989: 34.

Shakespeare, William. The Works of William Shakespeare. New York: Oxford UP.

Spong, John Shelby. Living in Sin?. San Francisco: Harper, 1988.

Suzuki, D. T. Zen Buddhism. Ed. William Barrett. Garden City: Doubleday, 1956.

Suzuki, Shunryu. Zen Mind, Beginner's Mind. Ed. Trudy Dixon. New York: Weatherhill, 1970.

Tao Te Ching. Trans. Stephen Mitchell. New York: Harper, 1988.

Thomas, Dylan. Under Milkwood. London: Dent, 1954.

Tolstoy, Leo. The Death of Ivan Ilyich. Mack.

Wallraff, Charles F. Karl Jaspers; an Introduction to His Philosophy. Princeton: Princeton UP, 1970.

Weil, Simone. Simone Weil: an Anthology. Ed. Sian Miles. New York: Weidenfeld, 1986.

Westfall, Richard S. "The Rise of Science and the Decline of Orthodox Christianity: A Study of Kepler, Descartes, and Newton." God and Nature. Ed. David C. Lindberg and Ronald L. Numbers. Berkeley: U California, 1986.x

Index

Italicized page numbers indicate extended treatments. Only selected references are cited for general subjects.

Abraham, 301

Abstraction, 147-50, 237-8

Action, *104-8*, 112, 116-8; and anti-empathy, 106; characteristic modes of, 105

Aesthetics, 54, 78, 124, 150-1; and religious practice, 234-5, 263

Ambiguity, 81; in abstraction, 149; and freedom, 214; and mysticism, 213-9. *See also* Mysticism

Anarchy, 121, 132, 275

Angst, 97

Anguish, *54-58*, 70; and religious practice, 234

Anticipation, 75,81

Apathy, 297

Appearance, social, 183

Asceticism, 139

Attachments, *see* Preconceptions, Detachment

Authority, 37, 60, 123, 296-7; and religious practice, 243-4

Authorization, external, 178-80

Beauty, 151

Beliefs, 35,49

Bible, 181-2

Big Bang Theory, 161

Certainty, need for, 34; and religious belief, 202, 243, 323

Chance, 4, 158-60: and reality of the supernatural, 166-7

Chaos Theory, 158-60

Cleared mind, *72-5, 293-305*; and activity, 117; and religious practice, 242, 286

Co-dependence, 111

Commitment, 324

Communication, 265

Community, sense of, 274, 276

Compassion, *see* Sympathy

Continuity, *273-92*, 320

Control, 6, *57-60*, 117; excess, 58-60, 73; and religious practice, 231; social, 129

Creativity, 74

Cruelty, 7

Cynicism, 128, 274, 284, 303

Death, 49-51, 67, 189, 242, 262, 326

Decisiveness, 115-6, 316, 330

Definitions, 16, 21, 102, 134, 157, 253-4, 258, 313, 324

Desire, 97-8, 112; and religious practice, 232

Detachment, 36, 61-66, 290; and empathy, 103; and mysticism, 222-3; and religious practice, 241; striving for, 65; and value, 173

Determinism, 4, 164

Discipline, 60, 71-2, 125, 136-7, 196, 314, 328; and mysticism, 223-4

Doubt, 13, *31-41*, 164-5, *301-5*; and cleared mind, 296, 298-9; confidence in, 39; and detachment, 65-6; excess, 37, 178; and fulfillment, 294; in modern life, 39; and prejudice, 135; release from, 177-84; and religious belief, 202-3; and religious practice, 243, 258-9, 323; tolerance for, 38-40, 302-5, 315

Education, 283, 301

"Emotion junkies," 126

Emotionalism, 122-8; and religious practice, 232-3, 245

Empathy, *101-18*, 137-9, 278-9; and cleared mind, 294; and detachment, 62; and language, 283; and self-righteousness, 137

Enlarged awareness, *11-16*, 71, 189, 244-5, 260-2, 290; and imagination, 82

Exclusiveness, 135, 277-8

Faith, 253, 322

Focus, 36

Force, 109

Freedom, 13, *66-9*, *317-21*; from attachments, 38, 62-3, 67; and cosmic imagination, 190; excess desire for, 67, 122-5, 132; and hope, 171; and imagination, 79, 82, 153; and God, 191

Fullness of life, *see* Integrity

God, *185-203*, 265-8, 299-301; accessibility, 285; anthropomorphism, *239-42*; and cosmic imagination, 191, 193-4; death of, 14-15; and enlarged awareness, 261; existence of, 17; and freedom, 191, 318-321; and humanism, 289-91; individual views of, 230; and literal-mindedness, 182; natural inclination to experience, 19; naturalistic concept of, 188; proof of 16-7; and value, 280

Guilt, 196

Haphazardness, 4. *See also* Chance

Happiness, 11, 14, 89, 139-40, 148-52, 163, 286

Hope, 170-2, 327-8

Humanism, 284, *287-91*

Idealism, 59, 129, 258

"If only," 113

Imagination, 14, *78-83*; cosmic imagination, *150-5,* 173, 189-94, 201-2, 264, 325; and hope, 170; and mysticism, 214; and opposition, 227; transcendental quality, 153; unifying tendency, 82-3,153; and word-symbols, *145-155*

Impatience, 108

Inactivity, 124, 126

Individualism, 122-4, 192, 273-5

Indulgence, 90-92, 125

Ineffability, 217

Initiative, 80, 266

Integrity, *133-40*, 163, 331; and the god-symbol, 323-5; and prayer, 319; and religious practice, 247-8, 259; and spirituality, 287-91

Joy, *see* Happiness

Judgmentalism, 94, 108-9

"Just when," 113

Justice, 109, 120

Language, 75, 281-3

Learning, 75-6

Literal-mindedness, 181-2, 214, 243

Love, 103-4, 111

Materialism, 14, 92, 95, 129

Meaning 4, *7-11*, 158-9, 167-9

Mechanism, 157-8, 160

Misfortune, 13

Music, 124, 226, 316; and religion, 263, 265

Mysticism, *213-224*

Narcissism, 96, 129

Nazi Germany, 6-7, 106

Objectivity, *see* Subjectivity

Openness, 14, 36, *69-72*, 76, *313-17*; and action, 107; and cleared mind, 296; and empathy, 102-3; and imagination, 153; and religious practice, 248, 259-60; and society, 131-2; and vagueness, 72

Opposition, 109, *225-8*; and religious practice, 244-7, 322; and television, 126

"Original sin," 258

Pantheism, 268

Passiveness, 98

Patience, 126, 137, 172

Peace, 203, 241; and God, 261, 265. *See also* Release

Index

Perception, 34-5; and detachment, 61; and hope, 170-1, and imagination, 79-80; and language, 282-3, and openness, 69, 80; and threats, 114

Perceptiveness. *See* Perception

Perfectionism, 6, 97-8

Physiognomy, 240-1

Prayer, 285-7, 318-20

Preconceptions, 35, 38, 102, 110, 327

Prejudice, 130, 135

Pride, 114; and religious practice, 233

Process theology, 4, 159

Productivity, 69, 71, 243, 317-8

"Psychologic body," *311-331*

Purpose, *see* Meaning

Quantum Theory, 158, 166

Rebellion, 183, 192, 273, 290, 297

Receptivity, 246-7. *See also* Openness

Release, mental, 195-6, 228; and religious practice, 239, 244, 257-8, 325-8

Religious practice, 4-5, *229-49*; destructive consequences, 17-9; nature of religious orientation, *251-68*; new forms, 15

Responsibility, 79, 130, 136, 164, 181, 191, 279-80, 293, 314, 328-9

Salvation, 194-6, 257

Science, 4, 20, 40, 188

Self-absorption, 12, *89-100*, 274

Self-centeredness, 324. *See also* Self-absorption

Self-denial, 64, 91, 99, 114-5, 195

Self-examination, 95-6, 220

Self-expression, 145

Self-identity, 148-9, 162, 165-6, 256, 276-7, 328; and cleared mind, 295-6

Self-image, 114

341

Self-righteousness, 130, 137, 182-3, 242-3, 246, 258-9; and integrity, 134-5, 165

Self-surrender, 99-100; and detachment, 63-5; and mysticism, 220-1

Self-worth, 280

Silence, 248-9

Skeptical, 5, 185

Slogans, 181

Society, *119-133;* and "correctness," 133; and television, 127

"Spectacle complex," 152

Spirituality, 3-5, 14-6, 284; and doubt, 303-4; and integrity, 287. *See also* Religious practice

Spontaneity, 284; and doubt, 303-4; and integrity, 287; and openness, 313-6

Subjectivity, of the God-symbol, 321-2, and objectivity, 20, 43, 196-7, 199-202

Supernatural, 4

Supplication, 231

Suspicion, 113

Sympathy, 109-10

Teleology, 188, 238-9

Television, 11, 125-8

Thankfulness, *43-52*, 119, 163, 330; and empathy, 103; and enlarged awareness, 189, 262; and religious practice, 266-7, 285-6; and responsibility, 136

Transcendent, 161, 166-7, 197, 255-7

Transcendental, *see* Transcendent

Transformation, sense of, 235-6

Trust, 303-5, 315

Truth, 4, *34-7,* 302

Uncertainty, 33, 38, 167

Index

Uncertainty Principle, 158

Unifying effect, 153, 238

Universe, *157-70*; and God, 187-8; origin of, 161

Unknowns, 159-62

Utilitarian, 194, 198-200

Value, *172-3*, *325-8*, 330; fundamental, 255-8, 266-7, 289; and god-symbol, 322; in interpersonal relationships, 279; and religious practice, 239, 253-4, 266-7. *See also* Meaning

Victimization, 120

Victor, George, 147

Violence, 130-1; on television, 127-8

Vulnerability, 49-51, 162, 221

Wonder, 12, 14, *43-52*; and cosmic imagination, 190; conscious effort toward, 44; contentment and joy, 44-5; of existence, 45-8: loss of, 44; and religious practice, 232, 235-7

Word-symbols, *75-77*, *145-50,* and cleared mind, 294-5: and external authorization, 180-2; inadequacy of, 77

Yearning-fulfillment cycles, 57; and religious practice, 232

Zazen, 73

Order Forms

To order additional copies of *God Unmasked; the Full Life Revealed*, send a check or money order ($24.95 plus $3.00 Priority Mail and handling, $27.95 total) made payable to:

NORTHWOODS CONSULTING
6107 S. W. Murray Blvd., Suite 351
Beaverton, Oregon 97008-4467

Please send a copy of *God Unmasked; the Full Life Revealed* to:

Date _____

Name _____

Street Address _____

_____

City _____ State _____ ZIP _____

Please send a copy of *God Unmasked; the Full Life Revealed* to:

Date _____

Name _____

Street Address _____

_____

City _____ State _____ ZIP _____